A How-to Guide for Love, Sex and Passion

Amazing Intimacy

*Create A Spectacular Marriage
In and Out of the Bedroom*

Doug & Leslie
GUSTAFSON

Individual, Marriage and Sex Therapists

Authentic and True Publishing

Lone Tree, Colorado
www.authenticandtrue.com

Amazing Intimacy, *Create A Spectacular Marriage In and Out of the Bedroom*
©2013 by Doug and Leslie Gustafson

Published by Authentic and True Publishing
9220 Teddy Lane, Suite 1500, Lone Tree, CO 80124

Printed in the United States of America

Visit our website at www.authenticandtrue.com

Cover design and layout by Steve Plummer

Library of Congress Control Number: 2013903796
ISBN: 9780989070041

The authors have written this book as an educational resource, not as a tool to be used for diagnosis and treatment. The information presented is in no way a substitute for consultation with a certified sex therapist, psychotherapist, or physician. Although the authors have carefully researched all sources to ensure the accuracy and completeness of the information, the publisher and authors shall have neither liability nor responsibility to any person or entity with respect to any loss, damage, or injury caused or alleged to be caused directly or indirectly by the information presented. Treatment of medical conditions, marital or emotional problems, and wellness should always be supervised by an appropriate licensed health care professional.

All case vignettes are drawn from the experiences of real clients treated by Doug Gustafson, MFT & Leslie Gustafson, MFT, although names and significant details have been altered to protect the privacy of those involved.

DEDICATIONS

Our profound thanks to all the couples in our practice, past and present, who have trusted us with perhaps the most sacred part of their lives, their marriages. Their desire to grow and transform their world together, to reach for more with courage and often fear, is a testimony to the power of the human spirit, to a God Who loves them dearly and to the blessings that come when you don't give up on intimacy. From you we have learned so much.

To our two boys, who have given us so much joy through the twists and turns of life. Our prayer for you is a life of intimate connections and endless love.

And finally, to our mom's, past and present, who continue to believe in us no matter what. If intimacy comes from the bonds of love, we have been filled up richly with your presence and prayers – and it has made all the difference.

DOUG & LESLIE GUSTAFSON

CONTENTS

A BRIEF STORY

W E REMEMBER WELL the days when our couple came to us, needing all our wisdom and help, and we began to understand their journey, their lives . . . unfolding before us.

They loved each other but like most newlyweds, they had to grow over time, learning what it really means to care, to create dynamic energy and sustain it, to love passionately in and out of the bedroom. The impact of raising a challenged son and an older son as part of a blended family, led to challenges – joys and sorrows merging into a symphonic rhythm not always predictable. Sometimes painful.

As with many couples we have known over the years, searching to get their relationship right and God-honoring meant tackling peaks and valleys, finding a way up the mountain when stuck and out of breath, when the dailies of life suffocated originality and enthusiasm.

Reaching into our therapists' toolkits and the willingness to pray didn't always move this couple toward greater joy, or rejoicing for that matter. Small walls from hurt feelings sometimes emerged, preventing closeness and the experience of uniting as one under God's watch. Small walls can grow and block vision and may sometimes seem insurmountable.

The definition of closeness they were looking for, the congruent love formed from a fabric of deep connection, was at times elusive. Yet their bond, a chord of love woven together by crisis, determination and destiny, kept them focused on the good they had. But each wanted more.

As with many crises, the latest one proved to be a turning point. A physical challenge presented an opportunity for him to see more clearly his vulnerability, need for connection and a new and more visible path toward loving his wife. She responded. It seems she had longed to be necessary to him and have something she could give him that was truly hers.

What grew out of several years of marriage, of getting stuck in finding a way to reach each other's heart and spirit in deeper ways, began to truly unfold. From their new beginning, we watched this couple forge a more meaningful vision for the life they wanted and knew they could create. They started to grasp the shortness of life and the future they needed to realize how to honor God and fulfill His purposes in their life together.

Each addressed their shortcomings more clearly, committed to maturity in their efforts to love more consistently and deal with their own past demons that had kept them locked up and insipid in their approach to connect and bond with each other.

They began, in earnest and with fierce effort, to reach out and pursue each other as if dating for the first time. They decided to have their own affairs – with each other. They realized to reach out in love, they had to demonstrate care and affection in ways never before. It actually seemed easier now that they had realized how vital they were to each other and how meaningful life with each other was.

They took on pleasure, in and out of the bedroom, as their personal responsibility, each promising to touch the other with consistent attention to their unique needs.

They found new and growing ways to affirm and reinforce their affection and respect for each other, with fresh ways to say "I love you and want you to know that."

And they both learned that at the foot of the cross, power came from supplication and humility. The spirit of their God became their life-blood. Reverence and awe became the well to draw from for true conviction and motivation to make a difference.

And so they wrote a book. About intimacy. This is our story. We hope to pass on the wisdom, conviction and learning we have gone through. In looking for and finding more.

Your potential lies ahead, only obscured by walls or lack of vision for what you can create and experience together. Open your eyes and look to the mountain tops. Join us in the journey of building a marriage with "Amazing Intimacy" – Your marriage.

PREFACE

W E BELIEVE MARRIAGE can be an exciting experience between two best friends – two lovers who share a heart-clenching journey of radical love, sometimes unspeakable joy and a deep, abiding passion. In fact, passion to the core, the kind that often takes you by surprise and leaves you wanting more –feeds the spirit and grows the heart in ways often unimaginable.

Creating this kind of love becomes an adventure that takes courage but also action – the type that builds love, creates energy and sustains deep bonds between two partners.

This doesn't happen by accident. Rather, true, abiding love is built on a model of care and affection that takes skill, undaunted persistence and an intentional pursuit between two lovers to grow the marriage into all it can be. And it takes a reliance on the incredible power of God and the love He sheds abroad in our hearts.

In the pages that follow, we will provide a model of hope for your marriage that inspires, encourages and instructs. And holds out a path that leads you down a road, perhaps one less traveled, bright with the light of love and bold promise – ultimately, part of God's design to create an awesome, vibrant marriage relationship.

That takes you one step closer to amazing intimacy, both in and out of the bedroom.

Doug & Leslie Gustafson

ACKNOWLEDGEMENTS

W E HAVE MANY people to thank and we can't find the words to express our deep appreciation to each and every one.

First, we thank our Lord and Savior who inspires us daily to live out a new life – who makes true intimacy possible with Him and in marriage and in all our relationships. He has sustained, grown and fed our marriage and is the true author of all that's amazing.

We want to thank our wonderful church, Mount of Olives, in Mission Viejo California and Senior Pastor John Steward – our friend and spiritual leader. You convinced us that the church is a place not only of worship, but a place to learn deep and practical truths – even about sex and intimacy. You gave us permission to dream and a belief that God would use us to impact the lives of your flock and others who hurt the most. And to Bill and Annie Harper, who came along side so many times with their love and friendship. You so often breathed life into our spirits, at times when we felt discouraged and needed support. We love you both. And to the wonderful staff at Mount of Olives. Your dedication to the gospel, to love and to healing makes the church what God intended it to be.

To our friend, colleague, life coach and professor, Chris McCluskey, MSW, CST, PCC. You have been an inspiration to both of us and your book on marriage, *When Two Become One: Enhancing Sexual Intimacy In Marriage,* has been given out to so many of our clients and forms some of the content in our book. It's yours and Rachel's book that was life changing for Leslie and sparked her desire to become a Christian Sex Therapist. Your commitment to Christ and what He offers to married couples, has been a foundation for us to live by and write about.

Thanks so much to The Institute for Sexual Wholeness and its founders and leaders Debra Taylor, LMFT, CST, Douglas Rosenau, PhD, Michael Sytsma, PhD and Chris McCluskey, MSW, CST, PCC. Your teaching and inspiration for bringing healthy, God- Designed sexuality to this culture and the Church today has been a Godsend as well as highly motivating and encouraging to Leslie who caught your passion.

To my team (Doug's) at Kaiser Permanente. You taught me so much about leadership and the passion to help those hurting emotionally. I have missed you more than you know. Leaving was one of the most difficult decisions of my life.

To Leslie's core group of therapists, whom she interacts with daily in their Psychotherapy Community Group online. Many of you who have become close and dear colleagues and confidantes in real life as well. Your support has been key and life giving. Thank you.

To Joe Jardine, a colleague and incredibly talented psychotherapist in California, for being the first reader, editor and a dear friend in this book journey. You are wise beyond your years and your friendship to both of us is priceless.

To our editor Nan Deyo and book designer Steve Plummer. Nan, your talent with words gives life to each paragraph. And Steve, your creative design surpassed our imaginations and gave our book the look and feel needed to visually match our belief in all we do and care about with couples. Bravo!

And to David Avrin, The Visibility Coach, for his direction and help with publishing resources. Your encouragement along the way has meant much to us both.

And finally, thank you to all friends and family who have heard us talk about this book for some time. Your patience, cheers and willingness to let Leslie vent along the way have been helpful indeed! More importantly, all the ways you have prayed for us and supported us in our lives and our marriage, has given us courage, inspiration and the will to finish. "Thanks" doesn't really capture how grateful we feel.

INTRODUCTION

"It feels good to be touched in all the right places by someone you love;
But what an amazing experience when they touch your heart and soul."

DOUG & LESLIE GUSTAFSON

Our Goal

DO YOU BELIEVE that marriage can be full of passion, life, inspiration and companionship?

That sex can be amazing, your bond with your partner airtight close, full of love and affirmation?

That you can experience each other as best friends and soul mates?

Marriage, as God designed it, should rock your world, take your breath away and bring life, promise and hope into your world.

We call this kind of marriage amazing – between the sheets and in the kitchen. A union of two souls into a tapestry of love, grace and purpose.

At a Glance

Yet building a passionate, loving connection in marriage doesn't happen by chance. Intimacy, constructed on a bedrock of passion, excitement and a deep bond of love, comes with intention and a road map for success.

We will provide that path, to motivate you and help create a vision that will give you an inside look at how to grow your marriage into a connection that is special, lasting and exciting.

So, *Amazing Intimacy: Create a Spectacular Marriage In and Out of the Bedroom* comes from our hearts, from what we strive for in our own marriage and what we have helped couples achieve in our counseling and coaching work over the past several years.

Intimacy can be truly amazing.

And it develops out of a willingness and deep desire to forge a relationship infused with love and passion and a courageous heart open to make any changes needed to accomplish this vision. And it comes from a commitment and profound belief that God orchestrates, through His wisdom and power, changed lives and compelling love between two people.

So again, do *you believe love between two married people can be full of passion, excitement and romance?*

Or are you someone who believes passion and romance are for dating lovers, vanishes shortly after marriage and only returns when you're on vacation and have a chance to let your hair down?

If that's what you believe, we couldn't disagree more. We hope to convince you otherwise. Amazing intimacy can happen, become the norm and last through a lifetime.

But an amazing marriage doesn't happen by accident. The complacency that permeates so many love relationships, in fact, causes love to deteriorate and even die. Yes, love can die.

So imagine with us for a moment. You are living a truly blessed life, your love for your spouse continues to grow and the passion you feel together, in and out of the bedroom, cuts deep into your heart and soul.

How does this happen? What ingredients in your behavior and beliefs created such a level of closeness and success – giving you a love beyond your wildest dreams?

We will answer those questions. We are sold out on hope and truly believe lives and marriages can move to higher ground – perhaps not imagined before.

We have identified 6 pillars or ingredients – we call them "attitudes" – that magnify the possibilities to grow and sustain an incredible love relationship. Both sexually and also outside the bedroom walls.

Our Audience

These attitudes are designed to inspire and provide direction and a deeper relationship for any married couple truly interested in growing their love for one another. Who desire to move beyond what they currently have and deepen their passion, commitment and the excitement they share. This includes a close look at sexual contact as well as all the ways we build connection in our love life.

In and out of the bedroom.

For all couples, whether you are struggling or seeking a more intimate, passionate bond together, we offer a way to understand deep and lasting romance. We offer concrete ways to grow, regain and sustain closeness and mutual desire.

All the principles or "attitudes" we elaborate on have the potential to create both growth and healing. Most importantly, without them, love fades and even evaporates from the connection two people share.

If you're interested in deepening your love for one another, creating more life and energy in your marriage and building your relationship on principles that keep you excited about your partner, this book and the 6 attitudes provides a path, a way of growing deeper in your loving bond and a way to ignite and even restore passion for one another.

We focus on real growth and change – meaningful, life changing truths that transform your life and take you to new levels. Not band aids that don't go beneath the surface to create real change.

For couples who are struggling and on the verge of divorce or despair, these principles can certainly help. This book, however, is not a substitute for those who truly need marital therapy. However, each theme we uncover in the pages to follow can act as an adjunct to the counseling process and help achieve the goals of turning your marital partnership around.

And if you are only one partner of a marriage and have an unwilling or incapable partner in building your marriage, this book does not eliminate you. These attitudes can help you with your own clarity and perspective around your marriage and how you might be able to effect change from your part.

Or perhaps you aren't sure about growing your marriage, whether it's even possible and whether or not you would rather keep things "the way they are." Hang in there. This book will open your eyes to possibilities and the potential to grow passion and love in your life. Read this with an open mind, then decide if it's for you. We are confident you will.

Also, you may find certain chapters more pertinent than others as they apply to your marriage today. Feel free to explore those sections most meaningful, perhaps skimming others that you feel you have a greater handle on currently.

Finally, this book provides a resource for therapists and pastors and others in the helping profession as an adjunct to the counseling and work you do with couples. It can serve as a cogent guide to give direction to the therapy process.

The Six Attitudes

We are convinced that integrating and growing all 6 attitudes has the potential to revolutionize your love relationship and build passion into your life. Let's look at each more closely.

We first take a look at the topic of "**Potential**" – examining what vision you have for your marriage now and in the future and how to move toward that picture. Couples seldom discuss this theme but need to. Thinking through what we want the marriage to be like and what this would mean in everyday behaviors and actions provides a compelling road map to achieving a strong, vibrant love life.

Next, we focus on what we call "**Presence**." We define this as the qualities you bring as a person – your own maturity and capacity to love – that provide the raw ingredients that create and maintain a strong marital bond. After all, the marriage is made up of a man and a woman who bring strengths and weaknesses into the relationship. We help you define them and give you a road map to provide direction for personal accountability, awareness and growth.

Next, we examine "**Pursuit**" – what we describe as a set of attitudes and actions that often characterize the dating period before marriage. Simply stated, we pursue one another with a variety of romantic and proactive behaviors that convince us we have a love worth marrying over. Yet, in marriage, we let go of the energy and drive behind this crucial theme. So we want to understand how to build it back into the habits and patterns that go into everyday marital life.

Our third "attitude" we call "**Pleasure**." Here we focus on the role of pleasure, both physical and emotional, that builds energy and passion into the marriage arena. We examine how to bring all kinds of pleasure into the relationship, including but not limited to sexual expression and release. We do take a close look at sexual intimacy as a God-created, unique way to bond and experience electricity in our partnership with our lover, our mate.

In our next attitude, we discuss the role of "**Affirmation**" in creating a more loving connection. Developing ideas about how to affirm one another and committing to behaviors that reflect this purpose goes a long way toward achieving patterns of affection, caring and trust in our love for our partner. Affirming one another can be the most powerful way we express care and interest in the life and being of our mate.

And finally, we examine the role of "**Awe**" in creating an engaging, vibrant married life. By awe, we mean developing a deep appreciation for God's design for marriage and His unique role in creating the possibilities for our love to grow and thrive. Standing in awe of God and His creation is a powerful internal attitude that causes us to reach out and involve ourselves in the magnificence of love as He created and defined it to be.

Ultimately, awe inspires us to live out a higher calling, to commit to the very best in our marriage and to rely on the spiritual resources God provides to make all this happen.

Keep in mind that this book is meant to be inspirational, informative and helpful in providing a model of intimacy that can rock your world together. In light of that, *Amazing Intimacy: Create a Spectacular Marriage In and Out of the Bedroom* should be read interactively. In other words, stop and reflect on all the questions to gain better insights into your life. Ponder the concepts presented in a way that creates understanding about what makes marriage intimate and exciting. Absorb each chapter prayerfully and ask for God's help in uncovering areas in which you need to grow or implement more consistently in your marital life.

The best use of all the concepts in this book requires a patient, open look at your life and the dynamics in your marriage. Spend the time you need to make sense out of your life and the partner you have been blessed with. And be open to taking actions that may even feel uncomfortable, unfamiliar or at times unclear.

We have designed this book to be motivational but also thought and action provoking. Whether you read it from the beginning or bite off smaller chunks to make the content more manageable, the effort you put in can produce amazing insights and results. Our prayer is for your growth, the kind that kindles a fire between you and your mate and can be sustained to the end. Amazing intimacy works that way.

Conclusion

We believe in life transformation. However, we are convinced that many settle for benign, vanilla-flavored marriages because no clear path has been set that leads them into new places where love thrives and passion explodes. Passion and deep connection have to be grown and nurtured.

Once we know the way and understand the ingredients that lead to passion, romance and a fulfilled marital life, we can begin the journey. A journey rocked by possibilities, unearthed through God's hand and wisdom and completed by our own determination to love more and to create a marriage only imagined.

We hope to be your guide, to offer help along the way and to watch as you soar. Intimacy can be truly fulfilling and reflect the intent God had when He made up the plan for two lovers to unite in the first place.

Our hope is that by His hand and your effort, you will look toward a future bound by hope and you will hear the echo of our voice and finally yours, claiming true intimacy with your lover you will both call "amazing."

Our first Attitude – Potential!

POTENTIAL

"Reach high, for stars lie hidden in your soul; dream deep, for every dream precedes the goal."
PAMELA VAULL-STARR

"We waste time looking for the perfect lover, instead of creating the perfect love."
TOM ROBBINS

Our Potential

WE WANT YOU to imagine with us for a few minutes – sit back and dream – of what you want your marriage to be like. Really like. Down to the nitty gritty, the fine points of how you get along, treat each other, express love and affection, engage sexually. How you're respected, cared for, supported. All of it. Don't leave anything out.

Now take this one step further. You are on a weekend getaway with your spouse. But no ordinary getaway . . . while there is fun and relaxation, you also spend a lot of time discussing and reaching conclusions about what you want your marriage to grow into over the next year, 2 years, 3 years and so on. You do this together.

In fact, you paint a clear picture of an exciting, passionate marriage that you want to create. The kind of energy and bond you hope to have with one another. You both identify the kind of sex life you hope for and would agree on, the way you want to display love and affection for each other, how to handle finances and children and how you want to convey deep respect and affirmation in your love relationship.

You develop clear mileposts and goals around where you are going, how to get there and the more immediate behaviors and actions you want to implement to get started and to emphasize your commitment to the partnership.

Now imagine you pray about each of these and feel that the direction you are headed in reflects God's best for your life, the kind of extreme love and care He hopes to create in you, individually and together. A spiritual life with key principles and practices that will add depth and meaning to the bond of love you have already established. Together, you develop the ultimate "getaway" – designing your marriage as you've always wanted for the rest of your life.

Realistically, most couples have never accomplished this. Never spent time planning and imagining – laying their hopes and dreams, however big and bold – down on the table of analysis and expectation.

Yet developing a path and plan for success in marriage is critical. Businesses that succeed have usually established clear plans for achieving marketplace advantage and financial profitability. Yet we often assume that our marriages will grow naturally and don't take work to clarify a vision and road to success.

PAUSE and PONDER

* **What do you want your life, your marriage to look like?**
* **Take some time to complete the Wheel of Life found in Appendix A. This will give you a clearer idea of how to shape**

personal goals, a vision for yourself and your marriage, and a visual picture or road map of the journey ahead.

True growth, spiritual and emotional, happens as a result of planned success – not fumbling around hoping love will conquer all with no thought or regard for directing our aim.

We hope to give you clear targets for creating an exciting and passionate life together. Each of our 6 attitudes helps you achieve the marriage and intimacy you hope for.

So our first attitude centers on a key ingredient for relationship success – developing a clear picture of what you want your marriage and love life to look like.

We call this potential.

This means assessing your true potential for creating a more meaningful, passionate relationship together. A picture to grow into, a marriage with a loving bond you can develop with the right skills and heart change.

The challenge can be daunting for some couples who may be struggling, easier for those who have achieved a stronger, loving bond. Dave and Sarah – a young couple struggling to find their way – exemplify the challenge of planning and designing the marriage you most hope for.

True growth, spiritual and emotional, happens as a result of planned success—not fumbling around hoping love will conquer all with no thought or regard for directing our aim.

Dave and Sarah

*Dave and Sarah came to us hoping for more. They had been mar-
ried for twelve years and had two children, ages five and nine.*

*Their current challenges centered on a waning intimacy, some inter-
mittent conflict and a growing experience of distance in the relationship.*

*Dave found that the demands of corporate life kept him both busy and
tired. At times, he would travel, adding literal distance between them for
sometimes a week at a time. This left Sarah alone with the kids and the
challenges of parenting by herself.*

*Sarah worked part-time as a physical therapist and so had some
flexibility with her son and daughter in terms of childcare.*

*Both described ordinary childhoods, although Dave's parents divorced
when he was eleven. He noted that his parents rarely displayed love and
affection and so the divorce, shocking in many ways for an eleven year
old, was no surprise.*

*Sarah noted her relationship with both parents was positive,
although she remembers her parents fighting a lot as she grew up.
They never hit each other but constantly bickered. She too remembers
little affection in the home, especially between mom and dad. Most of
the caring was directed to the kids.*

*In their dating and early in their marriage, both Dave and Sarah
shared a growing love and chemistry but agreed that their connection
with one another was now fading. Perhaps the stress of finances and two
children had created challenges neither had anticipated. They felt lost,
like a ship losing its compass, an experience they never thought possible.*

*Their sex life had also suffered. Making love was now a chore for
Sarah and Dave felt resentful that she no longer seemed to desire him.
Discussing the issue only created more stress and anger and so both
tended to avoid the topic.*

*Early in our work with this couple, both had trouble stating what
they truly wanted from each other. Neither had seen positive role models*

growing up in terms of expressing intimacy. Both Dave and Sarah were confused about what more they could ask for from each other, and expressed disbelief that love and marriage hadn't just "worked out."

Dave commented in one of our sessions, "I'm so disappointed. I thought our love would carry us through life. Now we're having to think about what our marriage is supposed to be."

Sarah replied, "Yes, I never imagined having to figure out how to get along and love each other. Isn't that supposed to just happen? Makes me question whether we truly love each other or not."

Stating what they wanted, directly and respectfully, was nearly impossible. It was like they didn't have the language or concepts needed to adequately describe what they truly hoped for. Dave was convinced that Sarah would never desire him again and Sarah believed Dave's growing insensitivity to her needs was cast in stone.

In fact, looking at their future together and defining a better, more hopeful day seemed risky. How could they communicate what they wanted without being shamed or turned down?

So dreaming about a new, more loving and passionate life together never happened. Instead, persistent conflict became the norm and their only way of communicating a desire for more.

When asked to describe a "vision" for their marriage, neither had any thoughts. They could hardly imagine getting along day to day, let alone conceptualizing a lifestyle of passion, intimacy and common goals. They both wanted relief, to move toward wholeness and peace, but had never thought about planning their love life together. Thought it would just happen.

So, Dave and Sarah – an uncommon story? Hardly. We have seen so many couples flounder in the abyss of darkness. Not just the kind of darkness that attaches itself to conversations, creating wounds and hurt. More than that. Darkness that leaves couples without a shore to sail to, bereft of hope, no direction or belief that love could or will ever prevail.

In our work with this couple, much needed to happen. But at the heart of it all, we focused on their dreams for love, for passion, for supporting each other and becoming soul mates, for deciding on a picture for their marriage that would rock their heart, soul and spirit.

In short, we zeroed in on their potential as a couple to create a loving madness, the type that heals wounds but also rockets you into a future of excitement, joy and togetherness. Their potential for maximum love.

Let's share some of David and Sarah's beginning thoughts about the kind of marriage they envisioned and what it felt like to create this picture of their future together. Their thoughts and list grew over time, especially as they continued to examine together their vision around all the themes and attitudes in this book. But here are their preliminary ideas.

Sarah

- I want to communicate openly, without getting defensive with one another.

- I want to go out on dates and hold hands again and show affection.

- I want to get away – just the two of us – once each quarter and renew our love and remind ourselves of the fun we can have together.

- I want David to really listen to me without assuming I want to hurt him or that I don't care.

- I want David to pursue me, without always feeling it's just for sex. I would like him to set up some, not all, of our dates and treat me like a date – such as opening my car door.

- I would like to have a more mutually supportive relationship around our personal goals.

David

- I want Sarah to believe in me, that when I work hard, it is for *us* and to communicate that to me.

- I want to have more fun together, even take up a hobby.

- I want to be able to discuss anything without fighting, even when we don't agree.

- I would like to enjoy our sex life together, like before. I would like to have an affectionate relationship and not have Sarah assume I always want sex.

- I would like to have fun and passionate getaways during the year by ourselves.

- I would like to have more couple friends.

- I would like to start going to church together and develop our spiritual life.

Now let's take a closer look at Potential and the many dimensions that it takes and see how to grow the skill of defining the marriage you most want.

What We Mean by Potential

Each of our lives consist of a rich story God uses to bring honor to Himself and that cultivates an unimaginable bond and relationship between us and Him.

In many respects, our lives are much like a novel, unfolding in chapters we create by how we live. Imagine writing this story or lifeline more intentionally – by looking at the horizon of life, defining what we want the future to be, and taking real steps to create that world for ourselves and our marriages. You can write a new story or re-write an old one.

Another way to say this is that we are all on a journey toward greater levels of personal growth and spiritual maturation. We haven't "arrived" at where we will be in the months and years ahead. So our lives represent a journey toward a *destination* made possible by *an ongoing* effort to grow and reach greater levels of maturity and capacity to love. Ongoing.

We can hope to arrive somewhere really special with the right path, focus and energy to complete the journey.

In light of this, each and every marriage relationship has a certain potential it can reach toward greater intimacy, closeness and excitement.

For all of us, that potential has only been partially discovered and realized.

How exciting! Our marriages can ripen, change, blossom and turn into a crucible where love, authenticity and deep connection abound.

Clearly defining what you want that future to look like becomes imperative. If you don't, you meander in life and you miss creating a chosen life. Life and circumstances will choose you and shape your relationships, including your marriage, if you let them. Do you really want the story of your marriage and your life to be written for you?

Each and every marriage relationship has a certain potential it can reach toward greater intimacy, closeness and excitement. Our marriages can ripen, change, blossom and turn into a crucible where love, authenticity and deep connection abound.

In discussing potential, we will set the stage for developing the remaining 5 attitudes – since each one involves the need to identify your vision for the marriage and how to create a new, vibrant bond around each theme.

For now, however, let's explore what it means to begin thinking about and identifying the kind of marriage you hope for – focusing on a new mindset that takes hope and possibilities and translates them into a clear vision for your love partnership. Both in and out of the bedroom.

Four Components

We want to highlight four components related to this dynamic principle of "potential" that help us understand the meaning of the concept and how to grow as a couple. We have identified four key themes. They are **vision, capacity to realize your dreams, commitment to wisdom and truth** and **urgency.**

We will look at each one separately.

Vision

First, potential encompasses what we think of as "vision." This centers on the need to cultivate a visual, verbal and written picture of what we want our love with our partner to look like – involving all aspects of our marriage.

Bill Hybels defined vision as "A picture of the future that produces passion." The vision you have for your closest love relationship should create energy and desire – it should produce *passion* and seem exciting to you.

It is vital that two people share deeply about what they want their marriage to look like. We want you to begin the process of defining the kind of love relationship you each want – what it would look like in terms of actual day-to-day behaviors, emotions, ways of relating and key patterns you share in how you communicate and reach out.

Here are a few significant questions to begin the process of defining your vision for your marriage. Keep in mind that your understanding of your potential and what you want to characterize your marriage will grow as you look at each of the 6 attitudes. At the end of the book, we encourage you to come back to some of the key questions and chapters to help you develop even further your ideas about the passion and marriage you truly hope for.

PA(II)SE *and* PONDER

❈ How would I describe my marriage in terms of closeness and intimacy?

❈ As we grow together in marriage, what do I want my marriage to look like in six months, one year, three years and even five years?

❈ How would our relationship be stronger and what would we be doing differently than today if we were at our target vision? What specific behaviors and patterns would we be seeing in our relationship at those different times?

❈ What changes can we bring into the marriage today that moves us toward a "picture of the future that produces passion?" What could we be doing differently "now" rather than later to deepen our love for one another?

So when we think of vision, we think of the picture of our marriage at a future time, complete with all the feelings, actions and love that would inhabit our partnership in deep and compelling ways.

Let's take a look at another way to bring this idea home.

The Miracle Question

We sometimes ask this question in counseling and coaching. Suppose you woke up tomorrow morning and your marriage had somehow completely developed in the way that you hope for. The changes are all encompassing, from how you manage money to the kind of sex life you share in the bedroom to how you talk and relate with energy and excitement each day.

What would that look like? What behaviors and changes would you see immediately? What would your loving behaviors look like? How would you talk to each other and how would you reach out and connect with your partner?

If you can begin to imagine what this looks like, you are on your way to defining the kind of marriage connection you truly want.

Throughout this chapter and at the end, you will have the opportunity to step into a process for identifying your vision for your life and marriage that will help you both determine points of agreement and where you might differ.

But know this. Without a specific idea of your mutual expectations and desires and an agreement to get there, with a true commitment to specific behaviors and a well-developed path to a deeper connection, it won't happen.

In fact, realistically, it can't happen without effort, design and a mutual commitment to create the marriage you both agree on and hope for.

. . . .

*Without a specific idea of your mutual
expectations and desires and an agreement
to get there, with a true commitment to
specific behaviors and a well-developed path
to a deeper connection, it won't happen.*

. . . .

Becoming Visionaries

Two lovers must think in terms of potential, possibilities and hope. We all need to continue to paint the picture of a brighter, more meaningful future. Otherwise, we cease to grow and become what God intended us to be.

Most marriages fail due to complacency, allowing the obstacles and circumstances of life to run the show. In a healthy marriage, two lovers need to dream together . . . about most everything, your love life, your kids, your communication, your spiritual lives, etc.

When we dream, we activate potential and kill complacency.

It is vital to develop an identity as a couple around the theme of keeping marriage alive by how you envision together – always mindful of creating love and passion and moving ahead toward a desired future. We never stop growing. Never!

Now that we have focused on the role of developing a clearer vision in our love partnership, we can get more specific about the next challenge – understanding and defining our capacity to grow into the vision we have identified.

Most marriages fail due to complacency, allowing the obstacles and circumstances of life to run the show. In a healthy marriage, two lovers need to dream together . . . about most everything, your love life, your kids, your communication, your spiritual lives, etc.

Capacity to Realize Our Dreams

Capacity to Grow

So our next principle focuses on a key dimension of potential – What capacity do you have as a couple to grow and expand what you have? In other words, what future relationship can you both reach for that comes from your desire, ability and potential to grow in your closeness, passion and love for each other?

You may be one of several kinds of couples reading this. You may, for example, be mature and wanting to build further on an already sturdy foundation. You may be a couple in conflict, ready for separation or simply apathetic. No matter where you find yourself, moving ahead into deep levels of satisfaction and connection means identifying and reaching a new potential in your future together.

The quality of your love life, sexual and otherwise, can expand and reach new levels of satisfaction and joy. Yet growth must occur for this to happen.

Think of building love into your relationship like training as an athlete. We have the potential to grow in our ability to accomplish a task or get better at a sport. But we often fail to think of love and affection developing in this way.

You can become a better lover and not just sexually. We can all grow in our ability to understand and express tenderness, care and affirmation in our love life. But as the athletic comparison suggests, it takes training and practice. We can't just *want* a better connection with our spouse. We have to *create* it and this often means learning how.

PA(II)SE *and* PONDER

❋ **How would I describe myself as a lover in my marriage? In and out of the bedroom?**

❋ **Do I have a picture of how I could become even more competent and effective in loving my spouse?**

❋ **What would be the areas of improvement and what exactly would I be doing differently as I grow in my capacity to connect with my partner?**

❋ **As a couple, what are our strengths in how we communicate care and tenderness? What more do we want in the future and what would this look like in our daily communication and how we reach out to each other? What key changes need to take place to get to the next level of passion and intimacy?**

Once you begin asking these kinds of questions, it becomes apparent that your beliefs, perspective and mindset play a significant role in establishing a desire to grow and change in life and marriage. Your "mindset" becomes a critical ingredient for growth and transformation. Let's take a closer look.

Mindset

Your potential to grow in your expression of love for one another, maybe even beyond your dreams, begins with a "growth" mindset. In other words, do you think of your life individually and as partners with transformation in mind?

Some people believe that love should just happen. It's the romantic thought of many that "If we really love each other, that alone will sustain us forever." This myth extends to life itself – that planning and developing intentional goals around growth and change aren't necessary.

We differ considerably and believe that we must be deliberate and focused on the prize to achieve lasting change. Our love relationships included.

PAUSE and PONDER

❊ **What do you believe about personal growth and change?**

❊ **Do you really believe that personal growth never stops throughout our lives?**

❊ **Do you believe in personal transformation and do you seek ways to promote that in your life?**

❊ **Have you developed a mindset about transformation that promotes habits and patterns that include personal insight and commitment to loving and living more effectively?**

❊ **Have you learned, as a couple, to dream together? Are you willing to begin a healthy process of looking ahead and identifying changes needed to create the marriage you most want?**

It is critical to begin to develop and commit to a mindset that prioritizes growth and change. Once we do, we can identify and focus on those principles that move us forward. That takes us to our dreams for a bigger, deeper connection of love and passion for each other.

Commitment to Wisdom and Truth

Once we establish a firm and consistent mindset centered on growth and transformation, we need to feed ourselves with the right truths; we ultimately need to seek out and surrender to principles outside ourselves that promote positive change.

For example, the principle of "honesty" and "transparency" in our communication with one another represents a vital principle for any healthy marriage. Without these components, your relationship will flounder. A commitment to openness in marriage represents a "truth" that isn't optional in building a passionate, intimate life together.

Another example would be "mutual respect." Without embracing one another respectfully, the quality of your marriage will struggle and most likely die. Violating this "truth" and the wisdom of applying this principle results in relationship disaster.

So a commitment to wisdom and truth takes us beyond our own ideas to a new realm of true relationship growth and health.

Many have defined these as spiritual in nature because they help us move ahead by adding power and depth to our lives by looking to higher sources for wisdom and power.

In other words, we don't make them up – they come from outside and feed our capacity to grow passionate love as we integrate them into our thinking and behavior patterns.

We want to be clear. True change happens because of applying principles and power beyond what our own human thoughts and emotions grasp. As couples hoping to create true passion and love for one another, we need to not only borrow from these truths, but turn them into our own personal source of power and wisdom to change and sometimes even heal.

We will explore this idea at length in our final chapter and attitude we call Awe.

> *True change happens when we apply principles and power beyond what our own human thoughts and emotions grasp. As couples hoping to create true passion and love for one another, we need to not only borrow from these truths, but turn them into our own personal source of power and wisdom to change and sometimes even heal.*

Two Perspectives

We have two ways of looking at our potential to grow as a result of commitment to wisdom and truth. First, we can identify principles drawn from truths that come from a higher source. Or second, we can look at concepts that focus on understanding the nature of wisdom revealed in Biblical truth. Let's look at each in turn.

External Sources of Wisdom and Truth

First, your marriage has the capacity to grow spiritually as you seek out divine truths and wisdom that may transcend your own limited understanding of love and relationships.

This involves recognition that to grow in our love for one another, we need to be "seekers" of information and principles that move us forward, that truly create love and passion.

We might, for example, read books on communication that focus on empathy – the willingness and ability to fully understand our spouse at all times. We would learn that, despite the kind of marriage we are hoping for, listening and truly understanding one another is a "truth" that no couple can circumvent as they seek to realize their potential together.

Ask yourselves a few key questions to get you thinking about this area of growth:

PA(II)SE *and* PONDER

❋ **Can you identity two principles, or truths, that every marriage needs to possess to build love and passion for one another?**

❋ **What three principles or values characterizing your marriage have helped you maintain your love for one another?**

Note that these significant growth concepts can be found in the writings of others who have explored key themes and reached conclusions you can trust. Ultimately, however, any real truth comes from God Himself.

Biblical Sources of Wisdom and Truth

Another way to pursue wisdom and truth involves a commitment to the divine revelation that comes from Scripture.

So, you might discover that God lovingly cares about His people, hopes that you will love each other in His strength and that this will involve the need to really understand one another and listen intently in the process of communication. In other words, empathy.

In this model, God is recognized as the source of all wisdom and truth and we are able to identify themes and principles that are taught in His Word that grow and shape our married life.

Our understanding of a God who embodies all truth and wisdom anchors us in how we interpret other writings, such as self-help books. The content would need to line up with God's Word because God is the source of all truth and wisdom and Biblical thought informs us of these principles.

Two significant questions would be:

PA◍SE *and* PONDER

❋ **How do you as a couple incorporate God's Word into your daily life and the decisions about what you want for your future together?**

❋ **Do you pray separately or together, seeking God's wisdom for how you get along and communicate love to each other?**

Summary

Our key point in all this centers on the need for all of us, in building our marriages, to identify and incorporate truths that stand on their own. They originate in higher sources than just our own sometimes limited perspectives.

Our final category centers on momentum – the energy couples must create and sustain to move toward a new day – to reach their potential to love each other passionately. We call it *urgency.*

Urgency

A sense of *urgency* or *desire* to love more deeply becomes a pivotal issue for true growth and change to occur. Urgency ensures moving ahead to a brighter future. We see so many couples who sit complacently and never reach for something more.

For some individuals, the sense of hope for newness has died and they have ceased believing in the possibility of real, lasting change. For others, they haven't had the tools or perspective about the need for change to drive them forward. Perhaps they have never learned how to set meaningful goals to intentionally carve out the life they desire.

Yet urgency, coupled with a strong belief that change is both possible and necessary, forms the cornerstone of realizing the real potential you have for a more positive, loving partnership.

Take some time now to look inside. Ponder some key questions that will give you a deeper look into your motivation, what you want and how important and urgent you feel about growth and change in your marriage. Share your thoughts on each of these questions with your mate.

PAUSE *and* PONDER

* **Can you imagine tapping into your desire for a new future in a way that creates momentum and promotes turning your vision into concrete goals?**
* **How motivated are you to live a different life, to have a vibrant, passionate marriage?**
* **What holds you back?**

One of the key ingredients of a meaningful relationship with God involves not only believing in His truths for life change, but also having a deep sense of urgency to advance spiritual principles into every area of our existence.

Final Thoughts

Potential involves the principle of change toward a desired future. As couples learning to love more deeply, we need to move forward with precision. Toward a future defined by passion and love, founded on the bedrock of truth.

We all have yet to reach our true potential to give and receive love. The journey lies ahead. The goal of creating a more meaningful, passionate married life as a reflection of our potential to rock each other's world should take center stage.

As we move ahead in the next 5 attitudes, we hope to more fully develop this theme as a vital ingredient of defining and moving toward your potential. We want you to create a love that is passionate, sustains itself in the storms and thrives beyond your imagination.

Now, let's look at our next attitude – *Presence.*

POTENTIAL
Review and Practice

Chapter Highlights

- Everyone's marriage has the potential to grow and blossom throughout a couple's life together. That full capacity for love and connection has only been partially reached. Or perhaps just begun.

- Clearly defining what we want that future to look like becomes imperative – otherwise we meander in life and we miss creating a chosen life.

- Potential encompasses what we think of as "vision." This centers on the need to cultivate a picture of what we want our love with our partner to look like, – involving all aspects of our marriage.

- It is vital that two people share deeply about what they want their marriage to look like. Begin to define the kind of love relationship you each want – what it would look like in terms of actual day-to-day behaviors, emotions, ways of relating and key patterns you share in how you communicate and reach out.

- Your potential to grow in your expression of love for one another – maybe even beyond your dreams – begins with a "growth" mindset. In other words, do you think of your life individually – and as partners – with transformation in mind?

- Once we establish a firm and consistent mindset centered on growth and transformation, we need to feed ourselves with the right truths. And so we ultimately must seek out and surrender to principles outside ourselves that promote positive change.

- A sense of urgency or desire to love more deeply becomes a pivotal issue for true growth and change to occur. Urgency ensures moving ahead to a brighter future. Otherwise, we sit in complacency and never reach for something more.

Exploring Together

- This week, spend time writing down the key ingredients of the marriage you want to grow into. Be specific, thorough and clear.

- Evaluate where you think you are in your marriage on each of these ingredients.

- What would it take to really grow into the vision you have for your love relationship?

- What challenges could get in the way of creating this vision for your marriage?

Enhancing Your Marriage

- Share your responses to the Wheel of Life exercise with each other. Discuss specific areas of growth as well as insights you gained about yourself and your hopes for the marriage.

- Develop a list of your top 2 or 3 goals for your marriage – areas that you hope to grow in the most over the next 6 months. Take a coffee break together this week and share these goals and dreams with your mate.

- Define how you would have to grow as a person to move toward these goals.

- What would you have to do as a couple to reach this vision?

- Ask how you can both support one another to reach these goals.

....

Pondering the Spiritual

- Do you believe God wants your marriage to thrive? And do you truly feel He will equip you both to make this happen, to help you create a vision for your marriage and reach it?

- Pray this week about your vision for your marriage. How can God help you move forward in your love for one another and help you both create the marriage of your dreams? What specific spiritual provisions does God bless us with to keep our focus on a better life? Include his Spirit, Word and how prayer influences direction and capability to achieve goals in our lives.

- What vision do you believe God has for your marriage? Include the kind of lifestyle you can create together, the love you share, the involvement you have with others who share your faith, and any other themes you feel honor God in the marriage relationship. Starting with 1 Corinthians 13, explore Scriptures you feel support the idea of a godly, God-honoring connection with your life partner.

- Pray with one another right now – asking God to honor your desire to build the kind of marriage that honors Him and expresses deep love for one another.

PRESENCE

What We Mean

IMAGINE FOR A moment that just by your very personality and character – your communication style, the ways you relate interpersonally, the insight and wisdom you bring into life, etc., – you have a high impact and influence on others. You make a big difference in their lives in positive ways.

In other words, people benefit from knowing you.

You are, at some level, a game changer in people's lives. You have the capacity to make others feel loved and valued by how you reach out to them and involve yourself in their worlds.

> *You are, at some level, a game changer in people's lives. You have the capacity to make others feel loved and valued by how you reach out to them and involve yourself in their worlds.*

With your spouse, you make them feel loved, prioritized and truly cared for. Because of the kind of person you have become, who you are and how you choose to bring love and passion into their lives – they are enriched.

At some tangible level, you "rock" their world and make a difference. We call this *presence*.

PA◍SE *and* PONDER

❋ Would I describe myself as someone who "makes a difference" in the life of my mate?

❋ Do I see myself as someone who has matured and reached a point in life at which I can influence others by the strength of my person and character?

❋ Am I influential as a person – in my most significant personal qualities – so that others benefit and feel impacted by knowing me?

❋ Do I work at growing the strength of my presence to love better and care more?

❋ Am I the kind of person capable of loving intensely and making my spouse feel valued and truly cared for?

These can be intimidating questions for all of us. But they are nevertheless vital to moving forward in our capacity to create a passionate love life with our partner.

What each of us have to offer – what we have deep inside that reflects our true potential to give love and bring passion into our partner's life – becomes one of the most important elements in building an exciting, dynamic loving partnership.

> Let us ask again, "Do you really know what you have to offer others and do you take action to impact lives by your presence and the power of your person?"

Every human being has the potential to dramatically impact another person by all the ways we love them; we can reach out to them and really shake up (in positive ways) their sense of being loved, valued and cared for, ultimately impacting their feelings of worth and self-esteem and even our own.

Have you uncovered that potential within yourself? Have you clearly unlocked the ingredients that provide personal power in loving your partner?

Understanding all the ways we can influence and empower each other as loving partners depends on knowing ourselves and growing in our capacity to love. It means finding ways to love more skillfully. It involves enhancing our desire to impact our partner's life – really tuning in and exercising those behaviors that reflect a strong presence and positive force in their world.

And it means becoming intentional in identifying and growing this kind of personal power in an effort to shape the love life we want most.

So our ongoing question for you and for your spouse becomes an encouragement to examine what kind of presence you bring into your married life and identifying where and how you need to grow. Let's take a closer look at what we mean by "presence."

Presence at its Best

We look at "presence" as the core of what defines you as a person, what you bring to the table in your marriage relationship in terms of your character, personality and capacity to give and receive love.

It includes the energy and emotions you bring into the here-and-now that are experienced by you and your loved one. As you show up for the relationship, the key becomes knowing and growing what you have to offer, to generate growth and aliveness in your loving bond together.

Simply put, "presence" is the "you" – your personality, strengths and weaknesses that contribute to the growth of marriage.

And we mean the real you – the hardcore inner strengths, your heart values and the actions you have cultivated as habits that reflect how you reach out in love and care to your partner.

I (Doug) had the privilege of working for Focus on the Family in their counseling department. I interacted occasionally with Dr. Dobson. He had a rich presence – warm, engaging and caring – much like he sounds on the radio.

His love for his wife was resounding and I believe God blessed his ministry as a result of the unique presence he brought into all his relationships.

. . . .

Simply put, "presence" is the "you" – your personality, strengths and weaknesses that contribute to the growth of marriage.

. . . .

I remember the first time I met Dr. Dobson, walking into his office on the third floor. His face and greeting were so warm I felt immediately at home. As he talked about ministry and the families and children that Focus on the Family tried to reach, his enthusiasm for life and helping others permeated the room.

Even his handshake and invitation to hear from us was so genuine that I'll never forget the experience. His smile and true desire to listen and know us was compelling. Dr. Dobson was a gifted man, anointed by God and he brought this warm presence into his whole life.

That I can still remember it today – 20 plus years later – speaks to the impact he had on my life.

Perhaps you can think of someone in your own history who gives you a personal example of the kind of presence you aspire to. Take a moment to reflect on that. Are you living that kind of presence with your spouse now?

Presence and Relationships

Relationally speaking, all of us are growing in our capacity to love and reach out to our mate. It is vital that we acknowledge our strengths, but also recognize any personal challenges we face in our abilities to care deeply and form deep attachments.

You will have an opportunity later to examine these personal strengths and challenges that you bring into your love life. But for a moment, reflect on your own relationship style and what you have to give your partner that creates love and value in this Pause and Ponder.

PAUSE *and* PONDER

❋ **What are your core strengths? (For example, I'm patient, loving, non-defensive, etc.)**

❋ **What issues get in the way of reaching out and loving your mate effectively? (Perhaps personal insecurities, not knowing how to reach out, defensiveness, etc.)**

We all have strengths and, yes, challenges that keep us from being fully engaged and present to impact our lives together. We all do. Each one of us needs to be honest about both our strengths and limitations in our capacity to love our partner.

Achieving the capacity to give and take in a relationship and to truly love each other requires that we build a life characterized by continued growth in our ability to give and receive love.

This capacity to love means we have become our own person. We become, or are becoming, who we were intended to be. In the field of psychology, we call this differentiation – a personal, emotional and psychological achievement that gives us a sense of wholeness apart from relationships and therefore a unique capacity to bring strength into the marital bond. It is coming into our own authentic individuality and realization of who we are deep in the center of our being.

Most of us, from time to time, wonder if we have truly grown up and are qualified to be successfully involved in a loving relationship.

· ·

Achieving the capacity to give and take in a relationship and truly love each other requires that we build a life characterized by continued growth in our ability to give and receive love.

· ·

We all need to honestly and accurately assess our level of maturity and what we need to do to love more consistently and with greater power and awareness. (See Appendix E "Have I Grown Up Assessment" for more ideas about this issue.) None of us have fully "arrived," so to speak, but we need to be in the process of growing for our relationships to also mature.

Spiritual Perspectives and God's Presence

So where do we get this idea about the importance of presence? From God.

Throughout history and today, God's involvement with His people includes His active presence and participation in their lives. We depend on knowing Him more and more deeply over time, who He is, what He stands for and how he loves us and others, to give our relationship with Him true meaning.

We often distort who God is and turn Him into an inaccurate version of what we think He is like. But overall, our spiritual growth depends on knowing Him more accurately and acting on that knowledge in our relationship with Him and those He entrusts to us.

Spiritual growth could, in some ways, be defined as a growing appreciation and integration of what we bring into our relationship with God and what He brings to us. Who we are and who God is becomes center stage in this growth process.

In addition, God equips us to grow and change in our "presence" with others. He influences us by His presence and power to become better people, to take on virtues such as love, joy, peace, long-suffering, patience, etc.

All these positive qualities represent God's work in our hearts and the transformation we have undergone and are undergoing that allows us to bring a brighter, more mature person into the world – and our love life.

He influences us by His presence and power to become better people, to take on virtues such as love, joy, peace, long-suffering, patience, etc.

Summary

Life represents an ongoing journey toward greater levels of authenticity and skill in making a difference in another's life. The quality of our presence – our person – becomes instrumental in achieving true intimacy.

There are three key themes or categories that allow us to better understand what is meant by presence and what it takes to grow and build our character and personal capacity to love more intimately.

We call these three the "Intimacy Triad." Let's take a closer look.

Presence and the Intimacy Triad

Ultimately, who you are matters – reflected in how others experience you and what powerful qualities you bring to the table to influence the caliber of life you share together.

We have developed what we call the "**Intimacy Triad**" – a key way of looking at this issue of personal growth and maturity.

These three key dimensions give us a paradigm of what it takes to grow personally and therefore, how to offer more in creating and sustaining a dynamic, successful marriage. These become foundational to all we discuss throughout the following pages.

Let's ask a few simple, yet powerful questions.

PAUSE *and* PONDER

* **Do you see yourself as someone who is becoming – someone trying to reach greater levels of depth and maturity in how you do life and relationships?**
* **Do you really value creating a deeper capacity to love others and make a positive impact in their lives?**
* **Do you believe God is working in your life to take you to new levels of transformation, impacting your ability to love, forgive and nurture your own person and relationships?**

One helpful way to look at personal growth and our commitment to develop a powerful presence in the life of our mate is to focus on three essential ingredients of the intimacy triad. These form a kind of map for how to think of your own level of personal maturity and capacity to really give in a love relationship.

These three are *personal awareness*, *the capacity to love* and *emotional maturity*.

As we walk with God and grow in His grace and the knowledge of His person, He touches all three of these. God is all about transforming our lives. He wants us to awaken to truth, love in mighty ways and grow in stature as His children.

In the next chapters, let's explore each of these three dimensions and absorb the reality that while we have a long way to go, God promises the grace and wisdom and power to move ahead. To become capable of great love and devotion to our life partner. To create a passionate bond with our mate that comes from personal strength and maturity.

We start with "Personal Awareness."

PRESENCE
Review and Practice

- We look at "presence" as the core of what defines you as a person, what you bring to the table in your marriage relationship in terms of your character, personality and capacity to give and receive love.

- "Presence" is the "you" – your personality, strengths and weaknesses that contribute to the growth of marriage.

- You are, at some level, a game changer in people's lives. You have the capacity to make others feel loved and valued by how you reach out to them and involve yourself in their worlds.

- With your spouse, you make them feel loved, prioritized and truly cared for. Because of the kind of person you have become, who you are and how you choose to bring love and passion into their lives – they are enriched.

- Understanding all the ways we can influence and empower each other as loving partners depends on knowing ourselves and growing in our capacity to love.

- All of us are growing in our capacity to love and reach out to our mate. It is vital that we acknowledge our strengths, but also recognize any personal challenges we face in our ability to care deeply and form deep attachments.

- God equips us to grow and change in our "presence" with others.

Exploring Together

- Do you see yourself as someone who loves effectively and deeply and touches the heart and soul of your mate?

- Who has most influenced you in your life and taught you what it means to love?

- In what ways do you see yourself growing in your capacity to love?

- At times, do you find it difficult to reach out in love? Can you identify some of your personal barriers to loving more consistently and tangibly?

Enhancing Your Marriage

- Make a list of 2 or 3 areas of personal strength – positive ways you reach out to your mate that come from who you are inside. Then, list 2 or 3 areas of growth – areas you want to improve in that would make you a better lover.

- Sit down with your spouse and share your list.

- Focus this week on one of these areas of growth, including how you reach out in this area to your mate.

Pondering the Spiritual

- When you think of presence, how do you relate this spiritually to your walk with God? Do you believe He wants you near, values your presence?

- When you think of spiritual growth, how does God empower us to love, to be more present and to grow in our capacity to connect with our mate?

- Pray this week about your strengths and weaknesses in your capacity to be present. Ask God to empower you to reach out and love more effectively and consistently.

- Do a personal study of John 15. How does "Abiding in the vine" inform us about the presence God wants us to have in our relationship with Him?

PERSONAL AWARENESS
– KNOWING OURSELVES
AND OUR MATE

General Thoughts

T HE RIGHT INFORMATION has the potential to create power in our lives. Imagine all the major decisions you make in life and ignoring the facts you need to make your best choices. If you're buying a car, for example, it pays to know market value, gas mileage and the price you should be paying.

And so it goes with our love life. We need to know the right information to give the kind of love that truly makes a difference. We need to embrace the facts and figures that teach us how to rock our lover's experience and infuse it with dynamic tenderness. A love that reaches out with the kind of quality stuff that touches the heart, bends the mind and endows the spirit with fire.

That means knowing ourselves and being aware of our feelings, thoughts, needs and wants. This sets the stage for a close, bonded relationship with our spouse. When we are aware of these parts of ourselves, it gives us a sense of who we are as individuals.

Our emotions, in particular, become part of the glue that binds us together; when we know and can share our feelings with our partner, we allow them to see who we are and what makes us "us." We must have a language that allows us to identify our emotions and a way to deeply share them with our mate to grow our love together.

Yet many people don't know how to identify and label their key emotions and feelings that come in many shades of mad, glad, sad and afraid. Most of us haven't practiced getting in touch with these key pieces of "information" and so we don't use them to relate and create understanding with our spouse.

And to be unaware means to be controlled by forces unknown, to surge ahead blindly, stumbling into the potential abyss of poor choices that don't build love and care and can in fact tear it down.

. . . .

We must have a language that allows us to identify our emotions and a way to deeply share them with our mate to grow our love together.

. . . .

In addition, our capacity to understand our emotions and reactions gives us insight into our partner's inner life as well. We can understand what they might be feeling and experiencing, what it is like to walk in their shoes. We call this empathy.

God, in fact, created us to be aware of our inner world of thoughts and emotions giving us the capacity to bond with our partner. Through thought and emotion, we draw close to God and those we love.

God's view of His relationship with His people centers on a kind of spiritual communion enabled by our capacity to know Him and experience Him from within. This connection with His being comes from how He has created us to feel, to experience emotion deeply and to use our thinking minds to know Him.

Too many people haven't learned how to know and trust their own feelings and emotions and, as a result, bring confusion into their love relationships. Many were not raised in families that taught how to appropriately express emotion or understand feelings. When we don't know how to value, attend to and express emotions, we can find it difficult to have empathy and understanding for our loved ones.

. . . .

Too many people haven't learned how to know and trust their own feelings and emotions and, as a result, bring confusion into their love relationships.

. . . .

Awareness of Ourselves and Our Partner

We used to watch the TV show, CSI. We enjoyed singing along with the song, "Who are you? Who? Who? Who? Who?" What a penetrating question. In this show, people reveal who they are by the nature of the crimes they commit. So it goes with love. We can be seen by our actions that say I value, love and adore you . . . actions that come from deep in the heart of a man or woman, generated from knowing ourselves and personal awareness.

> *So "who are you?" Do you really know yourself, your essence or core as a person and could you define this to someone else?*

Personal awareness means having clarity about who we really are, with our strengths and limitations. But it also means knowing who our partner really is – and *their* strengths and limitations.

In marriage, we can find ourselves hoping for a different version of the person we married and wanting to return to the fantasy version of the person we thought they were when we were first dating.

We need to grow out of this perspective of seeing ourselves and our partner through "rose- colored glasses" or an unrealistic lens. When we get to know ourselves and our loved one, we can gather a more accurate picture of who we are, how we love and what patterns we have developed that affect our key relationships.

It can be challenging to be real, to look at our own "good and bad" selves, but it far outweighs pretending, where no one feels known. It truly gives us the opportunity to have an honest and meaningful partnership with each other.

So the capacity to thoroughly know ourselves and our mate becomes essential. We all have strengths and weaknesses and being able to name our strong points and understand our limitations relationally has profound importance in developing a close, intimate marriage.

When we get to know ourselves and our loved one, we can gather a more accurate picture of who we are, how we love and what patterns we have developed that affect our key relationships.

Awareness and Your Body

Personal awareness extends to your body as well.

This may catch you off guard. We often think of personal awareness as extending to our thoughts and feelings but don't apply it to our bodies in a more thorough sense – knowing ourselves sensually and embracing our physical selves in all the ways God created us.

So, do you know your body?

Knowing what sensations and feelings you experience in your body and where, informs you about what causes you pleasure or discomfort or pain. When you become more aware of your body's experience, you are able to identify where you do and don't like to be touched, what feels good and what doesn't.

In the process, you gain a greater appreciation of how your body works, which can increase your confidence about your physical self. This insight can even improve your self-image. Knowing what brings you pleasure, and your willingness to identify blocks or inhibitions that get in the way of experiencing positive, bodily feelings, can also help you move toward a more open physical relationship with your spouse − and certainly a more intimate one.

So personal awareness is more than just identifying your inner emotions and thoughts − it also involves knowing your body and how to recognize physical sensations that bring pleasure to your life.

. . . .

When you know your body's experience, you are able to identify where you do and don't like to be touched, what feels good and what doesn't.

. . . .

Tim & Carol − Lessons on the Impact of Awareness

When Tim and Carol first came to see us, their marriage was in trouble. Their courtship had lasted almost two years, and included romantic getaways, a growing affection and what each thought of as a "deep" and certain love for each other.

The demands of raising a young family, financial concerns and three moves in the last six years created new pressure on this young couple. They found it increasingly difficult to talk about minor irritations and concerns. Both professionals, they invested more time in their careers than in building a more solid relationship. Both, in fact, felt "lost" as to how to create closeness; therefore, no real vision for the marriage had emerged.

Few conflicts arose while they were dating, and so Tim and Carol never developed a successful way of talking about their wants and needs and even their hopes for the relationship. They simply didn't have to, other than negotiating minor irritations and differences of opinion.

We asked each one what they most wanted from one another, what feelings they kept inside that they needed to share and how they nego- tiated hurts in the relationship before. Both indicated that they didn't really have too many conflicts in the first part of the relationship – and that they had never really discussed feeling "hurt" or asked each other what they wanted in terms of emotional comfort and care.

Our work with both of them centered on developing a language of "awareness" around what they were feeling and wanting from one another.

Both described their families of origin as guarded, where no one really talked much about needs and wants. They never learned to be aware of what they hoped for or how to talk about times when they felt hurt or neglected.

Tim's father was an alcoholic and his mother spent much effort trying to make sure his father was happy. C, and arol's family were missionaries who lived in zeal for their evangelistic work but didn't realize their children needed help expressing feelings and desires that came up in their development.

Tim put it this way, "I didn't think we really needed to talk about our feelings with one another. No one ever did that in my family and I thought a good relationship was one where you just know what the other person feels and needs."

Carol shared that, "I came from a Christian family and having conflict wasn't really all that acceptable. I used to cry at night when my feelings were hurt but never thought I could tell anyone. To say what I wanted and needed wasn't really OK for kids."

She further explained, "When Tim and I met, we got along so well. It was like we knew each other inside and out without having to say much of anything. So when I started to have hurts in the mar- riage, I didn't know what to do. It was kind of like crying by myself all over again. I wasn't supposed to be feeling these things and much of the time didn't really even know how to name the emotions I was experiencing."

So when Tim and Carol found each other, their initial years of dating seemed like heaven – little conflict and an increasing trust in one another that felt different than what they had experienced growing up. As Tim put it, "We thought we found in each other what we didn't get enough of growing up."

And perhaps, at some level, they did. Yet the growing demands of life created more need for skills that would capture their true feelings and needs for relational intimacy.

Because neither one had much experience labeling and identifying key feelings and needs, they ended up hoping the other would "naturally" know what the other one wanted. And so their worst nightmare ensued – feeling much like they did growing up, no one really knowing or finding out what thoughts and emotions or hurts seethed beneath the surface.

For both, learning the skills of identifying their basic needs for love, respect and attention created a new environment where love could grow and blossom. Their new attention to one another proved to be a powerful elixir for love to flourish.

Tim, for example, became increasingly aware of feelings of frustration and loneliness and times when he wondered if Carol really respected him. When feeling hurt or rejected, Tim practiced speaking up and telling his wife what he was experiencing. When he did this in a thoughtful, caring way, he was amazed at how she responded to him.

Carol also began experiencing her emotions more clearly and was able to begin identifying when she felt alone, abandoned or that Tim didn't seem to love her. When feeling these emotions, she started sharing them with Tim and he tried hard to hear her and listen carefully.

Both began creating a new type of dialogue together, filled with more specific emotions and the thoughts they were having about one another. Doing this in respectful, non-accusatory ways opened the door for greater mutual understanding and allowed trust to build!

We call this presence

> . . . *choosing to be fully involved with one another through sharing our deepest thoughts and feelings creates a kind of glue together . . . we stay informed about each other's wants and needs and so we grow closer.*

We bring an attitude of disclosure into each and every day – and even moment – of our lives together in which we tell one another what we want, where we hurt, and what we are feeling.

Love thrives when we strive to create a transparent and honest relationship and dies when we ignore, hide or deny our key needs with one another.

Yes, love can die, like an untended garden. At the same time, love can blossom and grow beyond our dreams with the right tools, heart and the choice to feed the marriage with energy and care.

For some, the challenge to explore their feelings brings up a lot of pain; it can become difficult to let go of anger and resentment and move forward. Yet for others, this opens the door to an expanded view of love and affection and two lovers can grow and deepen their love for one another in the process.

Awareness becomes the key. Without knowing what you feel and want, and without a willingness to express those very needs and emotions, love can never really blossom.

Love thrives when we strive to create
a transparent and honest relationship
and dies when we ignore, hide or deny
our key needs with one another.

Next, we want to explore one of the critical realities we need to be aware of and know about ourselves. All of us have a "bonding or attachment" style that determines the unique way we form loving relationships. In other words, you have a behavioral pattern or style that becomes a key ingredient in the personality of your love relationship. In the next chapter, we'll take a closer look.

PRESENCE &
PERSONAL AWARENESS
Review and Practice

- We need to have the right information to give the kind of love that truly makes a difference. That means knowing ourselves and being aware of our feelings, thoughts, needs and wants. This sets the stage for a close, bonded relationship with our spouse.

- Personal awareness means having clarity about who we really arc, – with our strengths and limitations. But it also means knowing who our partner really is – and their strengths and limitations.

- Choosing to be fully involved with one another through sharing our deepest thoughts and feelings creates a kind of glue together. . . we stay informed about each other's wants and needs and so we grow closer.

- To be unaware means to be controlled by forces unknown, to surge ahead blindly, stumbling into the potential abyss of poor choices that don't build love and care and can in fact tear it down.

- It can be challenging to be real, to look at our own "good and bad," but it far outweighs pretending where no one feels known.

- For some, the challenge to explore their feelings brings up too much pain and it becomes difficult to move forward and let go of anger and resentment. Yet for others, this opens the door to an expanded view of love and affection that allows two lovers to grow and deepen their love for one another in the process.

• Personal awareness extends to your body as well. We often think of personal awareness extending to our thoughts and feelings but don't apply it to our bodies in a more thorough sense – knowing ourselves sensually and embracing our physical self in all the ways God created us.

• We look at "presence" as the core of what defines you as a person, what you bring to the table in your marriage relationship in terms of your character, personality and capacity to give and receive love.

Exploring Together

• Do you see yourself as someone who is aware of your feelings and emotions?

• Do you find it difficult to share your feelings and wants with your lover? What gets in the way?

• Do you see feelings and emotions as unnecessary or vital pieces of information to share with your mate?

• Are you able to identify body sensations and do they give you information about what you are feeling and experiencing?

• Are you willing to become more aware of what you want, think and feel in your marriage?

Enhancing Your Marriage

• Take time and write down your personal commitment to identifying and sharing feelings in your marriage. Discuss your commitment with each other and why you feel this is important. Start a journal and record your feelings if you like.

• This week, wear a ribbon or bracelet on your wrist to remind yourself to tune into your feelings by asking yourself the question, "What am I feeling right now?" Use sensations in your body to help you discover what you are feeling as well. Do this as often as you can. At the end of the week, sit down with each other and share what you learned.

• Identify 2 or 3 times this week where you have had positive feelings toward your mate. Share those with each other.

Pondering the Spiritual

• Are you able to share your feelings with God? Do you believe He cares about what you think and feel? Read Hebrews 4:16. Reflect on what God hopes we will share with Him regularly. Do you believe this includes all our experiences, wants, needs and emotions?

• What do you believe God intends for us to do with our awareness of our thoughts, feelings and needs in marriage? Do you believe God created us to have these experiences in order to grow our love for one another? How does this work?

• Read Psalm 139:13-16. We are created in the image of God. Spend time praising Him this week for how we are

made. Acknowledge the way He has made us to know
Him and each other through our emotional world and
thought life!

PERSONAL AWARENESS –
OUR BONDING STYLES

Attachment – The Glue that Binds Us

YOU ARE IN a *relationship* with your spouse. Something binds you together as lovers, friends and companions and for some, soul mates. You are "attached" to each other.

Being attached to our lover, our life partner, is a good thing – assuming the bond is a healthy one. Part of "healthy" means we don't lose our individuality, our uniqueness and our personality in the process.

But what exactly do we mean by "attachment," by being "bonded" to another – our spouse.

For a moment, think of "glue." Glue or Velcro binds non-living substances together. The right glue, applied in the correct way and in the proper quantity, results in connection, unity and attachment. The stronger the glue, the tighter the hold.

And there are different kinds. Some glues work OK, but don't really stick. Others "stick" but you can't separate what you joined together. And some are just plain messy.

Relationships are no different. We need to think about how we discover, apply and sustain the right glue in our love relationships in order to insure that we create a loving, trusting bond together. One that works, allows for love to flourish and two partners to grow as individuals.

What this binding substance consists of and where it comes from becomes center stage in properly explaining the way two lovers in marriage unite. And more importantly, how they create lasting passion and intimacy in and out of the bedroom.

Let's take a closer look at the rich meaning behind this concept and examine your own bonding capacity and style.

We need to think about how we discover, apply and sustain the right glue in our love relationships in order to insure that we create a loving, trusting bond together.

The Story Behind Intimacy and Attachment Styles

If we remember what we experienced in our earliest days of childhood, it will help us understand the patterns we bring into our love relationships. Yes, we bring in patterns. A style. A way of connecting to our lover, ingrained over the years, aged like a fine wine.

We bring in a capacity to love and bond with another human being – forged through past and current experiences. In other words, how we love and what we experience in love with another has been dramatically shaped early in life into patterns we call our bonding style.

All of us have some kind of bonding pattern – the style of how we relate to others, particularly in our love relationships.

In the earliest chapters of our life, we are dependent on our caretakers for love, security and belonging. From these experiences, our type of "glue" is set. It is vital that we understand how we have been shaped by our journey, starting young and ending at today. We bring these early experiences, and later ones that build on them, into significant patterns that reflect our capacity to give and receive love. How well we bond.

. . . .

It is vital that we understand how we have been shaped by our journey, starting young and ending at today.

. . . .

A Closer Look

As children, getting our basic needs for love and attention met become as important as the air we breathe. We are wholly reliant and dependent on our parents to take care of us, to demonstrate love and affection and to make us feel valued and protected.

For those of us who have had our basic needs satisfied, the results are profound. We have a deep appreciation for our own worth and identity. In addition, we develop a basic sense of trust in others and an ability to develop meaningful relationships involving intimacy and connection with our spouse and other loved ones.

So imagine yourself as a child for a moment. You are full of life, feelings and impulses. If your parents embrace and love you, with all your new emerging thoughts and emotions, you develop a deep sense of trust in others and also yourself.

If your parents are sufficiently threatened, angered, or anxious about your emerging bundle of feelings, something happens inside of you to cope with their reactions. You will learn to do one or all of the following: disown your own emotional world, deny your needs for love and attention, withdraw into fantasies that preoccupy your life, hate yourself, or a host of other possibilities.

More importantly, you will develop core beliefs about your worth, perhaps negative ones, and struggle with knowing whether or not you can get your needs met in your key love attachments. "After all," you think, "if my parents couldn't accept and value my emotional world, I can't either – and probably no one else will." And you will not have learned how to love another human being because that starts with yourself.

All these early childhood experiences create what some researches call an "imprint" or set of internal expectations about what happens in our most significant relationships. We develop a set of beliefs about ourselves and expectations about what will happen with our spouse or partner in life. These are core beliefs that tell us what to expect in terms of getting and receiving love from others.

This "imprint" we develop in childhood forms a relationship pattern that we call our "bonding" or "attachment" style. This can be best thought of as your unique capacity to provide healthy and meaningful "glue" to the lover you have chosen to marry.

All these early childhood experiences create what some researches call an "imprint" or set of internal expectations about what happens in our most significant relationships. This "imprint" we develop in childhood forms a relationship pattern that we call our "bonding" or "attachment" style.

How We Attach – Personal Patterns that Define Us

And so each of us has a distinctive approach that guides us in our attempts to form intimate attachments. In practical terms, this individual "style" can be defined as the kind of "connection" you look for in your marriage or key significant relationships – and also the kind of connection you are capable of entering into based on your life experiences.

Interestingly, how we bond can radically affect the kind of closeness we seek with God and the ongoing spiritual connection with Him we look for through all the experiences of life. God seeks an abiding, strong bond with each of His children. When we come from a place of personal hurt and woundedness in our bonding history, it can dramatically affect what we expect of God, how we see Him, and how we seek after His person.

God takes us as we are and longs to be the healer and transformer of our pain. Understanding how we bond can help shape a path toward greater personal intimacy with our maker. Such is spiritual growth at its best.

> *In practical terms, this individual "style" can be defined as the kind of "connection" you look for in your marriage or key significant relationships – and also the kind of connection you are capable of entering into based on life.*

Ultimately, healthy "intimacy" doesn't happen by accident. It grows over time as we mature and develop. But the "style" we bring into our adult life defines how we behave and how we attempt to be close to another. It is vital that we understand our unique style as a starting point for further growth and change.

Let's take a closer look at the four bonding styles and how they affect our connection with our mate.

The Four Intimacy Styles

As we explore these together, look for yourself in each style.

How do you attach? What bonding patterns characterize you and the kind of glue you bring into your love life?

So, you have a style. Maybe you never thought of it that way, but you do. A – a relationship style forged out of the bedrock of early childhood experiences and reinforced by later relationships and events in your history. What's yours?

Let's take a closer look at each style. Remember that most researchers agree that there are four key styles. Most likely our key love relationships reflect one of these themes.

Below is a description of each intimacy style: The Secure Style, The Avoidant Style, The Insecure Style and the Disorganized or Chaotic Style.

The Secure Style

This individual has established consistent patterns of mutually satisfying relationships in their marriage or key relationships. There are typical ups and downs but overall, this person feels a sense of satisfaction, safety and growth with their partner that is consistent and predictable.

This person tends to come from a home characterized by warmth, consistent positive connection, healthy involvement and affection and likely feels a deep sense of self-worth and trusts their partner.

When two people in marriage bring a secure style into the relationship, they create a strong bond based on mutual trust, ability to communicate effectively, and resolve conflict without wounding one another. When hurt, they seek to understand, reach out and forgive. Anger is handled quickly and resolving disagreements paves the way for greater closeness and affection.

This person likely feels a deep sense of self-worth and trusts their partner, and tends to come from a home characterized by warmth, consistent positive connection, healthy involvement and affection.

PA(II)SE *and* PONDER

* ❋ Do you tend to form love relationships that are lasting, built on trust and stability?
* ❋ Do you enter your love relationships with a solid sense of self-worth, confidence and trust that love can flourish?
* ❋ Is your bond with your partner characterized by mutual trust, ability to communicate effectively and capacity to resolve conflicts successfully?
* ❋ Has your love for one another grown consistently over the months and years?

The Avoidant Style

With this style, relationship struggles tend to be based on the need to "avoid" the feelings and emotions generated in the marriage or partnership. Being avoidant means that while seeking close relationships in life, the person struggles with closeness and demonstrates a felt need to detach from others.

Most often, these individuals come from families where "distance" characterized the way their parents connected with each other and their children and where feelings were either unacknowledged or "swept under the rug."

A person bringing this style into the marriage is often seen as "strong" early on in the dating or marital experience. But down the road, what gets exposed is someone who struggles to know themselves and their own needs, denies those needs and so frequently doesn't see or understand the personal wants in their spouse.

They appear difficult to reach and their spouse often wants more than they are getting in terms of closeness and emotional warmth and expression.

PAUSE and PONDER

* **Do you tend to avoid feelings in your love life?**
* **Do you often find yourself detaching from your partner, withdrawing and avoiding conflict?**
* **Do you struggle sharing your wants and needs and instead tend to ignore them or sweep them under the rug?**

The Insecure Style

This person has established consistent patterns of ambivalence, anxiety and/or anger in their key relationships. Often, these individuals seek high levels of intimacy, acceptance and involvement from their spouses and are often preoccupied with the availability of their mate.

Relationship struggles tend to be based on their uncertainty about the bond they have with their lover. In other words, trust, consistency and belief in their own ability to be loved and the availability of their partner has somehow been compromised.

We find several unique styles – or subsets – in the insecure style. Each has a distinctive flavor with challenges particular to that style. These are the angry, the anxious and the invisible style.

The Angry Style

This individual has experienced and developed significant ups and downs in their key love relationships. This includes strong feelings of warmth but those feelings may be interspersed with anger and concern over whether their partner is really there for them or not.

This intimacy pattern often involves intense feelings of closeness, followed by frustration and desire to get away from their partners. The emotional connection, vacillating between comfort and anger, closeness and distance, often results in moods and behavior that can be quite unpredictable and intense.

This individual has experienced and developed significant ups and downs in their key, love relationships. This includes strong feelings of warmth but interspersed with anger and concern over the availability of their partner.

In childhood, receiving love and affection was often unpredictable for individuals with an angry style. Love may be there one moment but gone the next. Hence, the positive feelings of dependency are founded on a bedrock of uncertainty. With the feeling or belief that disconnection is inevitable and closeness doesn't really last.

This temporary nature of closeness and distance in childhood creates anger and the child feels helpless to resolve such conflicting emotional states.

The Anxious Style

This style holds a great deal of similarity to the angry style but relationship struggles tend to exhibit more anxiety around the temporary nature of love in the home, rather than anger.

What we often see with this style is ambivalence about the availability of a caregiver to really love them, which has carried into adulthood. Fear tends to surround relationships, with ongoing concern and anxiety about the other person's love for them.

The Invisible Style

A common offshoot of this style focuses on the individual who typically seeks to meet the needs of his or her partner, but not their own. They become "people pleasers." How others feel and what they want dominates this intimacy pattern. They take their anxiety about losing the love in the relationship and try endlessly to please their partner, hoping to keep their love. There may be significant relational needs that are denied, in favor of what their partner wants, and the relationship can be very "one-sided."

These individuals often experienced homes where they needed to meet the needs of their parents, rather than the other way around. Becoming "people pleasers" helped them cope and deal with their parents and also gave them a way, however ineffective, to get their own needs met.

> *There may be significant relational needs that are denied — in favor of what their partner wants, and the relationship can be very "one-sided."*

PA(II)SE *and* PONDER

* Do you find yourself "preoccupied" with how available or loving your spouse is?

* Do you consistently get angry or anxious because your spouse doesn't seem to care or to reach out to you?

* Do you often wonder if your spouse really loves you?

* Do you frequently feel like you sacrifice your own needs to meet those of your mate?

* Are you afraid to share your own wants and needs in the marriage and prefer to ignore them or sweep them under the rug?

The Disorganized or Chaotic Style

These individuals lack a unified, coherent style of attaching to others. They often feel "chaotic" inside and lack the experience of safety and comfort that are characteristic of more predictable, secure attachments to others. Hence, the pattern here involves significant anxiety and fear and confusion in relationships.

Some with this pattern attempt to control others in their love relationships. Others end up feeling victimized by their loved ones. Childhood may have been marked by parental unavailability and/or instability or abuse.

You may have been able to identify your "Intimacy Style" by the descriptions provided. However, if you would like extra help, fill out the "What's My Intimacy Style?" quiz in Appendix B.

What It All Means

Once we have an understanding of our intimacy styles, we can begin to appreciate how this drives us in trying to develop intimate attachments with our spouse or partner.

If, for example, we have a pattern of relationship behaviors characteristic of a "Secure Style," it has different implications than if we are "Insecure."

More specifically, those seeking intimacy whose "imprint" represents a particular style tend to attach themselves in ways characteristic of that pattern.

If your imprint, for example, is avoidant, you will seek a relationship with others but are likely to be distant in how you relate to that person. Often, a spouse will see this as strength, only to learn later in the marriage that the "avoidant" person is really unavailable to meet their needs. After all, they can only get so close and can't tolerate the affection and emotion that are needed in effective interpersonal life.

. . . .

More specifically, those seeking intimacy whose "imprint" represents a particular style tend to attach themselves in ways characteristic of that pattern.

. . . .

If, on the other hand, you are an "insecure" person in your marriage, you will have a style by which you are more preoccupied with the availability of your spouse. When you draw near, however, you may eventually withdraw and experience emptiness or anger. These emotional ups and downs begin to characterize your intimacy style and you will have few "stable" relationships in which getting and receiving love become predictable and satisfying.

If your basic imprint is "invisible," you likely spend most of your time trying to establish intimacy by pleasing the other person – by meeting their needs and paying little attention to your own. There is not much give and take, because your focus is on someone else's world.

If your style is more "disorganized," you have likely found yourself a victim in abusive relationships or perhaps being controlling in your interpersonal style. The disorganized person often has few meaningful relationships where love is experienced and given freely. Rather, you have probably come from an injured place in childhood. As a result, you bring those injuries into your intimacy style in a way that can bring chaos and unpredictability for you and your spouse.

So, what's your style and how do you see your own patterns playing out in your marriage?

Identifying your bonding style will help create a better understanding of what role you play in the relationship you have with your lover. This allows you to be more effective and to make changes if needed, and opens up a dialogue with your mate about some of the key ingredients that make up the personality of your love life.

The story of John and Katie – When the Avoidant and Insecure Styles Collide

And what a story this is. When they first came to see us, John and Katie were in turmoil. After 5 short years of marriage, Katie was ready to leave and John felt he couldn't do anything to stop her.

Simply stated, she wanted more. Over the last few years, Katie told us she had been "crying out" for more affection, care and involvement from John. After all, he had been so attentive in the early years of their dating relationship and even marriage. Now she expected the same but her experience was that John had changed.

John, on the other hand, told us he kept trying but couldn't seem to please her. He stated he loved her and didn't want the marriage to end but felt confused, angry himself and couldn't figure out why his wife was so unhappy.

Katie came from a home of six children. She is a middle child and explained that she never felt much attention come her way. Her parents were busy trying to care for all the kids and didn't have enough time or attention to go around. She described her early life experiences as feeling alone and unloved.

Her mom was caring, but seldom available and her dad spent most of his time at work. She wondered, even as a child, if she was really loved and, in adolescence, began dating, hoping for attention and focused on whether the boys loved her and would want her or dump her.

John, on the other hand, came from a home where feelings weren't ever validated or discussed. As the oldest of two, he felt he was expected to get good grades and to never rock the boat. He thought his parents loved him, but they didn't show much affection for him, for his younger brother or for each other in the marriage.

John learned that feelings weren't important and even when he felt hurt, he would never talk about this and would go on without resolution. His dad was busy with work, attended his sports events but seldom hugged him. His mom was less distant but didn't encourage him to express emotions and never asked how he was doing. John learned to ignore and even discount his own emotional experiences.

So Katie's wants and needs were foreign to John. After all, he was home and felt he was available, but didn't really understand feelings and wants and needs. He spent most of his life denying his own wants and so had trouble understanding what others need and what it meant to be emotionally available.

Katie, on the other hand, longed for someone to love her and be present and attend to her feelings and hurts. Over time, she became preoccupied with whether John loved her and if he could ever understand her and meet her needs for love and attention.

The pattern we see here is not uncommon. John's "avoidant" style collides with Katie's need for love and attention. Her "insecure" style causes her to focus on John's emotional and physical availability. In other words, is he truly present and will he love me?

Early in the relationship, John appeared strong and Katie interpreted his demeanor as a sign of stability and availability – only to discover that John has significant difficulty understanding what it means to be fully present, loving and emotionally connected in a love relationship.

John believes he is "available" and wonders why his wife is unhappy with him. After all, he hasn't changed much and, all of a sudden, he isn't enough for her. John learned early on to distance himself from his own emotions and so being empathic with his wife presents a real challenge.

As we identified their bonding style, both were able to recognize the kind of interpersonal dynamics and hopes they brought into marriage. Katie wanted constant reassurance of love. John wanted respect and acceptance without emotional investment.

Both began to challenge their assumptions about love and were increasingly able to develop realistic ways of working on their own limitations. John acknowledged his avoidance of emotion, including his own, and started learning about wants and needs and the feelings that accompany them.

Katie learned to have patience with John and how to improve her ability to ask for what she needed without heightened expectations about what her lover could provide. She became more accepting and less preoccupied with John's ability to love and accepted his slower learning curve in reaching out to her – without interpreting this as being unloved and uncared for.

Once they identified and understood their bonding styles, both John and Katie made several commitments to personal change. Some of the decisions they made to restore their love for one another went as follows:

John

- Begin trying to understand his own feelings, wants and needs without distancing himself from his own experience.

- Learn what Katie wants and needs. Explore how she feels. Respond to her needs with feeling and warmth.

- Take specific steps to ask how Katie is doing, what she needs from him and express care and concern.

- Respond positively to her requests for affection and holding.

- Develop his own personal plan for how to love and reach out to his wife. Select behaviors to initiate, such as more touch, asking how she's doing, practice listening to her feelings when she needs to talk, etc.

Katie

- Have patience with her husband as he learns the language of feelings and how to get in touch with his own emotions and hers.

- Try not to interpret his distance as lack of love for her.

- Clearly state what she wants and needs without pressuring John.

- Find out what he wants and needs in the relationship. Wait patiently as he tries to convey his thoughts, emotions and needs to her.

- Personally acknowledge when she is getting "preoccupied" with whether John loves her. Find gentle, healthy ways to communicate her anxiety to him.

- Learn to trust that he is growing without panicking about his availability.

Over time, both learned to work on their own attachment style. Katie committed to developing greater trust, to not rely on her own anxiety in her understanding of whether John truly loves her or not. John worked hard on his own "avoidant" style. He became much more responsive to his own feelings and needs by practicing self-awareness and asking his wife to share with him her feelings about the relationship.

Conclusion

So where do you fall in terms of your hopes and expectations about love from your partner? How do you seek out reassurance and connection from each other? What balance or challenges may reflect a bonding style different from one another and what growth do you each need to learn more about in order to connect in better, more fulfilling ways?

As you grow in your understanding of intimacy and what makes it amazing, we truly believe you can answer these questions with greater clarity and focus. And you can commit to realistic ways of growing your capacity to bond, connect and be an effective lover in your marriage relationship.

We desperately need to connect with each other in ways that produce amazing results – love unimaginable and sustainable over years of mutual enjoyment. How we bond gives us clues to the real magic God created in securing two people together for life.

PRESENCE AND BONDING –
END OF CHAPTER EXERCISE

What We've Learned About Bonding Styles

- You are in a *relationship* with your spouse. Something binds you together as lovers, friends and companions. You are "attached" to each other.

- Glue or Velcro binds non-living substances together. We need to think about how we discover, apply and sustain the right glue in our love relationships in order to insure that we create a loving, trusting bond together.

- How we love and what we experience in love with another has been shaped early in life into patterns we call our bonding style.

- This individual "style" can be defined as the kind of "connection" you look for in your marriage or key significant relationships – and also the kind of connection you are capable of entering into based on life experiences.

- It is vital that we understand our unique style in order to grow and change.

- If your bonding style is **"secure,"** you will have established consistent patterns of mutually satisfying relationships in your marriage. You have a positive self-concept and are capable of trusting others. When two people in marriage bring a secure style into the relationship, they create a strong bond of mutual trust, effective communication and ability to resolve conflict without wounding one another.

- With the **"avoidant"** bonding style, there is a struggle with closeness and a need to detach from others. Often these individuals come from families where "distance" was the way their parents connected with each other and their children and where feelings were unacknowledged or "swept under the rug."

- With the **"insecure"** bonding style, a person has established consistent patterns of ambivalence, anxiety and/or anger in their key relationships. Often, these individuals seek high levels of intimacy, acceptance and involvement from their spouses and are often preoccupied with the availability of their mate.

- With the **insecure/angry style,** there are strong feelings of warmth but they are interspersed with anger and concern over the availability of their partner.

- With the **insecure/anxious style,** we often see ambivalence about the availability of a caregiver to really love them.

- With the **insecure/invisible style,** there may be significant personal needs in the relationship that are denied – in favor of what their partner wants and asks for.

- With the **"disorganized"** bonding style, there is a lack of a unified, coherent style of attaching to others.

Exploring Together

- Describe, in your own words, your bonding style. What childhood experiences have shaped your bonding style?

- Take a piece of paper and write down your bonding style. Identify several ways this style has impacted your marriage over the months and years. Include strengths and challenges.

- How does knowing your style help you understand how to love and be loved more effectively?

- Identify several ways you want to enhance your way of attaching to your mate, including positive areas you already enjoy.

Enhancing Your Marriage

- This week, pick one of the ways of attaching to your mate mentioned above. Make a purposeful attempt to practice this with your partner. Check in with each other to see if they noticed.

- Take time to sit down with each other in a relaxed environment and celebrate all the ways you love each other. Write them out together. Give each other "high fives" for loving each other.

Pondering the Spiritual

- How we bond can radically affect the kind of closeness we seek with God. Evaluate the kind of relationship you have with Him in light of your understanding of your own bonding style.

- God seeks an abiding, strong bond with each of His children. How do you want to grow in your closeness with Him? What steps do you need to take to make this growth happen?

- Experiences from the past can keep us from connecting, bonding and loving in healthy ways. How does God seek

to provide healing when we have wounds from our past
that keep us from attaching and loving with trust and
security?

Our next leg of the stool in our Intimacy Triad involves our capacity
to love another human being. Obviously, the greater our innate, learned
and God-given capability to reach out and love another, the stronger
our bond with our partner becomes. Let's look more closely at this key
factor in marriage success.

OUR CAPACITY TO LOVE

Ingredients of Loving Our Partner

WE BEGIN THIS chapter with some key questions for you to ask yourself:

PAUSE *and* PONDER

❋ **"How would I assess my ability or capacity to love?"**
❋ **"Am I a loving person to my spouse?"**
❋ **"How does he or she know I love them? What proof do I offer through my actions and how I involve myself in his or her life?"**

Every person has a certain capacity to love another human being that can be strengthened and enlarged. Remember from our last chapter that our ability to love has been shaped by all of our life experiences, including (and some psychotherapists would say "especially") those in childhood.

Simply stated, if we were loved and affirmed deeply as children for the unique person we are, and if subsequent love relationships nurtured that same experience, our capacity to love grows and flourishes. We know how to love based on our early experiences of being loved and by later ones in other caring relationships. We can love because we were first loved.

On the other hand, if our personal experiences in relationships were filled with an absence or lack of love and affirmation, or even harm, we develop wounds and emotional scars and a tendency to self-protect and hide ourselves from others. Thus affecting our future love relationships. This often results in repeated attempts to heal our hurts with another person, hoping they will be able to repair what happened in our past.

We can love because we were first loved.

So let's get really honest. For most of us, the ability to experience and express love is a growth issue. We simply haven't fully developed this vital element of ourselves.

Your Definition of Love

Your definition of love and how you honestly assess yourself as a loving human being becomes critical at this point.

The capacity to love is created over time and must be cultivated and grown.

> *Love brings energy into the relationship, a kind of magnet that draws two people together. We need to understand love has many dimensions and be willing to develop and implement each one with our partner.*

Here are some ways of looking at "love" and evaluating where we stand on these key points.

Love:

Means cultivating a desire and habit of reaching out to our spouse with affection, respect and understanding.

Sets aside time with the one we love.

Involves the desire to know someone deeply and not just superficially.

Carries with it the experience of knowing, respecting and valuing ourselves.

Means choosing to reach out, to be involved with our partner, to care about how they are doing and finding ways to let them know this.

Conveys the perspective that we cherish our mate.

Brings fondness into the relationship.

Means honoring our spouse for their uniqueness and inner strength and personality.

Involves forgiving our partner for past and present hurts.

Means being spiritually and emotionally present.

PA◍SE *and* PONDER

* Spend some time reflecting on the above statements about love. How do you feel about each one?
* Do they describe your loving style?
* To what extent does each one represent an area of growth?

If it looks like love is a tall order, you are right. But a proper and growing understanding of love, a deep appreciation for all the ways we can reach out and bring love into our partner's life, and a solid commitment to love effectively is vital. And results in a dynamic, thriving marriage.

> *We must love and we must love well, with all our heart and effort. So defining the ingredients of "love" becomes essential. We encourage you to create your own "love is" list or add to the one above. Operationalize*

them and create habits of love that characterize how you reach out and touch your lover.

Communication

Loving and learning to love intentionally involves another key dimension and set of skills we call "communication." One way of operationalizing love. Love has to be translated into action. It must be communicated to the one we share our love life with – and effectively.

There are several essential elements of communication that we can grow in and integrate in how we reach out to our mate.

It is vital to look at communication through two distinct lenses. One focuses on your heart – the attitude and care and even tenderness you bring into your lover's life. We call these "heart conditions." The second centers on actual, specific communication skills.

. . . .

Love has to be translated into action. It must be communicated to the one we share our love life with – and effectively.

. . . .

All the communication skills in the world will not help if our hearts are cold and in an unloving place. On the other hand, having the right "heart," without knowing how to listen, speak clearly and utilize other key interpersonal techniques, dilutes our warmth and the care we are trying to convey. We will first look at the heart.

Heart Conditions

We want to focus on your heart – what you bring into your own life and that of your partner's that reflects deep, underlying beliefs about the worth and value of the person you married. All communication skills come up void or anemic apart from these heart conditions. And so they come first. More specific communication skills flow out of these heart conditions, which we will address later.

When we look at the heart, we are talking about the inner conditions of your life that allow you to reach out and shape each and every relationship you find yourself in.

Note that we call them conditions. We do this to emphasize that each of us has a heart with a certain condition, almost like the physical condition of the body. This implies, of course, that we can influence that condition and grow and enlarge our heart and therefore the kind of love we bring into the life of our partner and ourselves.

Think of these four heart conditions as legs of a table. Each one adds to our capacity to love and care deeply for our mate. In addition, they set the stage for a secure, sexual bond that allows for maximum enjoyment and energy. Indeed, they hold up the table and feed positive intimacy – in and out of the bedroom. Let's look at each one in turn.

Compassion

The bedrock of a thriving marriage comes from a heart of compassion for one another. The capacity for compassion comes from a belief that human beings are vulnerable and that our partner needs our grace and a tenderness that acknowledges the rigors of life, as well as our support and help to navigate life's demands and challenges.

Compassion has to do with an attitude of acceptance of your partner and, ultimately, yourself. Accepting one another, complete with flaws and limitations, becomes an essential element of mutual love and care.

John & Carrie – Lessons on the Impact of Compassion

When John & Carrie came to see us, they had been married about 15 years. They described their relationship as "hostile" and "conflicted." At the same time, they elaborated on the deep connection they had when they first married – and even the love they still experienced despite their growing distance.

Both described their lives as stressful, with job uncertainties and the challenge of raising an 11 year-old boy with ADHD. John and

Carrie were really struggling over the sometimes complex circumstances of life.

John complained that Carrie had distanced herself from him over the years. He had become jealous of her connection with their son and all the effort she put into that relationship. He loved his son too, but felt she had turned to their child with her energy and emotions, rather than the marriage.

Carrie agreed that she had withdrawn, but said that she had given up hope for a more supportive husband. At one point she exclaimed, "All he wants is sex — then everything would be OK."

Over time, the distance between them had resulted in a growing resentment toward each other, with intermittent times where they would connect and move forward. Yet even these positive times were eclipsed by their continually growing anger.

Neither partner wanted to give in and look at their part. Both looked at the relationship from the perspective of hurt and frustration — not what they could build together.

We remember distinctly, during one of our first sessions, John reaching out to Carrie in an unusual act of love and care. He grabbed her hand and, with a tear rolling down his cheek, told her how sorry he was for the tremendous pressures she was experiencing and that he was beginning to realize her need for support and encouragement.

That gesture opened the door for something dramatic in their subsequent sessions with us. It truly unlocked compassion between them and Carrie's very real sense that John cared about her and understood her hurt and struggles.

We explored the many dimensions of compassion over the next several weeks and found that their bond and love for one another resurfaced. Before long, they were flying on their own. Each began reaching out to the other with gestures of care and support, unlocking a vast reservoir of connection and bond in their married life.

Compassion heals.

Carrie recognized several areas about herself and her need to grow her compassion toward John:

- A need to reach out to him with loving touch, despite her resistance to being vulnerable. Some of her vulnerability was caused by the deterioration of the marriage while some was the result of; were growing up in a distant, emotionally disconnected home.

- How much she cared for John when she tried opening her heart to him and his needs.

- Her need to set aside her own anger in favor of reaching out to her husband.

- How her anger and resentment had caused her to "withhold" love.

John also recognized several issues about himself and his need to grow in his compassion toward Carrie:

- How he took sexual rejection as something personal, rather than a sign he needed to be softer and more affectionate with his wife outside the bedroom.

- How he needed to create a more empathic connection with Carrie, asking her where she struggled and the challenges that went into her day.

- How he had distanced himself from his wife due to feeling hurt, but also as a way to convey his anger and growing resentment.

- How he tended to blame Carrie for their problems rather than looking at his own challenges and resistance to greater involvement with his wife.

Compassion can grow as we focus on reaching out with grace and tenderness. At some level, this needs to be unconditional. Our spouse doesn't need to earn our compassion; we bring it into their lives as an act of respect, care and the realization that our partner deeply needs our acceptance, just as we need theirs.

God loves each of us without conditions. As His love flows into our individual experience, we have more to give each other, and this includes compassion based on our desire to reach out and give our mate a gift – the certainty that we love them for who they are, including all the plusses and minuses.

Are you ready to unlock compassion in your own life?

Take a few minutes to examine the role of compassion in your life by exploring Appendix C "Discovering Your Compassionate Self." Learning how to identify compassionate feelings and bringing intentional, compassionate actions into your lover's life, and even those of others, sets the stage for relationship success and fulfillment.

Our spouse doesn't need to earn our compassion. We bring it into their lives as an act of respect, care and realization that our love partner deeply needs our acceptance, just as we need theirs.

Forgiveness

Our next condition follows from the first and focuses on our capacity to reach out in loving forgiveness to our life partner.

One author defined forgiveness as "letting go of the search for a different past." We would agree. An attitude and capacity to forgive keeps us current in our loving relationships and prevents resentment from building up and infecting the marriage.

The willingness and ability to "let go" of infractions, hurts and imperfections becomes a cornerstone of a growing marital relationship.

Letting go means accepting the sorrow of another, not allowing hurt to seep into your emotional bones and inhibit your ability to move forward after disagreements. It means releasing yourself from feelings of revenge and control and releasing your partner to the One greater than you.

The best framework for practicing forgiveness centers on creating a loving relationship that processes hurts and disappointments on an ongoing basis.

In other words, developing a profound, healthy, passionate love means keeping hurts from building up. We simply must love in a way that regularly heals wounds, never allowing them to grow and take hold. We must continue to sustain positive emotions and experiences as the key characteristics of our love life, not as exceptions to the rule.

> *The best framework for practicing forgiveness centers on creating a loving relationship that processes hurts and disappointments on an ongoing basis.*

Warmth

This next condition is similar to John Gottman's idea of fondness. This capacity offers a compelling look at how our heart "sees" and even experiences our mate. Warmth comes from inside of us when we allow our pleasure and gratitude to radiate outward towards another.

When we bring radiating warmth into our love life, we bring a unique gift that creates the atmosphere and ambience necessary for love to grow.

In many respects, this involves a choice. We need to intentionally create positive feelings as we reach out to our lover with care and tenderness.

Ask yourself these key questions and evaluate your capacity for warmth and fondness.

PA(II)SE *and* PONDER

* **Would I describe myself as a "warm" person who is capable of bringing warmth into my lover's life?**
* **What feelings and behaviors become part of my experience as I bring fondness into the life of my mate?**
* **Am I able to generate warmth toward my life partner and does it create the kind of tenderness that propels me to reach out with caring behaviors, words and deeds?**

Surrender

This condition exemplifies an aspect of marriage that can't be ignored. To some extent, being connected to our spouse involves a surrender of our independence and acknowledgement that another human being depends on us for love and devotion. We don't lose ourselves in another person but we do give up certain choices and life styles that we held on to as a single person. Surrender comes from an understanding that our life is not just about us.

Yet it goes even deeper. The question we have to ask is whether or not we are willing to reach out and give ourselves to another, even when it means a sacrifice. In a very real sense, we surrender ourselves to the idea of creating a profound, growing love for our mate and make this an ever present, ongoing priority.

The question we have to ask is whether or not we are willing to reach out and give ourselves to another, even when it means sacrifice.

We choose to set ourselves aside for the betterment of another and for the greater good of the marriage, because our desire to sustain and make our marriage thrive outweighs our need to have our own way.

How These Work

Now imagine for a moment (even close your eyes and try to picture this) that your marriage has been defined by these four dimensions: *compassion, forgiveness, warmth and surrender*.

> *You can actually experience, even in your imagination, what it feels like to receive compassion and what it means to give compassion.*
> *You can think of compassion, forgiveness, warmth and surrender and how these have come to characterize each of your interactions with your mate. You can picture giving and receiving these as the foundation of all you say and do with one another, as if they are always in the background, orchestrating the way you get along together.*

If we could truly live them out, these dimensions would dramatically shape all our ways of being and each and every interaction we have with the one we love.

Think of these four legs of the table as structures that hold the table together and upright. An incredibly loving bond between two married lovers consists of a deep, abiding connection. And what holds them together and supports them are those four legs.

With compassion, forgiveness, warmth and surrender, we have the necessary ingredients for positive communication – that come from deep within our heart. But more importantly, we have the needed characteristics that allow us to develop a healthy, secure marriage. This sets the stage for romance and togetherness and becomes the cornerstone of great sex.

More on John & Carrie – Lessons on the Impact of Compassion, Forgiveness, Warmth and Surrender

As we worked with John and Carrie, we witnessed progress in a number of areas. Unleashing compassion in their interactions and attitudes toward each other set the stage for growth on several fronts – including forgiveness, warmth and surrender.

Resentment can have a way of festering and defining a relationship. Without resolution, it grows and continues its destructive path, and their anger toward one another didn't melt overnight.

What did happen was extraordinary. Once compassion entered the relationship, the walls began to soften, opening the way for a more deliberate forgiveness as they identified key hurts, took personal responsibility for their part in the wounds and sought mutual repentance.

Both began bringing warmth into their interactions. And certainly their surrender to each other, defined by a renewed commitment to love each other while letting go of their own demands in the relationship, made real change possible.

Some ongoing steps John took:

- He began to keep a journal where he documented his thoughts, behaviors and feelings related to showing Carrie *compassion, forgiveness, warmth and surrender.*

- He committed to developing new behaviors involving compassion as a way to reach out to her in fresh ways.

Some ongoing steps Carrie took:

- She made sure she involved herself more emotionally with John, surrendering to his need and hers for more closeness.

- She deliberately made sure that she didn't substitute her emotional bond with her son for her husband's.

Both committed to developing each of these heart conditions in how they reached out, the way they loved the other and the way they prioritized the marriage relationship.

In summary, these are major catalysts for healing and change that can be understood and put into action to have profound impact on your marriage. They help create a path for both growth and healing. Compassion, forgiveness, warmth and surrender offer ways of reaching out that ignite fresh change and offer the opportunity for transformation. They are vital *heart conditions* and, combined with the right communication skills, grow love and passion.

Communication Skills

Now that we have examined the "heart conditions" necessary to create breakthrough change and healing in marriage, we will focus on the second, vital area of communication – your actual skill set.

Using positive communication skills is a centerpiece of a growing, thriving marriage. Our skills in communicating thoughts and emotions to our spouse keep us connected to the life of another human being. And developing and practicing communication skills is also one of the quickest ways to improve your marriage sexually and across the spectrum of caring behaviors.

In looking at communication, we hope to uncover several communication skills necessary to build an intimate, mature and growing marriage. We call these "techniques." These "techniques" become the ways we develop a deeper connection with our spouse and involve words and behaviors that communicate trust and care for one another.

Communication Techniques

Once we continue to grow in our appreciation and implementation of our "heart" conditions, we will be creating the fertile soil for positive communication to take place. We can then add other interaction strategies that continue to create strength in the bond between two lovers.

We avoid beginning statements with the word "you" or that contain the words, "always" or "never," because "always is never always true" and "never is mostly sometimes." Read this again if you need to. In other words, blame and broad scale accusations simply destroy connection and trust.

Now let's review several specific ways to expand our capacity to grow together and communicate more effectively. We move from heart conditions to the actual skills needed to bring love into each other's lives through how we communicate.

Listening and Giving Feedback Non-Defensively

First, using non-blaming language and tone of voice, we tell each other what we are feeling and thinking in ways that invite dialogue. As noted, this means we communicate with respect, taking turns listening and giving each other feedback regarding what we have heard.

This may seem simple at first, but is often difficult to initiate. It requires us to be honest about how we sound – our tone of voice – when speaking to each other. Do we talk in friendly ways that appear open and non-defensive, or do we speak with a tone of voice that betrays a closed attitude and edge of frustration?

Are we always ready to "make our case?" Or, do we convey openness to what someone else is sharing before we try to organize our thoughts and reactions to what we are told?

Reflecting Back and Summarizing

This means giving feedback to our partner about what they said in order to clarify their meaning and show we understand the issue. This means we listen to all parts of the message – the content or words spoken and the tone of voice and body language – and communicate that to the person sharing. This helps validate our partner, even if we disagree with the message. A, and all this happens before we respond with our own thoughts and feelings.

Even when our partner expresses hurt and frustration, we need to have the ability to listen without shutting the other person down or criticizing them for feeling a certain way. This reflects an ability and desire to show each other respect, even when disagreeing.

So, listening non-defensively means we focus on understanding our partner's perspective, including their thoughts and feelings even if we disagree or feel hurt or angry. And we are not preparing our next response when someone else is talking in order to defend ourselves. We set our agenda aside to listen. We are indeed open to what they are saying and are really trying to understand the message.

Even when our partner expresses hurt and frustration, we need to have the ability to listen without shutting the other person down or criticizing them for feeling a certain way.

Choose to Stay Calm.

Another essential ingredient in good communication centers on how well we manage our emotions. In short, our ability to stay calm means creating a safe space where both can share openly without risk of being hurt or wounded. Listening in an open way means we manage and balance our emotions in order to listen more carefully.

Listening is much more difficult when our emotions are heightened. Sometimes it helps to take a time out from conversation so we can return to a place of calm before we re-engage, as long as this doesn't become a pattern whereby couples avoid interacting and never return to the topic.

Invite Additional Sharing.

This means we ask our partner, "Is there more you would like to share to help me understand?" rather than hoping the conversation will end or assuming they are finished. Couples who encourage sharing and dialogue, even on difficult topics, help create an attitude of openness and reflect a desire to create mutual understanding on any subject.

It is not uncommon for one or both partners to avoid bringing sensitive issues back up, hoping to avoid further conflict. This can be incredibly damaging because it conveys a lack of concern and care for resolving hurts that must be addressed. Instead, we live with the wounds or assume our partner will live with them, thus growing the hurt and potential resentment.

Honor and Protect Your Love Connection.

Strive to keep your bond with one another healthy and vibrant. Couples need to protect their connection with one another and to keep disagreements or anger from damaging that bond.

This involves a real commitment to mutual transparency while refraining from hurtful words and actions. Sometimes the bonds of love can be fragile and we need to deliberately protect our connection from getting broken or damaged.

Imagine just that – a heartfelt, determined commitment to keeping your connection with your mate growing and strong. Imagine that you protect it from deterioration and damage, much like a valuable treasure or property.

Couples who devote themselves to honoring their bond of love, keeping it from harm by destructive words and actions – all the while, reaching out in healthy ways – keep their marriage intact. They are able to disagree, have conflict and not wound one another.

Sometimes the bonds of love can be fragile and we need to deliberately protect our connection from getting broken or damaged.

Strengthen and Grow Your Love Connection Each Day.

This involves a purposeful focus and care in keeping positively connected, even when there is conflict. In other words, don't stop loving each other in real ways because an issue is not resolved.

As John Gottman has explained so well, we need to prevent the development of unhealthy patterns such as "stonewalling," avoiding one another, speaking with contempt or giving up on finding a positive resolution. Equally important, we must manage our emotions effectively, keeping extreme anger from leaking into our lives verbally and non-verbally.

Pay Attention to Your Communication Goals.

The goal of hurting or disrespecting your partner is never OK. Rather, the goal should always be to maintain closeness and to better understand one another with support and care for your partner, even during disagreements. Processing all of your feelings in a civil way keeps contempt, a killer of marriage, at bay.

When disagreeing, take turns expressing your side of the argument. When the other is speaking, give them your entire concentration and focus, knowing you will get a turn to speak. Try to understand each other completely, even if you disagree, and show care and respect for each other's point of view.

Be Aware of Your True Feelings.

Be willing to discuss feelings other than anger, knowing that anger is a secondary emotion.

Secondary means that there are almost always other emotions the anger conceals, such as feeling hurt or wounded. These need to be expressed in order to really understand one another.

So when angry, try to protect your interactions from expressing only frustration and focus on the underlying, true emotions being triggered.

When There is Conflict, Focus on Solutions.

Be ready to express your side of the disagreement and hear your partner's side but also be ready to explore outcomes and possible compromises. A person can win an argument but lose the battle. Think win-win. Win-win strategies focus on encouraging one another to express different points of view without criticism. Winning means maintaining the connection, not having the better argument.

Summary

Each of us brings talents, skills and heart to the table in our marriage relationship. We call this a person's "presence" and think of it as an ongoing area of growth in an individual's life. The more we grow emotionally and spiritually, the greater our capacity to love and to build a healthy life. Including our love and passion for our partner in marriage.

OUR CAPACITY TO LOVE
Review and Practice

- Every person has a certain capacity to love another human being that can be strengthened and enlarged. You are in a *relationship* with your spouse.

- We know how to love based on our early experiences of being loved and by later ones in other caring relationships. We can love because we were first loved.

- We truly believe that the capacity to love is created over time and must be cultivated and grown.

- We must love and we must love well, with all our heart and effort. So defining the ingredients of "love" becomes essential.

- It is vital to look at communication through two distinct lenses. One focuses on your heart – the attitude and care and even softness you bring into your lover's life. We call these "heart conditions." The second centers on actual, specific communication skills, "techniques."

- Think of these four heart conditions as legs of a table. Each one adds to our capacity to love and care deeply for our mate.

- Heart condition *compassion*: The bedrock of a thriving marriage comes from a heart of compassion for one another. Compassion has to do with an attitude of acceptance of your partner and, ultimately, yourself.

- Heart condition *forgiveness*: The willingness and ability to "let go" of infractions, hurts and imperfections becomes a cornerstone of a growing marital relationship.

- Heart condition *warmth*: When we bring radiating warmth into our love life, we bring a unique gift that creates the atmosphere and ambience necessary for love to grow.

- Heart condition *surrender*: To some extent, being connected to our spouse involves a surrender of our independence and acknowledgement that another human being depends on us for love and devotion.

- We move from heart conditions to actual skills needed to bring love into each other's lives through how we communicate.

- Communication skill #1: *Listening and Giving Feedback Non-Defensively.*

- Communication skill #2: *Reflecting Back and Summarizing.*

- Communication skill #3: *Choosing to Stay Calm.*

- Communication skill #4: *Inviting Additional Sharing.*

- Communication skill #5: *Honor and Protect Your Love Connection.*

- Communication skill #6: *Strengthen and Grow Your Love Connection Each Day.*

- Communication skill #7: *Pay Attention to Your communication Goals.*

- Communication skill #8: *When There is Conflict, Focus on Solutions.*

Exploring Together

- At the beginning of this chapter, we listed many ideas about what love means. Review them together and spend a bit of time adding to this list in your own words. What does love mean to you both in your marriage?

• Of all the heart conditions we outlined – compassion, forgiveness, warmth, and surrender – which do you find the easiest to practice in your marriage? Which do you find the most challenging? Take turns giving each other feedback on what you see your partner practice the most and what you would like to see more of from them. Be sure to affirm each other for the ways you have shown compassion, forgiveness, warmth or surrender and the positive ways that has impacted you.

• Communication skills are essential to a healthy marriage. Do the two of you like the way you communicate with each other? What strengths do you have in this area of your marriage? Of the list provided in this chapter, which one or two skills do you think would really benefit your marriage if you put them into practice?

Enhancing Your Marriage

• Schedule a time to get together this week for the sole purpose of talking. Really try to communicate in the most loving way possible. Be conscientious about being both honest AND caring. Don't bring up areas of conflict. Let this be a time of talking with the goal of enhancing connection, closeness and learning more about your lover – what they think, how they feel, what is in their heart.

• So, taking turns, allow each other time to express whatever you/they would like to talk about. Try to summarize back to them what you heard and check in with them to see if they feel heard. Notice if you both feel more connected after you have had this opportunity.

Pondering the Spiritual

- Focus on God's compassion, warmth and forgiveness. How does He show His love for us through each of them?

- How does God's Spirit enable us to exercise the right heart conditions and communication techniques?

- Carefully read 2 Corinthians 1:1-7. What do these verses tell us about God and how He comforts us? Do you let Him comfort you? Are you able to bring comfort to those around you? To your spouse?

- Spend time in prayer, asking God how to develop comfort and compassion in your life. How can you show this, in heartfelt ways, to your life partner?

Next we want to look at our final, yet key ingredient that goes into the mix in defining our presence. We call this *emotional maturity.*

EMOTIONAL MATURITY

So how mature are you? Ever been asked that question?

Ever wonder if you are grown up or do you sometimes feel like a kid who just hasn't gotten it all together?

N SOME WAYS these are kind of scary questions. But certainly ones we need to face.

We are all in a never-ending process of "growing up," despite our age and having moved out of childhood. Personal development continues forward, assuming we engage in a growth process as human beings. Not everyone does.

Imagine truly understanding the key ingredients of maturity, both emotionally and intellectually. And that in addition to understanding, we had a way of moving toward more wholeness and healthy ways of seeing the world that would vibrantly impact all our relationships. In other words, insuring that we continue to grow and mature.

We all have differing ideas of what constitutes "maturity." Some of these beliefs are common sense and some reveal deeper meanings behind how people develop and "grow up" and become capable of loving and being loved.

We are all in a never ending process of "growing up," despite our age and having moved out of childhood.

We want to focus on several dimensions of this important theme. We are hoping to provide a real grasp of how emotional maturity impacts our ability to bond and love our mate. And more importantly, we want to offer a roadmap to success – how each of us can focus on developing our own personalities and create an exciting life with our partner.

Once again, we use the analogy of "pillars' to look at each of the dimensions that form the basis for loving deeply. Some will overlap with other discussions we have focused on, especially those related to communication. We will repeat some key thoughts while applying them to the theme of maturity.

Pillar One- Managing Our Emotions and Being Open

So how do you do with your emotions? Are you up and down, steady, unflappable? Or do emotions get the better of you?

We all differ on our ability to keep our feelings in check. But more importantly, the question becomes how we use our emotions to create understanding and strength in our marriage.

Knowing and managing our own feelings is only part of the picture. Equally important is how to experience openness to our partner's emotional world. To all their thoughts and feelings that make them unique and often different than us.

Let's not miss the real heart of this issue. Our feelings, not just our thoughts, guide and direct our love life. We desperately need to embrace, understand and manage our emotional world. We need to be open to our feelings, to utilize them along with all our thoughts in such a way that they don't overwhelm our life.

We will look at two aspects.

Capacity to Understand Our Emotions

First, emotional maturity involves the capacity to understand our emotions without letting them dominate our will, our decisions and our interpretation of interpersonal events in our life.

That is, be objective. Know yourself and your emotions but don't let feelings alone dominate your thinking and what you ultimately believe is true.

Let's explain this further. We know, for example, that often the first interpretation we give events in our life comes from the feelings generated by that experience. For example, if someone cuts us off on the road, our fears are activated, anger can quickly kick in and we feel as though that driver did it on purpose. We may think "that the driver is an idiot." We have made two big "leaps in thinking" that may or may not be true. Yet our feeling world tells us to interpret the event only one way.

Professionally speaking, we used to think that our "thoughts" determined how we interpret the events and experiences we have in the world and that our feelings followed after we drew our conclusions. Current research suggests that often the opposite is often true. Our emotions have a great influence on how we construct meaning out of the events that happen day in and day out. Often our emotions happen immediately, before we have a chance to "think through" what is happening.

. . . .

Emotional maturity involves the capacity to understand our emotions without letting them dominate our will, our decisions and our interpretation of interpersonal events in our life.

. . . .

The implications of this for developing intimacy with our spouse are monumental. If we allow only our feelings to determine how we draw conclusions, we will not take advantage of our ability to think through situations and come up with different, often healthier interpretations.

We simply must take the lead. We have great personal power to love and rock the world of our partner when we understand and take control of our own emotional world.

This doesn't, however, mean we ignore our feelings; rather, we need to build personal awareness of our emotions. Our feelings become a source of information that contributes to our understanding of what goes on in our key relationships.

If I am feeling hurt or wounded, for example, it helps to identify the emotion and be willing to discuss my reactions with the person involved. This creates a potentially deeper connection and mutual understanding that grows love.

> *We simply must take the lead. We have great personal power to love and rock the world of our partner when we understand and take control of our emotional world.*

Keep in mind we are discussing emotional maturity and key dimensions that define how much we have grown in life. Awareness of our feelings and emotions varies from person to person. Yet it is a vital aspect of our ability to bring mature love into the picture. We simply must know ourselves, and the more deeply we do, the better.

The Gift of Openness

Second, and in addition to understanding our emotional world, we bring in a significant *presence* to our love relationship when we exhibit a disposition of openness to solving intimacy issues and resolving conflicts. We discussed this under our topic of communication and will apply it here to emotional growth and maturity.

One of the greatest gifts we can give another human being centers on our willingness to hear them . . . to reach out with attempts to understand them, including their thoughts, emotions, their inner experience. This takes openness to the being of another.

We don't mean to sound simply philosophical. Because nothing provides more growth and healing in a love relationship than cultivating a deep desire to hear one another. Without criticism or judgment.

This means we need to cultivate a non-defensive way of relating that encourages mutual self-disclosure and trust. We need to be able to set our assumptions and expectations aside to remain unbiased. We need to remain calm enough to hear what each other has to say.

How would you rate yourself on a continuum with openness at one end and defensiveness on the other?

. . . .

Because nothing provides more growth and healing in a love relationship than cultivating a deep desire to hear one another.

. . . .

Several questions help us understand our own level and capacity to relate non-defensively.

We'll examine a few of these. Spend some time going over each of these questions; they will tell you a lot about your own capacity to listen and stay open to your own experience and that of your mate.

• ━━━━• P A U S E *and* P O N D E R •━━━━ •

✳ **Are you able to listen to your partner without anger and irritation dominating your experience?**

* **Do you feel interested in his/her position or views or discount those different than your own?**

* **Do you listen with the intent of "waiting out" your spouse so that you can speak?**

* **Are you most concerned with understanding what your partner is saying or hoping they will understand you?**

* **Do you reach conclusions about conflict based on your own hurt without listening to your partner's point of view?**

* **Do you feel threatened about even the slightest conflicts and that you have to defend yourself?**

These are only a few questions that get at this vital theme. If you would like a better understanding of where you are on this issue, you can fill out the "Attitude of Openness" questionnaire in Appendix D.

When we are defensive, we feel a need to protect ourselves and see conflict as a battleground where we can get hurt, not as an avenue for mutual understanding and care.

Those high on the defensive continuum have real difficulty seeing any conflict as mutual problem-solving; instead, conflict is seen as a threat to their being and stability.

Yet our capacity for openness to our own experiences and tolerance of our spouse's, if different than ours, provides a key to relationship growth and health. This demands an actual awareness of our own wants and needs and the simultaneous acceptance of our mate's.

Remember, we are talking about "you," what qualities and characteristics you bring into your love relationships that cause growth. Or, conversely, get you stuck and that may even harm the relationship.

. . . .

Yet our capacity for openness to our own experiences and tolerance of our spouse's,

*if different than ours, provides a key
to relationship growth and health.*

We are talking about "presence," and linking this to the capacity to manage our emotions with our overall maturity. If you struggle in this area, growth toward greater insight and ability to positively impact your personal life and your experience with your spouse is needed.

Pillar Two - Empathy

Another sign of emotional maturity centers on our capacity to know and understand what our spouse may be experiencing. This involves knowing what they are feeling and thinking – their perspective on a given event or situation.

We do this by first having **empathy** for them. To show empathy is to identify with and vicariously experience another's feelings and experience. It means you emotionally put yourself in the place of another to gain a sense of what it is like to "walk in their shoes." We all have the ability to get outside of ourselves and be other-centered, at least to some degree.

One central feature of empathy focuses on our willingness to listen and understand our partner's thoughts and feelings. Even if they are different than our own!

We can choose to "set ourselves aside" for the moment, understand their perspective and find ways to honor their view of any issue. And again, even if it differs from our way of seeing things.

For example, when a husband (or wife) enters the house after a hard and long day at work, the potential for reconnecting happens, often setting the tone for the evening. The day may have been filled with numerous stressors, including a failed business deal or a colleague whose need to discuss their bad day kept interrupting his focus.

He likely comes home with a need for understanding and either time alone to calm down or a listening ear from his wife. By putting herself in his shoes, she may ask how he is really doing and take the time to listen and try to understand.

She might say, "It must have been frustrating to have a day like that when I know you were hoping that deal would go through." This would show him that she gets what he is going through and "feels his pain or frustration" (empathizes). This could well be the soothing balm to ease the transition back home and help each other begin reconnecting.

To show empathy is to identify with and vicariously experience another's feelings and experience, to emotionally put yourself in the place of another.

Perhaps she has come home from a hard day at the office or been burdened by household issues such as caring for the children and needs support and understanding. His ability to set his day aside and sincerely care about hers involves a decision to be empathic and to care at a meaningful level.

He might say, for example, "Wow. You've had quite a day too. Caring for the kids isn't easy" or "coming home stressed from work is a challenge," and therefore invite her to share more while showing he cares to know her experience, her thoughts and her feelings.

So, how do you rate yourself?

Are you someone who listens well, even if you don't agree, or do you shut the other person out, just waiting for your "turn to talk?"

Pillar Three – Involvement

Involvement. A simple word, yet rich in meaning. There is great power when two people in love discover how to stay connected; how to revolve around one another and be present in each other's space;

how to create a bond that tells the other they matter, that they are thought about and that they are important; how to be attuned to their lover in ways that can be felt and experienced.

Simply stated, to really love and enjoy one another, two people must experience an ongoing, persistent and meaningful connection with one another. This clearly involves a capacity to get outside ourselves in order to reach into the life of our life partner. To be absorbed in their world, interests and life. Without losing our own!

To truly love someone requires an ability to engage in the life of another, moving from a more self-centered place to one of mutuality and partnership.

There could be many ways to describe this dimension of maturity. We could call it other-centeredness, an extension of empathy described above, or simply the ability to set ourselves aside and clearly see and reach out to the life and needs of the one we love.

This is a very intentional way to love. Purposefully reaching out because of care and choice for the welfare of our lover means achieving a place of growth that allows us to sometimes even suspend our own self-interests and attend to theirs.

And being intentional means developing a mindset bent on creating love, affecting the life of our mate in positive ways and growing a deep, passionate connection that becomes the hallmark of our path together.

Being involved in an emotionally mature way doesn't depend on the behaviors of our spouse. We reach out to our partner out of the choice to love deeply. Not as a response to their actions toward us.

Being involved in an emotionally mature way doesn't depend on the behaviors of our spouse. We reach out to our partner out of choice to love deeply. Not as a response to their actions toward us.

When we think of the spiritual component of this kind of involvement, we think of God reaching into our lives and loving us. Not because of what we have done, but based solely on His choice to know us and care for us as our Father.

God desires a close union with each of us and takes the lead in offering and creating the energy and momentum for that to happen. He doesn't wait for us to respond. What a model of the love and care we can extend into the life of our mate! This truly defines love at its best.

Concluding Thoughts

Once we grasp the significance of the three components of intimacy - *personal awareness*, the *capacity to love,* and *emotional maturity* – we can appreciate the complexities of developing a passionate loving bond with another.

We can also begin to comprehend the possibilities of what lies ahead when we focus on developing and sustaining love from the perspective of our presence in the relationship.

We can't emphasize enough that the key to unlocking your real potential to create a fulfilling love and passion in your marriage centers to some extent on your willingness to grow and transform your own life.

Love thrives in the atmosphere of energy and aliveness generated from two people interested in becoming all that God intended them to be and in fulfilling their true nature and purpose in life.

For love to really grow and reach its peak, there must be an ongoing attention to the details of personal change. Love is a dynamic force, seeking to always break new ground and come into its fullness in the bond between two lovers. An idle life, devoid of urgency around our own maturity and capacity to be all we can be, leads to stagnation and complacency. The fertile soil of a loving bond can't grow in this dry desert.

We know we have been pointed and a bit confrontational about the importance of becoming emotionally mature. Our hope is that this ongoing emphasis leaves you motivated to continue your personal and very spiritual journey of growth and even healing in your life. Or perhaps, rather than continue, to start down this path in a way never before experienced. We hope to guide and direct you on that path toward love's ultimate expression between you and your partner.

Have I Grown Up Assessment

Before leaving, go to Appendix E and complete the "Have I Grown Up" Assessment. See if you can identify areas of personal growth that will provide some direction for your own future development.

EMOTIONAL MATURITY
Review and Practice

- We all have differing ideas of what constitutes "maturity." Some of these beliefs are common sense and some reveal deeper meanings behind how people develop and "grow up" and become capable of loving and being loved.

- 3 "Pillars" help us understand what we mean by emotional maturity.

- Pillar 1 **Managing our Emotions & Being Open**.

  › Emotional maturity involves the capacity to understand our emotions without letting them dominate our will, our decisions and our interpretation of relational events in our life.

  › One of the greatest gifts we can give another human being centers on our willingness to hear them. To reach out with attempts to understand them – their thoughts, emotions, their inner experience. This takes openness to the being of another.

  › Our capacity for openness to our own experiences and even tolerance of our spouse's if different than ours provides a key to relationship growth and health. This demands an actual awareness of our own wants and needs and the simultaneous acceptance of our mate's.

- Pillar 2 **Empathy**

  › Another sign of emotional maturity centers on our capacity to know and understand what our spouse may be experiencing.

› One central feature of empathy focuses on our willingness to listen and understand our partner's thoughts and feelings – even if they are different than our own!

- Pillar 3 **Involvement**

› To really love and enjoy one another, two people must experience an ongoing, persistent and meaningful connection with one another. This is involvement.

› To truly love someone requires an ability to engage in the life of another – moving from a more self-centered place to one of mutuality and partnership.

› Being involved in an emotionally mature way doesn't depend on the behaviors of our spouse. We reach out to our partner out of choice to love deeply. Not as a response to their actions toward us.

Exploring Together

- Spend some time reflecting on the three pillars of emotional maturity. How would you rate yourself on managing your emotions, your openness to your mate, your capacity to sustain involvement with your partner and ability to listen and create an empathic environment?

- Which pillars of emotional maturity represent strong assets in your love relationship? Which ones would you define as areas of growth?

- How intentional are you in staying involved with your lover? How do you do this?

- How well do you listen to one another on non-conflicted parts of your life? How well do you both listen when there is conflict?

Enhancing Your Marriage

• Sit down together. Take turns sharing with each other the highlights of your week. As the listener, make a pointed effort at really hearing what is being said and how your mate is feeling. Summarize what you have heard. When they are done, check in to see if they feel fully heard. If not, ask what more they need you to hear.

• Share with each other what you are thankful for in how you stay attuned to each other's lives. How would you like to feel more involved with each other? What would that look like?

Pondering the Spiritual

• How would you describe God's involvement in your life? How would you describe your involvement with Him? Do you picture God wanting a close relationship with you or do you see Him as more remote, watching events but not too concerned or involved in what's happening?

• How do your habits, such as Bible study, prayer, etc., reflect your involvement with God? What needs to grow in this area to really experience His love and closeness?

• Find three Psalms (such as Psalm 23) that you feel reflect God's involvement and empathy with His people – with you. How do these Psalms speak to your heart and remind you of His love and deep connection with you as His child?

PURSUIT

"If you tell me what you seek after the most, what you pursue in life and are most passionate about, you will have revealed the deepest part of your heart and soul."
DOUG & LESLIE GUSTAFSON

*"On my bed by night
I sought him whom my soul loves;
I sought him, but found him not.
I will rise now and go about the city,
In the streets and in the squares;
I will seek him whom my soul loves.
I sought him, but found him not."*
THE SONG OF SOLOMON, 3:1-3

As I (DOUG) sit in my kitchen, I'm looking out at the Rockies and wondering what it might be like to climb those tall, majestic snow-capped mountains. I imagine reaching the top, breathing the cold, biting air, the feeling of exhilaration as I camp atop a jagged peak and gaze over valleys teeming with life below me.

My mind wanders and for some reason I think of my good friend Bill, visiting his home in Southern California and watching NASCAR. Drivers traveling in circles competing for first place, hoping to stay alive, fighting for the crown of victory.

I turn my focus back on writing this chapter and Leslie and my hopes for helping you create and sustain a marriage beyond your dreams. I'm wondering how we can speak into your life, giving you the desire for more and the willingness to reach the peaks and summits in your journey toward a more connected, vibrant love.

What does each of these scenarios have in common? Choice – about what is most important to us, about what we decide to pursue in life. The man or woman seeking to reach the tallest mountains, the race car driver striving for first place and a writer wishing to promote better lives for others, all involve a decision to pursue some goal. To reach for heights they haven't found but hope to attain.

We call this drive, this desire to move forward and accomplish goals, this vision for what life can be, *pursuit* – what we go after, what we seek out, what we strive to attain.

Introduction

And so our next attitude we call pursuit. Simply defined, we will be looking at how two people actually pursue each other in a loving relationship – how we reach out and seek involvement with one another. How we attempt to truly touch our partner's life with tangible behaviors that say "I love you" and "You matter."

We hope to take you to the peak and to be able to look down over the roads and highways below, knowing you have achieved a better place with lasting care, love and passion.

And perhaps more than any of our six attitudes, this one takes center stage in the growth of the marriage. Why? Because pursuit represents a pivotal foundation necessary for love to really grow and thrive. Without pursuit, there is a real potential that love will wither and fade in power and scope. Maybe more than just a potential, but likelihood!

Imagine for a moment you are a NASCAR driver, a mountain climber or you are writing a book of your own. You get in the race car, but never step on the gas. You start climbing the mountain but sit down to rest and decide not to get up and journey ahead. Or you decide to write a book but never pick up the pen or sit behind your computer.

Obviously, nothing would ever happen. You would lose the race, fail to reach the peak ahead and never author a book. So look at love the same way. Can your love relationship flourish if no one ever steps on the gas to keep love alive and growing? We don't think so.

Without two people pursuing one another, love becomes stale and can even die.

We all pursue something or some things in life. Whether time with friends, reading, striving for financial success, or time "surfing the net," that pursuit defines us – who we are and what we care most about.

Therefore, one critical part of intimacy centers on knowing yourself as a pursuer.

This may sound confusing, but think of your marriage and the love you have for your spouse and the behavior patterns that define the personality of your relationship.

Now, imagine being pursued. What it feels like to have someone really care about you, want you and reach out to you in ways that convey love and involvement.

Do you pursue each other? Do you pursue your mate?

Jim & Karen

When Jim and Karen came to see us, they described a marriage of 16 years that had occasional conflicts around typical issues such as finances and raising their two daughters. But we soon found out that the key struggle centered on Karen's feelings of rejection and being unloved.

She described Jim as a successful businessman with whom she fell deeply in love during college. Jim would bring her flowers, take her on special dates and she felt "chased" and valued. A few short years into the marriage, however, the relationship began to shift. Jim became more engrossed in work; they had their first child and both focused on the "operational" concerns of raising kids and making money.

Over time, Karen felt alone and wondered what had happened to the passionate love they once shared. Jim didn't really pursue her romantically any longer. The gifts and special, thoughtful ways he communicated love, dwindled. Sex became more infrequent and seemed more out of obligation than the result of excitement and passion.

Karen couldn't figure out what happened and wondered if Jim was seeing someone else. She also questioned her own attractiveness, having gained weight since their last child. She caught Jim on the Internet a few times looking at pornography and concluded she couldn't compete with the young beauties he found there.

She confronted him and he denied any kind of frequent porn use but offered little reassurance about his love and desire for her.

Jim explained that when they had their first child, he suddenly felt like he wasn't wanted in the same way. Sure, Karen would give in to sex, but she was often tired and he didn't know how to change the ensuing boredom in the relationship. He didn't know what to do other than complain. Which didn't really help much.

As Jim noted, "I love my wife but she seems to want more and more from me. She knows I love her and yet she seems to want proof of that all the time. I feel like I'm failing her and yet I get busy and it's hard to remember to be romantic and treat her like I did when we were dating."

Jim came from a family with few role models regarding closeness and affection. His father worked late hours and never came to any of his sporting events or school functions. He remembered his father and *mother arguing frequently and found out later in life that his dad had a short term affair with his office secretary.*

Carol, on the other hand, came from a family where conflict was kept secret. She never heard her parents raise their voices with one another and so when they divorced in her teen years, she was shocked.

Jim and Karen's parents spent little time asking questions about their life or concerns. It was assumed that they were doing well and happy. And neither one had parents who modeled a consistent, affectionate relationship in their marital life.

So when Jim and Karen found each other, their attention to one another in their dating relationship was a brand new experience. Jim remembers being attentive to what Karen was feeling and needing from him. And he felt wanted, that he mattered and made a real difference in Karen's life.

And Karen remembers being more open about her feelings and her hurts from childhood. She would talk about her difficulties and experienced Jim as being caring and attentive. Their relationship was "working" and they both felt loved by the other.

Yet something happened early in the relationship that changed the course of their mutual experience. Attentiveness and trust gave way to mistrust and a lack of reaching out. Both kept waiting for the other to open their arms, yet suddenly neither took the first step to embrace their mate.

Jim actually believed that Karen no longer admired him or wanted him sexually and he didn't understand her need to "feel close" to him as part of their sexual encounters. Carol believed that she had somehow become less attractive and felt too vulnerable to offer her body to her husband.

Sex became awkward and neither had a way to discuss this without hurting or threatening the other person's sense of worth and value. Both assumed that sex and affection would simply continue without having an ongoing focus on creating passion in the marriage.

As Karen noted, "We seemed to have kind of a magical, dating relationship — like we found the partner of our dreams. We were close and we both found ways to prove that in how we treated each other. But something happened. It's like it just ended over time and we didn't bring it back — or know how to build that again. I end up hurt all the time and it makes sex hard to agree to."

Both Jim and Karen lost the "natural" pursuit that courtship creates and found that, later in the relationship, the daily decision to reach out to your lover takes a unique skill set, perspective and motivation. In other words, to sustain love, both partners need to develop the art of reaching out to the other, with genuine effort and consistency, to build and maintain passion and intimacy in and out of the bedroom.

Yet Jim didn't really know how to talk about his wants and needs for closeness and sexual contact and Karen didn't have the language necessary to discuss her need for safety and affection as part of the experience of intimacy. They ended up hurting one another in their anger and attempts to ask for what they wanted or complaining about what they weren't getting from each other.

To sustain love, both partners need to develop the art of reaching out to the other, with genuine effort and consistency, to build and maintain passion and intimacy in and out of the bedroom.

In order to repair their love and get passion to grow again, Jim and Karen made the following initial commitments to one another:

Jim

- Initiate many of the behaviors he used to do when courting his wife. For example, bringing her flowers.

- Choose a variety of behaviors to reach out to Karen, not to "prove" he loves her but to demonstrate his care for her coming from his own heart. Setting up their first date night in years was one initial step Jim took.

- A strong commitment to discontinue porn use.

- Show his concern for how she's doing by asking her about her day, listening attentively and finding ways to help more with the kids.

- Paying attention to Karen's emotional needs and learning how to think about sex as both an emotional and physical connection.

Karen

- Once again, being more open about her feelings and not withdrawing.

- Willingness to initial sexual contact. To explore how to use her femininity to make Jim feel more wanted and also to get in touch with her own desire for sex.

- Reaching out to Jim with small behaviors such as affection, asking him about his day and reinforcing her respect for him as a worker and provider.

- Remembering to get her emotional needs met by her husband and not just by the kids.

Continually pursuing one another in the marriage relationship, sustaining the energy we find in courtship, often gets overshadowed by the demands of daily living and the belief that love simply continues to grow without effort. As if we no longer need to pursue one another. Like we jump in the race car, hope to finish well, but never step on the accelerator!

When we do find partners who have continued to love each other deeply, we see patterns of reaching out that reflect a consistent pursuit of the other. These couples have developed the capacity to know themselves and how to successfully share their hearts with one another, to stay informed about what they need and want. And so, consistent and ongoing movement toward their partner has stayed central in the relationship.

Most of us are familiar with "pursuing" our partner during the earlier, more romantic stage of our relationship – during courtship. But so often, one or both partners become complacent and stop those behaviors that indicate real interest and even fondness for the other. The new demands of daily living create, as noted before, a need for relational skills that may have never been practiced or fully developed.

So love can die. This may sound dramatic, but our deepest relationships need to be constantly cultivated and nurtured in order to stay alive and grow.

At its core, pursuit involves reaching out and toward our partner, leaning into them, not leaning away, with the intent of loving them in positive ways – to grow the relationship and closeness we have with them.

When we do find partners who have continued to love each other deeply, we see patterns of reaching out that reflect a consistent pursuit of the other.

A few key questions help us get closer to what pursuit looks like in your marriage. Take time to reflect on and answer each one.

PA(II)SE *and* PONDER

❋ **What does pursuit look like in your marriage?**

❋ **Over the months and years of marriage, what has changed in the way you pursue one another?**

Each of these questions helps us see what's happening in our marriage. Do we both engage in high levels of pursuit, similar to dating? Or have those patterns diminished, disappeared or seem to have been forgotten?

The Challenges of Pursuit

When we think of pursuit, we look at how it applies to all the ways we reach out in love and care to our mate inside and outside the bedroom.

Yet clearly, the willingness and ability to pursue one another with consistent acts of love can hit roadblocks. For some, stepping into a place of true involvement becomes a challenge. And while it may have been easier to pursue your lover in the beginning of the relationship, this somehow becomes more complicated and difficult to unleash later on.

Common Challenges

There are several challenges we face in our ability and willingness to pursue a closer relationship with our life partner. Or to have them pursue a closer bond with us.

Some of them can be deeply rooted in past experiences and inhibitions about being close and vulnerable to another person. Other reasons center on habits and ways we let go of growing our love due to inattention and or perhaps not knowing how to reach out.

So let's take a look at several related areas that present common challenges for two lovers to initiate and sustain pursuit of one another:

- Imbalanced relationship patterns.

- Past wounds from childhood.

- Unresolved hurts in the marriage.

- Undeveloped interpersonal skills.

- Lack of personal insight.

- Addictions and other personal challenges.

- Lack of understanding how to pursue each other.

- Struggle with Becoming an Individual

Imbalanced Relationship Patterns

Yes, the patterns of how we love can become imbalanced, out of sync and in need of adjustment. One such pattern we call the "Pursuer and the Pursued" (discussed earlier in our section on bonding and attachment). That sounds like a title for a Western movie, yet it reveals a significant challenge to couples trying to build love.

So what exactly do we mean? In this pattern, one partner commonly reaches out to the other, while the one pursued distances themselves from contact. We call this person the "avoider."

We commonly find that couples experience a lack of balance regarding this theme when applied to "desire." Frequently, one partner pursues the other one sexually or emotionally while the other withdraws. And so patterns develop that keep couples frustrated and that can potentially hurt.

Let's explore this further, related to a couple's sex life. Often, the partner who has a greater awareness of their desire for sexual contact puts pressure on the one who has lower awareness of their desire. So, at some level, the one with "lower desire" ends up retreating in order to maintain some kind of balance.

In addition, the one pursuing rarely gets to know their partner's wants and desires (instead of their own) because they are typically overshadowed by their own experience of want and need. And the one being pursued never has the room to get to know their own level of desire or their experience of their own unique wants and needs that are separate from their mate's. Why? Because they often spend more time "fending off" their spouse than learning to go inward to discover what is important to them physically and emotionally.

In the extreme, one can turn into a "sexual bully," demanding sex and attention and minimizing the partner's wants and needs. This can move the bullied one into becoming scared and giving in to their partner's sexual demands in order to get sex over with, while the inevitable consequences of resentment – loathing their partner and having an increasing desire to flee the relationship – build.

The person who pursues often feels anxiety about backing off. After all, "If I back off, I may never have sex."

The good news is that if the pursuing partner learns to back off, and the withdrawing partner learns to be more in touch and assertive with their own desires, there is a good chance of learning new patterns and breaking the cycle of frustration.

Space becomes created between both partners that allows them to have their separate feelings and wants and come together in mutual decision about their sexual intimacy. This causes a shift so that both feel more enlivened and empowered in the relationship when it comes to experiencing sexual closeness.

The good news is that if the pursuing partner learns to back off, and the withdrawing partner learns to be more in touch and assertive with their own desires, there is a good chance of learning new patterns and breaking the cycle of frustration.

In addition, if the patterns stays stuck in this place, the one with "low desire" never has the opportunity to learn that sex can be about them – what they need, what feels good and what they hope for from their mate. They never get the opportunity to answer these crucial questions since they are always trying to bury desire in fending off their pursuing partner.

An important part in all this is for the pursuer to learn how to pursue for the purpose of greater emotional connection, not just sexual gratification. And to get to know their partner more deeply, whether there is sexual contact or not.

Past Wounds from Childhood

No one grew up in a perfect home. Yet some parents struggle to meet the emotional and stage-related needs of their children on a consistent basis. We all have a profound need to love and be loved.

If adequate love and nurturing fail during childhood, we not only live with hurts and wounds, but may even take those into our adult love relationships.

We can, for example, hope our partner will heal our heart. In other words, we seek relationships that somehow "make up" for the absence of love and affection we grew up with.

Or we may live with a fear of intimacy. This happens when our adult relationships resurrect needs we may have buried from childhood and our subsequent fear that, just as before, they will be unmet. Hence, we live in the past and we develop the expectation that our adult partner will act like significant others in our family of origin.

Carrying unresolved past wounds keeps us from experiencing the present. It's as if we can't live beyond the hurts that define our inner emotional world. Moving into a place of intimacy with a loved one requires us to see our partner in a fresh, healthy way. Not as a ghost from the past.

Moving into a place of intimacy with a loved one requires us to see our partner in a fresh, healthy way. Not as a ghost from the past.

Unresolved Hurts in the Marriage

Some couples fail to adequately resolve hurts and wounds that occur in their relationship with one another. Over time, these create patterns that keep two people protecting themselves from further hurt, rather than cultivating and growing their love and pursuing each other.

In marriage, we all need to process conflict and disappointments and to do so in a way that opens the relationship up to growth and fulfillment.

Much like wounds from the past, hurts in marriage keep us afraid of intimacy and create expectations of future hurt, from which we protect ourselves. Fears and hurts leave us unable to experience our present partner as safe and can lead to a guardedness that shuts out openness to affection and bonding.

Lack of Personal Insight

We all have varying abilities to tune into our emotions and keep negative emotions from interfering with our key love relationships.

The skills necessary to understand and handle our inner emotions become essential ingredients of interpersonal success.

Much has been written recently on "emotional intelligence" – a way of looking at how adept we are in understanding our own emotions and those of others. Knowing our feelings and personality issues that help us or hinder us from connecting with and pursuing our partners becomes essential in the development of an intimate bond.

Addictions and Other Personal Challenges

Obviously, addiction to alcohol, drugs, food or pornography nearly eliminates our ability to be in a loving, growing marriage because these are typically pursued as most important. In addition, problems with depression, anxiety and other mental health imbalances can have a similar effect, as they consume our inner life.

The need to grow past addictions and personal problems with mood and anxiety becomes essential if we are to grow deeply in our love for another.

Lack of Understanding of How to Pursue Our Mate

Many of us grew up never learning how to pursue another person in a love relationship. We may have few role models and, many times, no learning experiences where we were taught specific ways to love another human being.

We may have no way to conceptualize pursuing another person with the intent of growing the bonds of love and marital harmony. In fact, this may even be the first time we ever thought about it.

Struggles with Becoming an Individual

A key component of a successful love life often centers on the maturity level of both partners, as we have discussed before. Both lovers need to have achieved a sense of independence, of standing on their own two feet, apart from the other. At some level, we are all on a continuous journey of emotional, psychological and spiritual growth. Prioritizing our own growth as a person becomes essential to insure that our marriages become and stay healthy.

When we think of maturity, we touch on a cornerstone of individual emotional health. Imagine your childhood as a journey of self-definition, where you develop a solid sense of your own identity. Apart from those around you.

Healthy families grow children who have confidence in their own abilities and personalities, giving them the courage and skills to successfully face the challenges of life.

A differentiated or mature person, therefore, possesses an appreciation for their uniqueness and worth and can face life with growing effectiveness because of a firm belief in themselves as competent and special. This person has grown up and away from their family of origin with confidence and trust in their strengths as a person.

The other side of the coin is someone who struggles with being an independent person or has a shaky belief in their own identity and ability to handle the challenges of life. We often see this manifested as low self-esteem and problems of worth. We also find this in someone who feels they don't really know themselves, having what we might call an unclear personal identity.

Someone who has not yet become their own person will struggle with self-esteem and often looks for a partner to make them feel whole. Thus, the marriage carries the burden of holding that person up and trying to make up for what didn't happen in childhood.

Conclusion

Any of these roadblocks to intimacy must be addressed in order to pursue one another with a deepening love and affection. And any of these challenges will potentially compromise love in and out of the bedroom.

How to Pursue Your Spouse

Let's switch our focus to a look at how to think of developing habits and even a mindset around pursing our spouse. After all, the effort to grow love has to be spelled out for many of us, and we can all benefit from tools and skills that keep us in a place of momentum. Where we continue to grow our passion for the love of our life. So often, pursuing one another hasn't become a habit and we need skills and beliefs that help us create a way of relating that incorporates this key attitude.

So how do we learn to "chase" our lover with passion, energy and renewed romance? Remember how natural this used to be? We got excited about one another, hormones and adrenalin kicked in, and we pursued. We went after the object of our affection. At least most of us did.

Something in marriage changes all that. First, the expectation that love just grows on its own makes us lazy, thinking all will be well without focus, initiative and effort. Second, we get used to each other. The "object of our affection" becomes more ordinary. Less exciting. More predictable.

All that needs to change. A profound shift needs to take place. We need to move, as lovers, toward our mate out of our own initiative. We need to draw from our own internal well of care and adoration. N, not because our spouse has "triggered" excitement, but because we produce it from our own heart, soul and personal energy. We can't expect our spouse to produce that quite so automatically as he or she used to.

Using the NASCAR analogy once again, imagine you are sitting in the driver's seat. The race begins. What makes you think you will have a chance at winning? Several factors come into play – your competitive nature, desire to win, driving skill, the status and monetary value of finishing first, etc. Most of these reasons center on your own heart and motivation to succeed.

A profound shift needs to take place. We need to move, as lovers, toward our mate out of our own initiative. We need to draw from our own internal well of care and adoration.

Or take climbing mountains. Getting to the top means preparation, a desire to experience nature, the thrill of making it to the end, the sense of victory or achievement and the exhilaration of standing at the top and looking at God's creation from above.

Both of these examples require us to look deep inside at our motivation, confidence, focus, desires, etc. And so it goes in loving our life partner. We need to draw from our internal motivation, skill set, desires and dreams. From this deep well, we reach out and pursue the one we love.

So let's begin the ascent. Let's examine the landscape from above. Let's step into the race car of passion, turn the engine on and hope to experience the thrill of winning.

There are numerous ways or paths that give us direction in pursuing our spouse. Each involves a need to examine our hearts and set concrete, behavioral goals that lead us in the direction of greater closeness. Let's look at several ideas on how to pursue our partner with deep love, passion and effort!

Look In The Mirror – Take Responsibility for Reaching Out

Taking responsibility means making a clear commitment to impacting your spouse's life in positive ways. In other words, we can make specific choices to love and honor our mate – in word and deed. We can think of ways to impact their world through our knowledge of what makes them feel loved, valued and cherished.

This responsibility means we need to examine all the ways we do or don't show up for the relationship that keep us more or less involved with our life partner.

Imagine for a minute that your loving style is convincing, penetrating, can't be missed, and hits the mark with your lover. You reach out in a way that can't be denied and comes from careful thought, planning, insistence and a commitment to actions that create love and connection.

Given this, you might ask several key questions that help you reflect on and evaluate your capability to love this intentionally. A few of these questions need to be thought through before moving forward. Take some time to Pause and Ponder.

PAUSE *and* PONDER

* ❋ Would you describe yourself as someone who reaches out in specific, concrete ways to touch the heart and soul of your mate?
* ❋ How do you do this?
* ❋ Do you have a thought-out or habitual (even if it's unconscious) way of loving your partner? Or is it hit and miss?
* ❋ Or do you wait for your spouse to initiate love and care before you respond? Are you always a "responder" or do you "initiate?"

Identifying how we love, our style, our patterns, how consistently we reach out to our husband or wife, is so important. This kind of honest evaluation allows us to see more clearly where we need to grow in our capacity to love and make a difference in the life of our mate.

Spend some time reflecting, journaling, writing about each of these questions. Develop an initial plan to improve and excel at loving and reaching out to your lover. Identify specific behaviors that move you forward in really pursuing your lover.

Develop - Developing Your Own Style of Loving and Caring

Once you take an honest look at your own level of personal responsibility in developing love in your marriage relationship, you have a better idea of just how intentional your loving style has become. And we truly mean an "honest" look. Be real with yourself. Otherwise, you may find it difficult to find a meaningful way of advancing the passion in your marriage.

You can examine whether or not you have identified specific behaviors that you know will help create meaningful connections with your spouse. As we discussed earlier, in our section on bonding and attachment, we sometimes think of this as the "glue" in the relationship. In other words, for couples to feel loved and bonded together, it takes glue-like actions – mutually rewarding and relationship building behaviors that grow and keep us closer to one another.

So the question becomes, do you create glue? Do you have intentional ways you bring passion, energy and positive caring into your lover's life that result in deep connection and a true lasting bond? Review the list of challenges earlier in the chapter.

> *Are there areas of growth that you need to identify and commit to that have kept you from loving more effectively?*

Love truly grows when two lovers develop an intentional, deliberate and consistent love style, with a series of conscious decisions to reach out in passionate and caring ways to our life partner.

We are committed to helping you think more strategically about how you love and also guiding you in the process of improving or developing your own style of reaching out and loving your mate.

Act – Ultimately, We Must Reach Out.

As simple as this sounds, in the marriage relationship, sometimes loving thoughts and feelings never get translated into tangible actions. And remember that loving connections come from consistent behavioral patterns. Not from sporadic, infrequent "I love you" statements on holidays or anniversaries.

Think about your own style and whether you regularly identify actions that build love, behaviors you have recognized that you know create lasting glue and are effective in convincing your partner you really do love them.

Do these actions get translated into consistent patterns?

. . . .

Loving connections come from consistent behavioral patterns. Not from sporadic, infrequent "I love you" statements on holidays or anniversaries.

. . . .

Create - Focus On Creating a Loving Experience

Love isn't all about emotions and feelings. But without the affection, care and tangible actions that move each other emotionally, love can't really thrive. Loving one another means being consistent in actions that say "I love you," "You really matter," and "I want you to know that and feel that."

Reflect on a time or chapter in your married or dating life when your emotional connection was really clear and alive. Take time to reflect on and answer these crucial questions. These will provide insight into how things were, are or can be.

PA(U)SE *and* PONDER

❊ **What created this emotional climate?**

❊ **What were each of you doing to make this happen?**

❊ **What behaviors kept your relationship growing?**

❊ **What positive feelings did you have for one another and how did you sustain these?**

Love grows and stays alive, pulsating with life, when we build experiences that keep it fresh and that communicate to our lover that they are valued, appreciated and cared for.

Notice the "when we . . . ." We must take personal ownership of how we bring these feelings of love into our lover's life. The actions and attitudes necessary to grow love come from within and through our actions, are translated into real life passion.

So a penetrating, personal focus on how to rock the world of our mate, how to generate passion and excitement toward him or her by our actions, is the stuff from which love is born and sustained.

Now let's bring all this home with some tangible exercises that will help you put a plan in place. That will start the adrenalin and excitement flowing again and provide a road map for growing and sustaining true passion in your love life together. Remember, your life together is a "love life." You are not robots, not just brothers and sisters. You are a gift from God, designed for mutual communion and explosive excitement for your life in marriage.

PURSUIT
Review and Practice

- By pursuit we mean how two people actually pursue each other in a loving relationship – how we reach out and seek involvement with one another. How we attempt to truly touch our partner's life with tangible behaviors that say "I love you" and "You matter."

- Continually pursuing one another in the marriage relationship, sustaining the energy we find in courtship, often gets overshadowed by the demands of daily living and the belief that love simply continues to grow without effort. Like we don't need to pursue one another any longer.

- So often, one or both partners become complacent because they don't feel like doing it and stop those behaviors that indicate real interest and even fondness for the other.

- At its core, pursuit involves reaching out and toward our partner, leaning into them, not leaning away, with the intent of loving them in positive ways – to grow the relationship and closeness we have with them.

- Yet clearly, the willingness and ability to pursue one another with consistent acts of love can hit roadblocks. These include:
  - › Imbalanced relationship patterns.
  - › Past wounds from childhood.
  - › Unresolved hurts in the marriage.
  - › Undeveloped interpersonal skills.

- › Lack of personal insight.

- › Addictions and other personal challenges.

- › Lack of understanding how to pursue each other.

- › Struggles with Becoming an Individual.

- So often pursuing one another hasn't become a habit and we need skills and beliefs that help us create a way of relating that incorporates this key attitude. All that needs to change. A profound shift needs to take place. We need to move, as lovers, toward our mate out of our own initiative. How?

  - › Take responsibility for reaching out. – We can make specific choices to love and honor our mate – in word and deed.

  - › Develop your own style of loving and caring. - Do you have intentional ways you bring passion, energy and positive caring into your lover's life that result in deep connection and a true lasting bond?

  - › Act – Developing a style where you regularly identify actions that create love.

  - › Create - Focus on creating a loving experience. Loving one another means being consistent in actions that say "I love you," "You really matter," and "I want you to know that and feel that." This creates the positive experience of being truly valued and cared for.

- We must take personal ownership of how we bring these feelings of love into our partner's life. The actions and attitudes necessary to grow love come from within, and by our actions, get translated into real life passion.

Exploring Together

- Take an honest look at your style of loving and reaching out. Do you make clear choices on reaching out to your spouse with love and affection?

- List several behaviors that characterize how you show and build love in your marriage.

- Take some time to talk with each other about how you pursued each other during dating and whether that has changed over the years or months of marriage. Have the ways you pursue each other changed over the years?

- Ask what specific behaviors you would like each other to do that would show you are reaching out and loving each other. Add these to your list.

Enhancing Your Marriage

- This week, each of you choose two behaviors from your partner's list that you would like them to focus on. Both of you, purposely and consistently put into action the behaviors requested by your partner every day. Be faithful to your own pursuing and try not to "keep score" on how your spouse is doing. Enjoy those times when your spouse reaches out to you and appreciate them by remembering them throughout your day.

Pondering the Spiritual

- Scripture speaks to the reality that God relentlessly pursues us. He wants us in an abiding relationship with Him that involves our total commitment, adoration and praise. Whether we look at the Old Testament or New

Testament, the personal stories we find unfolding always involve God's desire to have ALL of us. And He goes to great lengths to reach into our lives and remind us of His presence, power and care for what happens each moment of each day.

• Spend time this week in prayer, thanking God for the life He has given you – the marriage partner He has given you. Reflect on His amazing love and how He pursues us for His glory and for our blessing. Commit to pursuing your mate with the love God gives you and the power to carry out compassion and care in their life.

• Open your Bibles to the Old Testament. Find examples of how God pursues us and loves us. Read, for example, Deuteronomy 10. This describes God's love for His people and how He set His love and affection on them. Spend time in prayer praising God for His amazing love and affection.

• Read Romans 5:8. Reflect on how God set His love on us, even though we didn't deserve such grace and affection. Praise Him for loving you and for what the love He hopes you will give to your mate, knowing how you are loved by Him.

Next, we shift gears and begin a close look at physical intimacy. All we have learned so far contributes greatly to our appreciation for how awesome sex can be. How unbelievable God's creation of sexual union is. How amazing bodily intimacy, combined with a deep emotional, even spiritual connection, can truly be.

PLEASURE

"Pleasures lie thickest where no pleasures seem...
There's not a leaf that falls upon the ground
But holds some joy of silence or of sound,
Some spirits begotten of a summer dream."

Laman Blanchard

"I Wonder...Man and woman...Created by design"
A Poetic Musing

WONDER...

What God was thinking, what hopes He had for each – man and
woman – when He first brought man into the world and decided being
alone wasn't OK? What must have gone through His divine mind?

I wonder...

What God-thoughts are like. What crossed His mind when He
reached into His unfailing love, His desire for each of us to experience
goodness and a thriving life and made us male and female? He must
have known our need for touch, for connection, for a lasting place in the
heart of another. His design.

I wonder...

How long it took to come up with "woman." The compliment of man, the needed ingredient for love to abound, for loneliness to exit the stage, for synergy to be realized.

I wonder...

Does God ponder? Did it take Him long to see human need for what it is? After all, He created us and so the ingredients of human experience and feelings He put within us. For us to realize and experience and rejoice in.

I wonder...

Where He came up with His plan for human touch and belonging? How He knew so well the heart-felt desires of our nature and being. Created after His image. His being within us.

I wonder...

How He must have smiled at the penultimate meaning two lovers would be able to bring to their passionate bond – reveling in the experience of knowing each other deeply . . . man and woman able to magnificently applaud their lover and the delight in knowing the special spirit each brings into their awesome union.

I wonder...

How, in His great love and wisdom and desire for our best, He thought of the greatest ingredient to bind two lovers together, the antidote to keep us enthused about our journey in marriage, the balm for our souls...
... Pleasure

Pleasure

Made to touch, to know each other deeply, to grasp through human experience the expression of love...by our desire to make our lover feel good.

A simple, yet majestic concept only God could have manufactured.

With pleasure, we say, "I want you to feel me deeply and the love I have for you. I am placing your happiness in the foreground of my mind and, with pleasure, I'll prove that to you."

Pleasure can also be a loaded, controversial topic in many ways. For some, pleasure means sin or hedonism we shouldn't focus on. For others, pleasure and fun are a way of life. Many have given up on finding pleasure in marriage. Somehow, it seems like an impossible attainment.

The word pleasure, too often, brings up feelings of guilt. It's as if seeking pleasure is not OK, "selfish," as if we should feel uncomfortable with it. We even use the term "guilty pleasure" to describe something that feels somehow "too good." This is so unfortunate. These kinds of beliefs hinder, not help to enliven a marriage.

You see, God gave us, in our bodies, minds and emotions, the ability to experience pleasure and the capacity to give and receive pleasure and pleasurable sensations. He created us to bond together around positive connections that relate directly to our willingness to bring energy and excitement into bodily and emotional touch.

The experience of pleasure grows a marriage, sustains love and becomes a meaningful way to assess how love explains itself in the unique bond of two people seeking to love each other. Consider these thoughts as we journey ahead.

PA(U)SE *and* PONDER

❋ So how would you define the word pleasure? What comes to mind when you think of the need for pleasure in your marriage?

❋ Do you believe it forms a vital ingredient in marital happiness?

❋ Can you imagine building a loving partnership with your spouse by creating a greater experience of mutual pleasure?

Grasping the role of "pleasure" in creating and sustaining love gives us a unique and vibrant way to think about how we connect with our partner. Cultivating pleasure in marriage gives us a desire to draw toward our partner, not away.

Often, marriages that have grown stale, upon investigation, have all but lost the sense of joy that comes from doing things together and that satisfy our need to feel good. Often, one of the quickest ways to jumpstart a bland marriage is to add a contagious energy, a vivid passion and a noticeable infusion of pleasure and even fun activities into married life.

> *Cultivating pleasure in marriage gives us a desire to draw toward our partner, not away.*
>
> *Using pleasure becomes one way to unite, to gravitate toward a kind of mutual involvement that satisfies and adds life to the relationship.*
>
> *So one of our ultimate goals, if we want to transform our marriage, centers on our capacity to bring pleasure into each other's life – physically and emotionally.*

In the bedroom, the issue of pleasure takes a front seat and we will be discussing specific ways to bring this kind of energy and passion into the sexual relationship. But more on that later.

Right now, we will focus on other dimensions of pleasure that create lasting strength and connection in our love for one another.

Pleasure Explored

We want to help you shape and define the culture of your marriage – growing your love for one another – by creating an exciting, passionate life. One that is filled with pleasure. These are marriages people want to stay in.

So have you ever thought about this before? Spend a few minutes thinking about the "culture" of your marriage. Yes, your marriage has its own culture or personality.

PAUSE *and* PONDER

❋ **How would you describe the personality of your marriage?**

❋ **What do you want your love relationship to look like?**

❈ **What kind of energy and pleasure have you, as two lovers, created together?**

Relationships that feel good are protected from looking outside and being vulnerable. It is critical and important to develop a home life that's enjoyable, where you are enhancing and cultivating ways to impact each other's world with "feel good" experiences.

We think there are three ways to think about this; they provide a basis for growing pleasure in your partnership – "Developing Sensuality," "Creating Fun Activities Together," and "Focusing on the Good."

So let's have some fun now and look at these in more detail. Remember, you can choose to change your marriage by deliberately bringing positive, pleasurable connections into your love life. You can define and create the culture and personality of your partnership.

Developing Sensuality

Our first theme centers on "sensuality." When we talk about sensuality, most people think we are going to discuss sexuality. Yet there is much more to consider than just the bedroom experience, which we will get to later. So what does the word sensuality mean?

We define sensuality as all the ways we highlight our physical senses, the ways we focus on, observe and experience the fullness of touch, taste, smell, sound and sight. Let's explore each.

Touch

Touch is so important. There are way too many marriages that are starving for affection and have succumbed to mere co-existence – a platonic type of relationship devoid of real excitement, resembling roommates or brother and sister. How sad. This doesn't have to be so.

Touch is a vital, basic need present the moment we come into the world and a doctor's hands pulls us from the womb and places us in the arms of our mother. From the skin to skin contact in the warmth and safety of our mother's embrace, we feel loved. We literally *feel* loved.

Touch reassures, touch comforts and touch lets us know we exist. When you first started dating, you likely touched each other a lot. Some couples can't take their hands off each other when they first start dating. Slowly, over time, because no one really knows how important it is, or hurts create walls and resistance, two lovers reduce or almost discontinue this kind of reaching out.

Some people struggle with being touched due to abuse or neglect in their histories. Touch can feel scary and or unfamiliar. It may take time and practice for some couples to learn to "take touch in" together. But the enjoyment of touch and its benefits can happen.

Touch is a vital, basic need present the moment we come into the world and a doctor's hands pull us from the womb and places us in the arms of our mother.

So let us ask you,

When you wake up in the morning now, do you lean over and curl up into your husband's arms, do you kiss each other, pat each other on the rear, and hug each other before leaving home?

Do you hold hands when out together, play footsies when at the beach, or engage in any of the thousands of ways we can touch that convey "you are special and I want to be connected to you?"

These all send the message we are happy to be with the one we love and are willing to fully express that care through the God-given expression of touch.

Taste & Smell

So how do we heighten and create taste and smell so that is pleasing? And how does it help marriage?

When we think of taste and smell, food often comes to mind and the many flavors and scents that go into our bodies and surroundings. We eat together, sharing the mutual experience of taste and aromas and the enjoyment that comes from creating time for this sensual activity. This is why so many dates involve going out to a nice restaurant and sharing time around the pleasure of food.

Can you imagine coming home at the end of the day, having planned to cook a sumptuous master-chef meal with your loved one – where you both dive into the experience of creating something together you will both later feast on – all the while feeding each other little bites of lobster or garlic mashed potatoes along the way?

After all, some have said it all starts in the kitchen. What a difference in your married life if there are times like these when you bask on simple pleasures together.

But what about the bathroom? There is opportunity there too for delighting in pleasing smells. How about a bath with your sweetheart, filled with aromatic bubble bath, bath salts or soaps and perhaps yummy smelling candles aglow around you? Relaxing together among soothing smells fills our memory banks with positive, fragrant associations to our partner. For it is true; when we smell good, we want to be closer to our partner and we remember them as pleasing.

So this discussion naturally moves into the topic of personal hygiene. In two words, It Matters! Being conscientious about our own smells and trying to stay clean, fresh and aromatic, perhaps with some lovely perfume or intriguing cologne, can go a long way. We are not talking about being overly particular and cleanliness is not really next to Godliness, but when we consistently smell good or distinct (in a good way), our lover can come to identify us with our pleasing smell and long to be around us as a result. Our individual odor can be quite powerful.

Sound & Sight

Our world, as God created, is full of sounds and sights that are amazing. We see and hear a world around us and it affects us profoundly. Being in spaces that are aesthetically pleasing, colorful and beautiful, enliven our senses and give us joy. This is one reason why we go to the beach, the mountains, the theater – places where our senses are heightened by what we see and hear.

Is your home a pleasing place to be? Does it look like you want it to look? Are you surrounded by things that make you feel good? Do you sometimes play music of your choice that soothes your heart and soul?

More personally, are the words you say and the tone of voice you use pleasing to hear? And are you easy on the eyes because you try to look good and be attractive to your bride or groom? Have you stopped trying or do you still aspire to look "hot" or sexy like you did in the early days of your relationship? How we sound and look are important ways we can cultivate a pleasing sensual experience with each other.

Creating Fun Activities Together

Our next way of developing pleasure involves creating fun activities together. When we think of fun, what often comes to mind is excitement, relaxation, no stress, laughter and other words that describe a sense of letting go and enjoying the moment. Not to mention the fact that "fun" is good for your health and overall well-being.

Simply put, couples who enjoy spending *fun time* together make a clear statement – that they appreciate and have a positive connection with their loved one based on the synergy or energy they create together. Having fun is a kind of connection that is different from planning a budget and less interesting events that we share in life.

Bringing positive energy back into our marriage means creating mutual interests, getting outside our comfort zones and even trying new experiences together. The message is that we value and believe in our life together and that we can build excitement and aliveness into our shared life – a chemistry so often present earlier in our marriage.

What a statement to make – I love you, you are fun and we, together, are fun and have an interesting life in each other's company.

Here's one practical suggestion to get you off and running. We call this the "fun jar." Whenever either of you think of something you have never tried before, something that sounds exciting to do, such as a place you'd like to visit or an activity you'd like to try, write it down and put it in the fun jar. When any symptoms of boredom start to set in, you have an antidote. You can draw from the jar and go for it.

We remember one couple struggling with this who discovered a mutual desire to spend time at a nearby beach town. While she window shopped, he enjoyed looking at small book stores. They would often go into the art shops and look around together, discuss mutual art interests and then diverge into separate ways for a while.

Bringing positive energy back into our marriage means creating mutual interests, getting outside our comfort zones and even trying new experiences together.

Their trips to the beach became creative, picking dinner spots at the end of the day or sitting in the park watching people go by and wondering what kind of relationship couples had together based on their looks or how close they seemed to one another. They even liked to look at people passing by and decide what animals they reminded them of. They were very fun people and they just needed direction in how to cultivate fun in their marriage.

And it all started when the husband placed his idea of day visits to small beach towns in the jar.

Fun has to be built into our married life, however creatively. When we do, we make a clear statement of love for one another and our belief that our relationship has life, aliveness and excitement. We create positive memories we can reflect on and that remind us of how good it feels to be with our lover and friend.

Focusing on the Good

Finally, it is critical to focus on what is good in each other.

Let's start with this question: What characterizes your thoughts each moment of the day? Do you have a positive outlook and way of viewing life events and your married life together?

The right mental perspective makes a difference. If we look for the good in life, in our mate and in each of our experiences, we have a much greater likelihood of creating joy and positive energy around us.

In dating, for example, in the beginning, all we really see are the wonderful traits in each other – the cute way she walks, the funny jokes he tells, the nice smile we see when he totally "gets" me, the way she treats other people. We see the good in our partner but often, this somehow disappears over time.

Imagine for a minute that all the positive thoughts you had about each other when dating simply continue throughout your married life. What a difference that would make. Yet so often the "cute" and "fun" traits we once smiled over become sources of irritation and we no longer grin when we see them. His "meticulous" ways become "fussy" and her "delightful laugh" becomes a "cackle." What a shame.

If we look for the good in life, in our mate and in each of our experiences, we have a much greater likelihood of creating joy and positive energy around us.

We need to purposefully look for the good in our partner and to practice noticing those traits that float our boat and that we find valuable, interesting and even exciting. For these experiences of pleasure to happen, we need to have a certain mindset when we go into them. Looking for the good in our partner and in our experience as well is that mindset.

So creating fun activities and being playful, being kids together, releasing the inner child, goes a long way in creating a mutually satisfying life together, influencing the very personality of that life.

Final Thoughts

We need to bring pleasure into our marriage – regularly. The experience of bringing pleasure into each other's life through a focus on sensuality, having fun together and focusing on the good in our mate, cultivates a passionate bond. And all this starts outside the bedroom.

Couples who truly enjoy one another and find pleasure in their shared life protect their bond of love and enhance all the other aspects of their life together.

PLEASURE
Review and Practice

- With pleasure we say, "I want you to feel me deeply and the love I have for you. I am placing your happiness in the foreground of my mind and with pleasure, I'll prove that to you."

- The word pleasure, too often, brings up feelings of guilt. It's as if seeking pleasure is not OK, "selfish," as if we should feel uncomfortable with it.

- God created us to bond together around positive connections that relate directly to our willingness to bring energy and excitement into bodily and emotional touch.

- Grasping the role of "pleasure" in creating and sustaining love gives us a unique and vibrant way to think about how we connect with our partner. Cultivating pleasure in marriage gives us a desire to draw toward our partner, not away.

- Relationships that feel good are protected from looking outside and being vulnerable.

- Three ways to develop pleasure in your marriage are Developing Sensuality, Creating Fun Activities Together, and Focusing on the Good.

  › Developing sensuality - We define sensuality as all the ways we highlight our physical senses, the ways we focus on, observe and experience the fullness of touch, taste, smell, sound and sight.

  › Creating fun activities - When we think of fun, what often comes to mind is excitement, relaxation, no stress, laughter and other words that describe a sense of letting go and enjoying the moment.

> Focusing on the Good - If we look for the good in life, in our mate and in each of our experiences, we have a much greater likelihood of creating joy and positive energy around us.

Exploring Together

• When you think of "pleasure," what comes to mind? Do you have any blocks or negative thoughts about experiencing pleasure? If so, what can you do to push them out of the way?

• In what ways do you bring pleasure into your married life now?

• Are you aware of bringing sensuality into your partner's life? Fun? And do you focus on the good in your mate?

• Talk with each other about what you think the "culture" of your marriage is. Especially regarding pleasure. Describe it. How would you like it to be? What can you do to make your marriage more pleasurable?

Enhancing Your Marriage

• Sharing good feelings together is so important for a vital marriage and we can do this by heightening our sensual experience. Below is a "senses" list. Take a moment to write down the things that you enjoy experiencing through your senses.

Touch	Taste	Sound	Smell	Sight
E.g. Velvet Skin	Chocolate	A Trickling River	Vanilla	A Sunset

- Plan a date using your sensuality list from above. Try to incorporate a few of each of your favorites. For example, using the above suggestions: Going to the beach with a velvet throw; a vanilla candle and chocolate and wine in tow to watch a beautiful sunset.

- Start a "fun jar" and jot down fun activities you would like to do together. Whenever you think of something new, write it down and jar it. The ultimate experience – A fun jar date coupled with some of your five senses.

- Make a conscious effort this week to focus on the good in each other. Purposefully look for the good in your partner (and yourself, and your life). Notice how it helps you feel better in mood and towards each other.

Pondering the Spiritual

- We are made in God's image. Spend time reflecting on God's intent in creating pleasure in your life and that of your marriage. Why do you think He did this?

- Thank Him for the gift of pleasure.

- Spend time reading the Song of Solomon. What does it teach us about pleasure and God's design for pleasure in our love life?

Next, we move into the bedroom and explore the role of pleasure in creating and enhancing sexual intimacy.

PLEASURE AND
SEXUAL INTIMACY

*"Intimacy is not a destination but rather an unfolding story
of how we love – ourselves and another human being."*
DOUG & LESLIE GUSTAFSON

Pleasure And Sex

T'S EVERYWHERE.

What a sexualized world we live in. Sex is everywhere. Just go through the check-out line at the grocery store and take a look at the magazines with half-naked women, men with bulging muscles and articles promising six secrets for turning your lover on.

Maybe you could skip this chapter, spend $5.95 on the latest informative magazine and discover all the wonderful mysteries of igniting passion in the bedroom. What a deal!

The latest version I scanned talked about candles in the bedroom, going slow, touching parts other than erogenous zones, flirting at dinner to create a seductive mood, turning her on with bubble bath . . . and the list goes on. What pearls of wisdom; what gems we have been living without. Treat her/him nicely and you may get lucky? Wow. Never knew. What magnificent advice.

But wait. Maybe there's more. Don't run to the grocery or bookstore just yet.

On a more serious note, making sex a vibrant, exciting part of our love relationship means understanding the process of love-making, how our bodies work, and the knowledge and skills needed *to feel confident in our sexuality* and our competence as lovers.

Your grocery store tabloid or favorite magazine won't help out a whole lot in this department. They are more concerned with selling copies than being accurate and informative. Also, sexual intimacy is complex and most sources don't fully understand how deep, meaningful physical contact really works.

Perhaps there is no greater challenge than learning to love one another deeply and expressing this physically, naked and vulnerable in each other's arms.

We plan to unlock the potential you both have to touch each other's mind and heart in the various forms of sexual contact that make marriage so unique.

We know that God declared two lovers to be "one," and the act of sex seals that deal. Something dramatic and awesome happens in the act of sex. We were meant to express love, culminating in sexual climax. A grand union with deep meaning and implications for building love.

We also recognize that openly talking about sex may be new territory for many couples and perhaps a bit scary or awkward. With that in mind, we encourage you to read the next two sections of the book aloud with each other to increase your comfort and ease and take your marriage to a new place of intimacy. We will be using both accurate scientific and descriptive language to talk about the anatomy of our bodies and the process of intercourse.

This may be a good time to talk with each other about what language you currently use to describe your genitals and what language you would like to use in your own sex talks together. Some of us have playful nicknames such as "Pete and Virginia"; or euphemisms like "down there", "secret hair"; or tolerable slang used for body parts or the act of sex itself. Couples vary here – some using more scientific terminology like "vagina and penis."

Just getting used to speaking about our "private parts" is a growth area for many. Some of you might even have checked out or went "ewww" when we used the word genitals. So, come on back, and join us again and hang in there. If you would like anatomical pictures to increase your understanding, *A Celebration of Sex* by Douglas E. Rosenau, PhD is a great resource.

Evan and Lori

When Evan and Lori first came to see us, they had just celebrated 11 years of marriage. They met as colleagues in their chosen profession and fell in love a few short months after they began dating.

Evan was a robust "man's man" and delighted in courting his wife. She had never been cared for as consistently as she experienced with Evan and believed he loved her deeply. He was "sweet and affectionate," traits she had never experienced in any man she dated and very different from the detached father she was used to as a role model.

Both decided to wait until marriage to engage each other sexually, a commitment they were able to keep despite their growing affection for one another.

Neither Lori nor Evan had much sexual experience prior to marriage. Evan had a few brief relationships that resulted in touching and pleasure to the point of orgasm – but never intercourse.

Lori's dating experience consisted of one longer term relationship but little physical contact. Although there was some genital touching, her boyfriend eventually pressured her to have intercourse. She refused and he finally ended the relationship after over a year.

Evan and Lori's first sexual encounters after marriage were fueled with the excitement and anticipation expected in their early relationship. They had an interest in one another's bodies and their initial sexual experiences grew out of this curiosity and care for one another.

Over the first year, however, their sexual contact became somewhat stereotyped and predictable. Evan typically reached orgasm quickly and Lori didn't have a chance to experience a longer time in the bedroom — she couldn't reach orgasm herself. In fact, she wasn't even sure she was supposed to.

Eventually, sex became unrewarding for her and her interest in physical contact began to wane. Evan, on the other hand, enjoyed these new sexual experiences and didn't know his wife was struggling to enjoy their time. He wondered about her "inability" to orgasm and thought maybe something was wrong with his wife's lack of sexual responsiveness.

Neither partner brought up their feelings about what was happening. Both were too anxious and didn't know what to say to describe their anxiety and dissatisfaction with how sex was going.

Lori's disinterest in sex grew and eventually Evan became more and more angry about their lack of physical intimacy. He began blaming her even more and complaining that their love was diminishing. He concluded that her lack of sexual desire was her problem. Deep down, he was afraid that he wasn't measuring up or was inadequate in some kind of way. Yet he had little ability to understand his feelings and it was easier to get angry and blame his wife for her disinterest.

Lori, on the other hand, had very little understanding of sex and how it was supposed to go. During premarital counseling, their pastor suggested that they wait to have sex until the honeymoon and both agreed this was important. Yet he never explained much about how sex works and so provided little understanding of the mechanics and emotions that go into successful physical intimacy.

At some level, Lori believed that Evan was the man of her dreams who would sweep her off her feet and that sex would just come naturally for both of them.

Both Evan and Lori had nowhere to go with their feelings, frustra-
tions and disappointments. Their fights became more frequent, even
though they couldn't really determine what their anger was about and
why they had become so hostile to one another. They reached an
impasse and wondered if they should have ever married one another.

Our work with Evan and Lori centered on a thorough look at their attitudes about sex and their understanding of how a vibrant sexual relationship develops. We explored at length their hopes and expectations of one another, their understanding of how their bodies work and a close look at how to bring sexual energy and passion into their marriage as a whole – before the bedroom door opens.

Evan, for example, learned that Lori's deeper connection to her sexual feelings and passion depended on his patience and attentiveness to her basic needs for closeness and affection. We examined his excitement during dating, how he intentionally "courted" his wife with key behaviors that impacted her feeling of being special and worthwhile.

We explored how these same behaviors need to continue in marriage and how men can shape their wives' confidence that the act of sex is embedded in a deeper overall relationship of trust and connection – enhanced by how we treat them daily.

And we focused on developing his understanding of how women respond physiologically during the sexual experience and how to pay attention to signs and clues that she is feeling close, safe and cared for during the act of sex itself.

Finally, we helped him understand how his own sexual excitement needs to be centered in a deeper understanding of how intimacy develops out of the bedroom and how this sets the stage for romantic energy and passion when the touching begins. Not only for Lori but also for himself.

With Lori, we also examined her understanding of the sex response cycle, how to ask for what she needs from her husband in and out of the bedroom and a deeper appreciation of how her body, as a woman, reacts during sex. This educational piece enhanced her grasp of the "fun" of sex, how she can affirm her husband's masculinity and need for sexual closeness that is more easily triggered than hers.

We helped her get in touch with her own femininity and sexual feelings, recognizing that, for many women, the process can take longer than for men. Most women don't know how to reach inward and feel sexual with much ease.

We explored her attitudes about sex, her understanding of how great sex enhances all other areas of intimacy out of the bedroom and how to reach out to her husband in ways that invite him to know her and love her physically.

We helped both Lori and Evan develop a way to process their feelings toward one another, including their anger and disappointments, and how open, transparent communication would help them heal and find ways to stay close and connected. We helped them embrace a plan for closeness and connection outside the bedroom and how to honor and prioritize their sexual life together as they learn new skills of how to please each other physically.

We share this story because it provides a dynamic look at the intricacies of creating a vibrant, passionate relationship, intertwined with physical touch and desire, a need for deep communion and a shared excitement about life together. Sex and pleasure form real ingredients in the story of a successful love picture. Their story gives us an inside look at their relationship, a not uncommon history that many others have experienced. Some of the themes, if not all, may resonate with your own experience.

And so we divide this section into the various components we believe will add both knowledge and skills to your understanding of sexual pleasure.

Initial Considerations

In a few moments, we'll examine several distinct physical and emotional aspects of the sexual experience that will be broken down into phases. Kind of a Sex 101 – mechanics and all. We hope to teach, preach and inspire you to love explosively, tenderly and competently through exposure to biology and the complex emotions that make sex and plea-sure abound in your love connection.

But first, a few considerations that need attention. These set the stage for our in-depth look at how to understand and achieve maximum, sexual fulfillment.

Presence Revisited

Grasping the role of pleasure in your sex life begins with a look in the mirror. With your clothes on and eyes wide open. An honest, some-times gripping confrontation with a few foundational elements that help create exciting possibilities when we strip naked and embrace our lover in spirit and touch.

These will parallel and, to some extent, repeat concepts we developed earlier in the attitude we called *presence*. They are worth elaborating on in the context of this section on sexual pleasure and excitement.

Pleasure – It All Starts With Me.

First, we need to embrace our individual capacity to experience plea-sure and be honest about what gets in the way . . . in other words, your ability to be a pleasure-giver and pleasure-receiver in the arms of a safe, committed lover. Some, for example, have difficulty integrating pleasure into their lives and so have challenges bringing pleasure into their rela-tionship with their life partner.

Take a close look at a few key questions to get us started.

PAUSE *and* PONDER

❋ **Are you open to giving pleasure to your bride/groom?**
❋ **Can you imagine being pleasured and feeling good about the experience?**
❋ **Do you like the idea of being fondled, of fondling and mov-ing your partner and yourself into sexual orbit?**

Sexual orbit? OK, maybe we got carried away but hopefully, you catch the drift. God created pleasure as a super glue in our connection with our mate. We need to learn to be sticky and enjoy the process.

The Differentiated Self

What a mouthful – differentiation. Yet secondly, we need to ask the critical question of whether we have two individuals capable of being in a close, intimate relationship. This is the needed starting point of growing an exciting, sustained version of lasting passion.

It is vital that each partner comes to the marriage a "whole" person or is in a process of growing into a mature individual with little interference from past wounds and hurts that haven't healed. A mature person has "differentiated" – in other words, has achieved some level of psychological wholeness and isn't looking for a mate to "complete" them.

Someone who has "differentiated" has grown up. This person isn't looking for someone to rescue them and doesn't engage in manipulative games to get what they want. They are able to give and take in the partnership without strings attached.

Someone who has grown in their individual identity is able to identify their wants and needs. Their personal awareness of their feelings and ability to empathize with others gives them a platform from which to love another human being.

We can't overemphasize the need for personal maturity and the potential this gives a couple in their intimate and sexual relationship.

Physical sex involves an intense form of giving that is itself embedded in a kind of vulnerability that makes maturity critical.

Along those lines, we can look at any individual and wonder how much or how well they have cultivated "self-care" into their lives, even apart from what happens in their key love relationships. Do they stand on their own two feet, able to experience joys in life based on an independent identity? Do they take care of themselves, bringing personal fulfillment and pleasure into their own lives without complete dependence on others for happiness?

When working with individuals experiencing depression, for example, we often advocate bringing fun into their lives and also adding exercise to their daily routines. In other words, finding concrete ways to get pleasure and even fun onto your personal calendar.

Physical sex involves an intense form of giving and is itself embedded in a kind of vulnerability that makes maturity critical.

For all of us, we need to think in terms of managing our emotions and developing ways to bring positivity into our daily lives. Imagine asking yourself daily, "What would feel good to me today?" If that question seems foreign or perhaps selfish, chances are you have not cultivated the skill of adding joy and pleasure into your day as a habit or practice.

Experiencing the Now

Third, another vital aspect of this has to do with our ability to experience the moment. In other words, when I'm in the moment, do I make it a point to experience it by centering or tuning into my own experience with all five senses – sound, smell, taste, touch and sight?

Many people struggle with "going inward" to enhance their own experience just for themselves – people often think this is selfish, perhaps even hedonistic or just odd.

Yet if I can't experience pleasure and good things and know my feelings and senses, it becomes a real leap to imagine how that's going to work in the bedroom. In other words, how can I "let go" and experience myself and my partner sexually if I struggle to know my own feelings and sensations – to enjoy them, value them and appreciate them?

We might call this mindfulness . . . the ability to know myself and my experience moment by moment. My capacity to reflect on all the feelings and thoughts and sensations that come my way as part of being a person created in God's image.

A mindful approach to life means I consider what is happening now, not later, or even yesterday. It means I can tune in to what I know about my body, my emotions and beliefs and filter out distractions that keep me from being present. Knowing what's happening right now gives me that ability to bring my body and mind into the presence of my lover, feel deeply and give generously. I have resources because I know myself and enjoy the joys of being a human being.

Men versus Women

An aside worth noting has to do with the different ways men and women experience their own sensuality and sexual selves. For men, generally, being in touch with their sexual self comes more easily than for women, as they experience their physical sex drive more often and it feels "closer to the surface."

Often, women need to warm up and unearth their sexual feelings in order to get in touch with themselves sexually, to recognize their sexual self, to feel their desire and arousal, including sensations in their body, and their overall sense of wanting a sexual encounter.

Often, women need to warm up and unearth their sexual feelings in order to get in touch with themselves sexually, to recognize their sexual self, to feel their desire and arousal, including sensations in their body, and their overall sense of wanting a sexual encounter.

So it helps women to think of finding ways to get comfortable, to engage in forms of self-care and ease their way into the experience of their own sensuality where they can feel "sexy" and ready for physical intimacy.

Sometimes women need to give themselves permission to experience and enjoy sexual feelings and their bodily expression due to negative messages they received during their developmental years. Many busy women today even find value in reminding themselves to think about sex during the day, to keep their "mind in the game" so to speak.

Men, on the other hand, typically need to slow down and get in touch with their emotional side, in addition to their desire to have physical sex. This means embracing parts of themselves they don't necessarily want to recognize such as a "needy side" or wanting to be comforted and supported by their mate. Being emotionally vulnerable can be very challenging for many men as they see it as weakness. Truth is, it takes strength and courage to be vulnerable and open with real feelings.

So each individual in the marriage needs to explore the ways they get in touch with their sensual side. Once this happens, physical expression becomes richer and easier to achieve in the bedroom.

Men, on the other hand, typically need to slow down and get in touch with their emotional side, in addition to their desire to have physical sex.

Presence and the Capacity to Love

Next, great sex and therefore amazing intimacy comes from a deep capacity to love.

Maturity means a capacity to bond in the relationship without fear and without closing off in the process. Transparency, openness and trust become essential ingredients for closeness and each person in the marriage has to have reached a place where they can give themselves to another human being.

In addition, great sex in the bedroom comes from the growth of the relationship itself. Not only does the marriage require two grown-ups, but the connection two people enjoy needs to have grown over time. The marriage needs to be characterized by a close, intimate bond without fractures and without any factors that diminish trust and care for one another.

A healthy marriage provides the safety for two people to share their emotions and dreams with one another, rather than an unsafe place where openness leads to hurt or rejection or fear.

Two lovers committed to personal, relational and spiritual growth can come together and experience deep and profound enjoyment in sexual contact with one another. Sex can be fun, exciting and even inspirational.

With the foundation of growth and personal maturity in place, the next step in developing "amazing intimacy" centers on how to create and forge together passionate sex that is satisfying and exciting and vibrant.

Two lovers committed to personal, relational and spiritual growth can come together and experience deep and profound enjoyment in sexual contact with one another. Sex can be fun, exciting and even inspirational.

Yes, we mean create. We all need to understand and implement a comprehensive model that enhances, develops and builds an exciting physical life together. So let's get to it.

Ins and Outs of an Explosive Sex Life – Including the Real Nuts and Bolts

The experience of marriage needs to be passionate – in and out of the bedroom.

Historically, we turn to the work of Masters and Johnson, who studied in detail the different phases of sexual encounter and response. In doing so, they focused on the biological aspects of the sexual contact cycle, including initial phases of arousal leading to eventual orgasm.

In their cogent and thorough look at these stages, Chris and Rachel McCluskey expanded on these phases and developed a more comprehensive look at the sexual response cycle that included more than mere biology.★ They constructed an insightful and spiritual look at the stages of sexual expression to include the emotional, psychological and spiritual aspects, emphasizing God's creative work and design for men and women in a committed marriage relationship.

We will draw from this work, as well as Masters and Johnson's, in developing four phases of the sexual response cycle. This includes our perspective that God created this magnificent design for those in a permanent, marital bond.

So buckle your seat belts. Here's how it all works. An amazing design, brought to you by God and given as a great gift for two lovers to dine and feast on as they create explosive, courageous love together. In harmony, passion gets translated from body to spirit in an awesome, swirling journey of contagious desire and skillful embrace.

Phases of Sexual Intimacy

Yes, there are phases that go into the lovemaking experience. An understanding of each phase can help couples experience, cultivate and gain mastery of how to bring brilliant passion and priceless pleasure into the naked bedroom of shared love.

★ Adapted with permission of Fleming H. Revel from *When Two Become One: Enhancing Sexual Intimacy In Marriage.* Copyright ©2004 by Christopher & Rachel McCluskey.

PLEASURE &
SEXUAL INTIMACY
Review

- How to make sex a vibrant, exciting part of our love relationship means understanding the process of love-making, how our bodies work, and the knowledge and skills needed *to feel confident in our sexuality* and our competence as lovers.

- This may be a good time to talk with each other about what language you currently use to describe your genitals and what language you would like to use in your own sex talks together.

- Sex and pleasure form real ingredients in the story of a successful love picture.

- We need to embrace our individual capacity to experience pleasure and be honest about what gets in the way.

- It is vital that each partner comes to the marriage a "whole" person or is in a process of growing into a mature individual with little interference from past wounds and hurts that haven't healed.

- Physical sex involves an intense form of giving and finds itself embedded in a kind of vulnerability that makes maturity critical.

- Another vital aspect of this has to do with our ability to experience the moment. This means I can tune into what I know about my body, my emotions and beliefs and filter out distractions that keep me from being present.

- For men, generally, being in touch with their sexual self comes more easily than for women, as they experience their physical sex drive more often and it feels "closer to the surface."

- Often, women need to warm up and unearth their sexual feelings in order to get in touch with themselves sexually, to recognize their sexual self, to feel their desire and arousal, including sensations in their body, and their overall sense of wanting a sexual encounter.

- Men, on the other hand, typically need to slow down and get in touch with their emotional side, in addition to their desire to have physical sex.

- Great sex and therefore amazing intimacy comes from a deep capacity to love. Maturity means a capacity to bond in the relationship without fear and without closing off in the process.

- In addition, great sex in the bedroom comes from the growth of the relationship itself. Not only does the marriage require two grown-ups, but the connection two people have needs to have grown over time.

- Two lovers committed to personal, relational and spiritual growth can come together and experience deep and profound enjoyment in sexual contact with one another. Sex can be fun, exciting and even inspirational.

- With the foundation of growth and personal maturity in place, the next step in developing "amazing intimacy" centers on how to create and forge together passionate sex that is satisfying and exciting and vibrant. Yes, we mean create.

- There are phases that go into the lovemaking experience. An understanding of each phase can help couples experience, cultivate and gain mastery of how to bring brilliant passion and priceless pleasure into the naked bedroom of shared love.

Our usual sections on "Exploring Together," "Enhancing Your Marriage" and "Pondering the Spiritual" will be at the end of our chapters on all 5 phases.

We begin with "Atmosphere."

ATMOSPHERE

What It Means

THIS STAGE REFERS to the setting. Where sexual intimacy takes place. Where we – a make sure we organize our time and efforts to establish a meaningful environment for great sex to occur.

When we spend time thinking about when and where sex occurs, we help facilitate each person's ability to get into the mood and more importantly, to fully surrender to one another emotionally and spiritually and physically. We start warming up the sexual engines. Some people balk at the idea of "planning sex." It seems somehow unromantic or lacking spontaneity.

The problem, however, with not setting specific time aside is simply this: As a relationship matures and the responsibilities of life increase, sex can end up taking a back seat to other activities. Sexual tension can result, building frustration. Over time, consistent patterns of physical contact that are vital to sustaining a passionate marriage diminish.

Remember that in the right setting, two people in a loving, committed marriage can give themselves over to one another with abandon. The right atmosphere sets the stage for enjoying each other's body and for creating a safe setting where vulnerability, playfulness and excitement can grow.

Imagine for a minute all the various "atmospheres" we take for granted in the many activities of life. Let's take golf. Suppose the golf course is built near an animal habitat with tigers and lions. Kind of silly but imagine this. Right atmosphere? Don't think so.

Or picture your favorite spot for meditation, or perhaps a picnic with your lover, constructed right next to a major freeway. Wouldn't really work.

And so it is with two lovers, about to embrace one another naked and vulnerable. Lovers who need maximum focus and attention. One man and one woman who must center themselves in utmost transparency, find their sensual sides and potentially ravish each other with affection and sexual abandon. Atmosphere becomes critical.

The right atmosphere sets the stage for enjoying each other's body and for creating a safe setting where vulnerability, playfulness and excitement can grow.

With the right atmosphere, passion can grow and even mushroom, leading to mutual pleasure and enjoyment.

So exactly how to we go about creating this ambience, this stage of sensual possibilities, a carefully constructed love cave? OK, maybe this language is a bit out of hand but this is my (Doug) favorite chapter.

A Closer Look at the Making of Your Sensual Tent

The McCluskey's point out several practical ingredients that enhance this phase they call "atmosphere." These include setting adequate time aside; blocking out distractions; locking the door; developing positive patterns of initiation and even the language we use to ask for physical intimacy; growing anticipation by preparing our mind and thoughts for the surrender that goes into love-making; the necessary ingredient of mutual consent, both in agreement that this is a good time for closeness and sexual contact.

Let's look at how one couple turned sharp corners in their understanding of designing and creating mood, lighting and the right atmosphere, when all seemed impossible to fix.

Dave and Patricia

It all started with children. Bless their hearts. Barge in when you're naked, demand more attention than a five alarm fire and wear you out morning, noon and night.

They have an uncanny ability to extract all the energy you have and flush it down the drain of potential sexual arousal and leave you in bed, praying for relief, downright ragged and snoring.

Then they smile, you melt and the next morning, it starts all over again. Meanwhile, another sexless day of hoping tomorrow will be different.

Dave and Patricia, married 8 years, madly in love and passionate about their sexual contact and its frequency. What happened?

The busyness of life, the endless energy needed to raise kids, supplanted their deep connection and replaced it with fatigue, deadlines, and a need to build a life with careers and all the other usual suspects that fill up our time and calendar.

Dave, of course, was the first to complain. He loved Patricia and enjoyed their sex life immensely early in the marriage. With some differences in sex drive, they managed to work out those bumps and developed a frequent and spirited bedroom pattern that left both satisfied.

Dave's growing dissatisfaction with their physical life mirrored Patricia's growing angst around their lack of meaningful time together. She would complain that their connection had grown more distant. Dave agreed but usually focused on renewing their bedroom time as an antidote.

Patricia insisted on the need for more time out together without the kids and made efforts to find babysitting. Yet this was somewhat infrequent and so "going out" together became intermittent at best.

Although they began to argue more in the relationship, many of their disagreements centered on the issue of the frequency of sex. Even the quality of their physical contact diminished. Sex became something rushed and often more to console Dave than the mutual pleasure they used to enjoy.

Sex meant finding brief time frames when they could lock the door, jump under the covers and finish before interruptions. Mood, lighting, candles, bubble baths before sex, all good ideas but shoved under the rug of expediency. "Let's hurry" became the motto. After all, lions were prowling around, the freeway noise was considerable and the goal, well, orgasm had to happen as fast if possible.

Patricia wanted more quality time and began feeling used during sex. Like she wasn't the object of love and care but simply needed for sexual release. Dave insisted this wasn't the case but didn't know how to jump start a new day and resolve the walls they had created between one another.

In our initial time with Dave and Patricia, we discovered that the fractures in their marriage had resulted more from the fast pace of life and having children than more serious wounds and challenges.

They desperately needed to talk about how their relationship had grown apart, without arguing and blaming one another. This proved to be somewhat easy, since their love for each other was still fresh, although beneath the surface.

The sensitive issue centered on their battles over sexual contact, especially frequency. They simply didn't know how to put the pieces back together again and resurrect their passion for one another.

It didn't take much for repair to happen. We discovered their physical connection for one another had indeed been strong. What it needed was the proper focus and attention to reignite what they once shared so effectively.

Although we discussed intimacy and the many dimensions of sex that make it special, our primary focus centered on getting them to set time aside and create a sexual atmosphere that honored their love for the other and their capacity for mutual passion.

As an assignment, we had both structure a "love evening" over the course of two weeks. For Dave, we instructed him to design the following scenario:

Dave

He was to pick a night mutually agreed on to engage in intercourse. He needed to make it special, to treat his wife in ways she would feel emotionally as well as physically valued. He told us she loved candles, especially vanilla scented ones and so we assigned him the task of finding new candles to lace the bedroom with. We also instructed him to find babysitting, knowing he could drop the kids off at his parents for the night.

At least two days before the special evening, Dave was told to begin "courting" his wife with flowers, cooking her dinner or any other "touchy-feely" behaviors he used to do to woo her. We asked him to focus on all the ways he would "give" to her that night, such as rubbing her back and preparing a bubble bath to start the bedroom experience. We instructed him to access his softer, loving self and treat her like a princess several days before engaging in sex that evening.

And finally, we gave him instructions to think of all the ways he treasured his life partner and tell her verbally or in a note why she is so special on the day of their rendezvous. Our assumption was that Patricia, like most women, needed to feel safe and free to be vulnerable. After all, the woman is the one "entered into" during intercourse and this creates more need for a man to build a safe haven, a room with passionate energy but still safe.

Patricia

For Patricia, we instructed her to open her heart to Dave's advances in any way she could, knowing she too wanted physical intimacy. We asked her to come up with special music and even sexy clothes she knew Dave liked and that made her feel personally attractive. We asked her to rest that day, to take a nap if necessary to prepare for their evening together. Then we instructed her to find her passionate, feminine self and to imagine how she would bring her charm and sexual electricity into the bedroom experience.

As you might guess, the evening went well. But our advice didn't center on creating one spectacular night. Rather, we were hoping to drive home the message that love and sex get created out of the right ingredients – from thought-through stuff that sends chills up a lover's spine – because your partner invested in sight and sound, aligning all the components of a sexy room, an invitation from the heart and a naked-ness that began days before the fireworks even started. Atmosphere. The right emotional temperature from two lovers who become mindful of what turns the other on. And the stage that gets set where lovers convene and bring pleasure with just the right walls, ceiling and ambience to say I want you, love you and no other.

Let's ask you similar questions:

PAUSE *and* PONDER

✵ **Are you ready to build atmosphere into your sex life?**

✵ **Ready to seek out the right sights, sounds and ingredients that send romance to the next level?**

✵ **Spend some time in fantasy imagining how you would create just the right sensual, safe atmosphere for love making to flourish.**

Follow some of these thoughts and ideas in this chapter to get started.

ATMOSPHERE
Review

- This stage refers to the setting – where sexual intimacy takes place – and making sure we organize our time and efforts to establish a meaningful environment for great sex to occur.

- When we spend time thinking about when and where sex occurs, we help facilitate each person's ability to get into the mood and more importantly, to fully surrender to one another emotionally and spiritually and physically.

- With the right setting, two people in a loving, committed marriage can give themselves over to one another with abandon. The right atmosphere sets the stage for enjoying each other's body and for creating a safe setting where vulnerability, playfulness and excitement can grow.

- The right atmosphere can include setting adequate time aside; blocking out distractions; locking the door; developing positive patterns of initiation and even the language we use to ask for physical intimacy; candles and mood lighting, even the right music; growing anticipation by preparing our mind and thoughts for the surrender that goes into love-making; the necessary ingredient of mutual consent, both in agreement that this is a good time for closeness and sexual contact.

This sets the stage for the next phase, Arousal.

AROUSAL/EXCITEMENT
AND PLATEAU

Getting Into the Right Space

S
O WHAT TURNS you on? We mean this with the greatest respect.
Arousal means knowing ourselves, what creates sexual excite-
ment for us and how to grow the experience.

This phase involves the crescendo of passion, the build-up of sexual
energy, and sets the stage for eventual climax. Because so much happens in terms of vulnerability and the need to let go of inhibitions,
this stage can often be the one where breakdowns occur.

- -

This phase involves the crescendo of
passion, the build-up of sexual energy,
and sets the stage for eventual climax.

- -

A focus on being one and experiencing mutual pleasure needs to
happen eventually, yet first begins with close attention to our own
experience of building excitement and our focus on emotional and
bodily arousal. Having the goal of striving towards orgasm can, and

often does, shut down the natural unfolding of the sexual response. Orgasms can't be willed; they must be surrendered to once there is adequate build-up of arousal.

Here we find the ultimate in personal vulnerability. Stripped naked and becoming more and more aroused, it is the time to get in touch with our personal experience of desire, sexual need, sensual feelings in our body and even erotic potential (we will talk more about that in a later chapter). Arousal starts inside our own body, mind and spirit. How to cultivate that, without interfering inhibitions, takes center stage.

We need to tune into our bodily sensations and allow pleasure to build.

So this phase, arousal, becomes a kind of centerpiece for experiencing deep sensual feelings, responding to our own arousal with openness and allowing excitement over what we are experiencing to grow.

Indulging ourselves with our own positive sensuality, feeling sexual and uninhibited, embracing our bodies and ability to enjoy physical sensations, become of skills we need to cultivate. For some, the seemingly "self-centered nature" of the arousal phase can be a stumbling block that seems somehow not morally okay. But it is more than okay. It is a relishing and celebration of what God has created to allow pleasure to occur in ourselves and with our lover. Letting ourselves truly grab hold of and experience the fullness of arousal is an exclamation point to God's incredible gift of sex.

So this phase, arousal, becomes a kind of centerpiece for experiencing deep sensual feelings, responding to our own arousal with openness and allowing excitement over what we are experiencing to grow.

Imagine for a minute that your inner life consists of many rooms you step into that hold the thoughts and emotions you want to experience in that moment. You might have a room with computers, notebooks and pencils to enhance your productivity and careers.

You might have a space that your children inhabit, where you love and parent out of skills and heart you develop in effectively raising and nurturing them along.

Now picture a room, a space, where you feel relaxed, sexual, sexy and even erotic. What's in that room? What do you have to create to get there and stay there, to engineer that personal space where you can absorb yourself in moments, one after the other, of sensual delight and sexual want?

Picture a time when those ingredients were in place. What was that experience like? How did you filter out distractions to stay in touch with your physical desire and sexual self? Was there music, incense, or other props that made a difference? What did you do in your thought life and even fantasy life to get yourself into that sexual space, that room filled with longing and anticipation of the joy sex can bring?

So how do we get out of the other rooms and into the sensual, sexual room we need to really experience awesome sex? For many, it can start with shaping and enhancing our mind – getting our thoughts in line to create the proper stage to feel and experience sex. But ultimately, the task centers on how to eventually get out of our mind and into our bodies.

What does this take for you? Let's explore some key thoughts and questions.

PA(II)SE *and* PONDER

❋ **What kinds of images, past experiences and settings allowed you to create a highly charged, sensual place for you that took you out of thinking and into the sexual feelings that heightened your state of arousal?**

❋ **What turned you on physically, allowed you to relax and step into an experiential world that felt sexy, desirous of gratification and moved you toward orgasm?**

❋ **How did you filter out distractions to stay in touch with your physical desire and sexual self?**

Unfortunately, many turn to experiences like pornography to create this space. Men especially are driven toward visual forms of stimulation, not realizing that the sensual place they need to find must come from within, or from the visual appeal of their wife, not from external forms of input that artificially get him in touch with his own sexual, erotic self.

Some of the kinds of things you may want in your mind are images or fantasies that can help move your body into a heightened place of sexual arousal – perhaps memories of other times you made love to your partner that were very exciting or places where you felt particularly warm and relaxed, sexual, sexy and wanting your lover. All of these kinds of images can move your body into increasing arousal and readiness for the next stage.

Arousal and Reaching Out

In addition to creating the right "space" and finding our own personal sense of being sexual and sensual, arousal results from creating passionate energy through how we reach out and embrace one another – physically and emotionally.

In other words, through touch and embrace, even with our eyes, we can stimulate one another, but also become more closely connected to our own passion and excitement, thereby growing arousal.

This can vary from person to person. Growing sexual excitement and experiencing that in body and emotion happens as we sink into a more personal, sensual space but also what we allow to develop as we touch, embrace, gaze at and fondle one another.

The goal here is to increase our sense of sexual arousal as we experience all of our senses during foreplay, as we touch genitals and non-genital areas and "bask" in the presence of one another, naked and exposed.
It is here that all the senses, sight, sound, taste, smell and touch come into
play. If we are open to the experience of being sexual with our mate, we
deepen our own internal sense of positive sexual energy.

For some, being more assertive in how they reach out sexually creates
a heightened state of arousal. Touching, feeling and looking into your
lover's eyes might be ways to grow your energy and sense of excitement.
As you touch and reach out, you create a deeper connection to your
own sensuality and desire.

For others, a more passive place where you experience the touch and
embrace of your lover gets you more excited and sexual.

*The goal here is to increase our sense of
sexual arousal as we experience all of our
senses during foreplay, as we touch genitals
and non-genital areas and "bask" in the
presence of one another, naked and exposed.*

Couples develop differing patterns around who is more aggressive or
if they are equally demonstrative in the lovemaking process. As long
as passion builds for both, differing patterns are fine. These have to be
worked out so that the experience is reciprocal, even if one is more
"forward" than the other.

In addition, the process of getting aroused is not necessarily a "linear"
experience. In other words, there may be starts and stops in reaching
full excitement and preparation for orgasm.

Oftentimes, men and women differ here. Frequently, men experience
arousal as a linear, uninterrupted experience from point "A" to point

"B." Excitement and sexual energy are experienced as a continuous event, with no slowing down or differences in feeling during the process.

Women, on the other hand, often find that to achieve maximum arousal, the experience is often less "linear" and involves more variation than a direct path to orgasmic release. Understanding each other and the process of arousal for both lovers helps each tune into and enhance each other's experience. Men, for example, may need to slow down and enjoy the shifts in energy and excitement his wife may be feeling.

Both lovers need to recognize that arousal has a magic and brilliance all its own. Increased excitement and arousal are embedded in a unique, fulfilling process that shines all by itself and creates an awesome intimate connection. In fact, orgasm isn't always the chief goal in lovemaking.

The hallmark of the arousal phase centers on creating passion, developing loving energy and enjoying sexual excitement as two lovers embrace each other in emotional and physical touch. The few seconds of final orgasm become icing on the cake. Yet the process of getting there can be more fulfilling than the orgasm and release that follows.

Frequently, men experience arousal as a linear, uninterrupted experience from point "A" to point "B." Women, on the other hand, often find that to achieve maximum arousal, the experience is often less "linear" and involves more variation than a direct path to orgasmic release.

Ultimately, creating arousal involves pleasing each other with embrace, touch, eyes, and any expression that depends on getting close to our vulnerability, to our sense of what it means to be naked in the presence of another and letting them in. We learn, with body, spirit and mind, how to create true pleasure, to saturate the moments together with a union that God calls "oneness." And doing it in a way that arouses sexual passion.

It means letting go, becoming immersed in the joy of the other's presence, body and mind and emotion. It requires men to think through how to build excitement in focused, pleasing ways with their lover, intent on creating a bedroom experience where she feels wanted and prioritized – safe and loved.

For women, it may mean embracing a lover who is stronger, who will enter her and how to be inviting, sensual and open to his masculine power – not afraid or unable to experience her own sexual, feminine being.

During this phase, identified as excitement and plateau by Masters and Johnson, couples experience growing passion and the need to become vulnerable to one another. Physically, significant body changes occur at this time. For men, the penis becomes engorged and erect with increased blood flow, testes enlarge and 60% of men experience erect nipples. For women, vaginal lubrication occurs, breasts enlarge, the outer lips (labia) become enlarged and bright red, the clitoris lengthens and eventually retracts and the vagina expands. Nipples also become erect. For both, skin flushes, blood pressure and heart rate increases and muscles tense.

Technically, a woman's body is ready for entry at this time. That said, without adequate clitoral stimulation, it is the rare woman (approximately 30%) who will be able to orgasm. The clitoris is the major pleasure center for women and exploring together the kind of touch and/or who will be touching this area is important. Some women require clitoral stimulation while entry is occurring while others need it in preparation for entry. Also, sometimes the thrusting of the penis will allow for the clitoris to be rubbed, which can also provide stimulation that promotes increased arousal. It is thought by many that the other 30% of women are experiencing stimulation in this way during the act of intercourse itself.

Knowing yourself, your body and how you experience sexual feelings is critical. There are no sexual "experts" in the bedroom. When there is comfort and safety with your partner, a lot of this "getting to know" each other can happen as you explore and discover together in this phase. Sex is adult "play" and abandoning ourselves to be free like children to try things out and experiment can go a long way.

Back to Dave and Patricia. In addition to helping them create the right atmosphere to get back into a deeper sexual connection, we had them both focus on specific ways they could create positive sexual energy together that night – a passionate "arousal." They both came up with creative ways to make this happen:

Dave

With some help and coaching, Dave was able to work at getting in touch with his desire for his wife, apart from the excitement of penetration and orgasm. He wanted to "stretch the night out" and linger with his wife for a long time, before intercourse even happened. He started by imagining the ways he could enjoy her body without touching her breasts or vagina. He pictured himself stroking her face, her stomach and even her legs. He decided to offer a back rub and try to enjoy the sense of touching her skin, without jumping right away to thoughts of entering her.

He committed to watching her breathing, to see what made her feel good. And in the process, try to stay in touch with his "closeness and affection" for her and how this impacted his sexual desire for his wife. While all this was happening, he wanted to experience his own sense of power, the strong feeling of being erect and how he could bring this power to her in gentle ways. Dave felt that all this would help him get in touch with his softer side, to feel growing passion, and that delaying intercourse would add to the experience later on.

Patricia

Also with help and coaching, Patricia made several decisions about what she wanted to experience and how to generate arousal. She enjoyed being more passive during sex but decided she needed to really connect with her own sensuality during the process. She even imagined touching herself sexually, while Dave explored her body in his own way – adding to the sense of her own responsibility to find her pleasure zones and feel OK about being sexual.

She sometimes had guilt about being sexual as a woman and wanted to replace this with an attitude of embracing desire as something positive, not negative.

She also decided to let Dave know, through eye contact and by touch, that he was stimulating her. She felt this would add to her own sense of femininity as she communicated that she liked being fondled and ultimately "taken." This was a new approach to Patricia, who often shut out her own feelings and her own recognition that she could be "sexy" and stimulate a man.

Needless to say, their determination to create the right atmosphere but also take responsibility for enhancing their own connection with sexual desire and create their own arousal paid off. The experience led to further encounters where they both experimented with what might be possible in growing their own, and each other's, arousal at this stage.

AROUSAL
Review

- Arousal means knowing ourselves, what creates sexual excitement for us and how to grow the experience.

- This phase involves the crescendo of passion, the build-up of sexual energy and sets the stage for eventual climax. Because so much happens in terms of vulnerability and the need to let go of inhibitions, this stage can often be the one where breakdowns occur.

- This phase becomes a kind of centerpiece for experiencing deep sensual feelings, responding to our own arousal with openness and allowing excitement over what we are experiencing to grow.

- Indulging ourselves with our own positive sensuality, feeling sexual and uninhibited, embracing our bodies and ability to enjoy physical sensations, becomes a kind of skill we need to cultivate.

- It is important to focus on what turns you on physically, allows you to relax and step into an experiential world that feels sexy, desirous of gratification and moves you toward orgasm

- Some of the kinds of things you may want in your mind are images or fantasies (non-pornographic) that can help move your body into a heightened place of sexual arousal - perhaps memories of other times you made love to your partner that were very exciting or places where you felt particularly warm and relaxed, sexual, sexy and wanting your lover.

- In addition to creating the right "space" and finding our own personal sense of being sexual and sensual, arousal results from creating passionate energy through how we reach out and embrace one another – physically and emotionally.

- The goal here is to increase our sense of sexual arousal as we experience all of our senses during foreplay, as we touch genital and non-genital areas and "bask" in the presence of one another, naked and exposed.

- Couples develop differing patterns around who is more aggressive or if they are equally demonstrative in the lovemaking process. As long as passion builds for both, differing patterns are fine.

- We learn, with body, spirit and mind, how to create true pleasure, to saturate the moments together with a union that God calls "oneness." And doing it in a way that arouses sexual passion.

- The hallmark of the arousal phase centers on creating passion, developing loving energy and enjoying sexual excitement as two lovers embrace each other in emotional and physical touch. The few seconds of final orgasm become icing on the cake.

- Creating passion means letting go, becoming immersed in the joy of the other's presence, body and mind and emotion. It requires men to think through how to build excitement in focused, pleasing ways with their lover, intent on creating a bedroom experience where she feels wanted and prioritized – safe and loved.

- For women, this may mean embracing a lover who is stronger, will enter her and how to be inviting, sensual and open to his masculine power – not afraid or unable to experience her own sexual, feminine being.

- Physically, significant body changes occur at this time. For men, the penis becomes engorged and erect with increased blood flow, testes enlarge and

- 60 % of men experience erect nipples. For women, vaginal lubrication occurs, breasts enlarge, the outer lips (labia) become enlarged and bright red, the clitoris lengthens and eventually retracts and the vagina expands. Nipples also become erect. For both, skin flushes, blood pressure and heart rate increase and muscles tense.

- That said, without adequate clitoral stimulation, it is the rarer woman (approximately 30%) who will be able to orgasm. The clitoris is the major pleasure center for women and exploring together the kind of touch and/ or who will be touching this area is important.

- Knowing yourself, your body and how you experience sexual feelings is critical. There are no sexual "experts" in the bedroom. When there is comfort and safety with your partner, a lot of this "getting to know" each other can happen as you explore and discover together in this phase. Sex is adult "play" and abandoning ourselves to be free like children to try things out and experiment can go a long way.

As passion grows, the stage is set for our next phase, Apex.

APEX/ORGASM

S O WHAT EXACTLY is an apex? Imagine you decide to take up mountain climbing. You train, learning all the necessary skills and decide on your first mountain. On the way up, you have several stops along the way. You enjoy the surroundings, the progress you've made and the excitement over accomplishing each step up the slopes toward the top.

You may even decide to slow down, or discontinue the journey ahead, satisfied with the hike and all you've experienced so far. If you continue and reach the mountain's peak, you feel the exhilaration of the unparalleled view and all you have seen on your way up. That is the apex of the trek to the end point, the top, the climax of the hike.

Great sex is like that. The apex, conclusion, final chapter, etc., means you surrender to an end result that makes all the effort, passion and energy make sense. Even though the experience getting there has been wonderful, intoxicating and unforgettable. Climbing the mountain, the process of getting there, creates the excitement and satisfaction. Reaching the top is the final icing on the cake or the flag atop the mountain.

The arousal stage means we climb the mountain and experience the awe and majesty and accomplishment that makes the trek meaningful to begin with. The arousal phase sets the stage for feelings of passion and sexual energy to eventually spill over and reach the summit – the Apex. Here, two lovers hopefully experience a profound sense of surrender to each other.

Biology, Men and Women

The ability to allow one's senses to flood with sexual energy and passion becomes the centerpiece of eventual surrender and orgasm.

Often, women require a slower build-up of sexual arousal, as we have said before, with adequate time to settle into the experience, relax and feel and enjoy the emotional connection for this to happen. Pressure from the man at any point, whether subtle or overt, can derail the natural flow of a woman's arousal response.

Women's bodies are continuing to enliven as heart rate, blood pressure and breathing increase. . So men, patience during this time is indeed a virtue and appreciation of the unique differences in our arousal response and God's unique design in us goes a long way here. As does a "ladies first" principle.

Men, on the other hand, can tend to be less aware of their own emotional needs for closeness and connection and more aware of their physical experience. So sexual climax can happen more quickly and without a slower growth of sensual feelings or apparent need for emotional connection. Research tells us that with active thrusting, men can orgasm in under two minutes. So learning to pace oneself and enjoy the ebb and flow of the plateau and arousal phase is a nice antidote to climaxing too quickly.

The old adage, "men are like microwaves, women are like crock pots" still applies. Some men may need help learning how to monitor and manage their arousal so they can stay emotionally and physically present longer and not "leave the party early" so to speak.

At climax (the shortest phase), our body's tension builds as our minds relish the experience and spontaneous release and orgasm occurs naturally and reflexively. Our bodies were designed for this. We can "enjoy the ride." Here, we experience the surrender and oneness that God intended with His creation of sexual connection. This union or communion of heart and soul reminds us of the very real spiritual aspect of sexual intimacy – the two becoming one.

We need to note that having synchronized orgasms as a goal can get in the way of satisfying sex. It is the rare couple who can manage this kind of feat as the mere energy end effort it can take might easily kill the mood and growing arousal. Men's and women's different pace in arousal lends itself more to having orgasms close together or one after another.

It is also noteworthy to mention that female and male orgasms are different in that men have a refractory period, which is a period of time the body needs to recuperate. For younger men, this can be a few minutes and for older men, this may mean a few hours or days. Women, on the other hand, can be immediately ready to orgasm again as there is no refractory period for them. So check in with your wife, guys. She may be ready for more.

When we think of the incredible connection we create with sexual surrender and intimacy, we see the power of a healthy sex life to bond us together and further the strength of our marriage relationship.

It is out of the positive mutual experience of passion and eventual climax that we enter the next phase, afterglow/resolution.

Feeding Each Other's Desire – The Heart of Love

One way to think of orgasm, in addition to biology and creating sexual passion, centers on our desire to move each other deeply through this truly unique, God-given encounter. Surrounded by love, erotic connection and passionate embrace, we generate an intense experience in each other. We do our part to touch each other emotionally, sensually and passionately, hoping our lover will sense our eagerness to bring them pleasure and excitement.

That is why we call this lovemaking. We "make love" through heart, mind and body, by our desire to see our lover explode with feeling and joy from the body's response to touch and sensuality.

This is why the connection outside the bedroom is so important. When we ignore growing love outside the bedroom, making love in the bedroom makes no sense. Lovemaking involves the whole relationship. Sex simply solidifies what is already magnificent in all areas of the relationship.

When we think of arousal and orgasm, we can't leave out the synergy created by two lovers who become best friends and soul mates in their clothes, in their ups and downs and in their daily grind.

> *That is why we call this lovemaking. We "make love" through heart, mind and body, by our desire to see our lover explode with feeling and joy from the body's response to touch and sensuality.*

Take orgasm all by itself. Here we have an intense physical and psychological experience that saturates our inner life and body, even for a few moments. How odd to believe we can move each other to that pinnacle and never create "orgasms"- spontaneous loving moments- outside the bedroom.

What do we mean by that? Arousal and orgasm, in an emotional sense, need to be part of our world before we ever undress. Bringing flowers, respecting and appreciating each other with notes of thanks and hugs and touch, flirting playfully with each other, calling and saying "I love you," all speak to the many ways we bring arousal into daily life and touch each other with mountain top experiences. Lovemaking becomes the parallel, albeit unspeakably unique, expressions of energy and desire that fastens itself to all our interactions and ways we rock our lover's world – before the bedroom door opens.

So, the apex becomes the point where desire explodes with a final exclamation, evidence that you have been influenced from head to toe by the one you love. Without a true lover in the mix, you have created nothing but biological release. With your lover, you have told a story bound by chapters of physical touch, relentless desire and a keen knack for generating bodily magic.

You have made love. In God's vernacular, you have become one.

....

APEX
Review

....

- The apex, conclusion, final chapter, etc., means you sur-render to an end result that makes all the effort, passion and energy make sense – even though the experi-ence getting there has been wonderful, intoxicating and unforgettable.

- The arousal phase sets the stage for feelings of passion and sexual energy to eventually spill over and reach the summit – the Apex.

- The ability to allow one's senses to flood with sexual energy and passion becomes the centerpiece of eventual surrender and orgasm.

- Men, on the other hand, can tend to be less aware of their own emotional needs for closeness and connection and more aware of their physical experience. So sexual climax can happen more quickly – and without a slower growth of sensual feelings or apparent need for emotional connection.

- At climax (the shortest phase), our body's tension builds as our minds relish the experience and spontaneous release and orgasm occurs naturally and reflexively - our bodies were designed for this.

- This union or communion of heart and soul reminds us of the very real spiritual aspect of sexual intimacy – the two becoming one.

- We need to note that having synchronized orgasms as a goal can get in the way of satisfying sex.

- It is also noteworthy to mention that female and male orgasms are different in that men have a refractory period which is a period of time the body needs to recuperate.

- One way to think of orgasm, in addition to biology and creating sexual passion, centers on our desire to move each other deeply through this truly unique, God-given encounter. Surrounded by love, erotic connection and passionate embrace, we generate an intense experience in each other. We do our part to touch each other emotionally, sensually and passionately hoping our lover will sense our eagerness to bring them pleasure and excitement.

- We "make love" through heart, mind and body, by our desire to see our lover explode with feeling and joy from the body's response to touch and sensuality.

- When we think of arousal and orgasm, we can't leave out the synergy created by two lovers who become best friends and soul mates in their clothes, in their ups and downs and in their daily grind.

Now, our final phase, "Afterglow."

AFTERGLOW/RESOLUTION

This is a time to linger and enjoy the experience that just took place. Not only do two lovers experience sexual release, decreased tension and increased relaxation (sometimes making it a bit too easy to fall asleep), but they have just joined together in an incredible statement about their love and mutual desire for one another.

Two have become one. Emotionally and biologically, two spirits and bodies have joined together in a union created by God that is unlike any other experience.

Afterglow becomes a time to celebrate that experience. At this time, both lovers have the opportunity to reflect on, silently or verbally, what just took place as their bodies return to their original state, or to just linger and hold each other. This can be a time of mutual praise or intimate statements about their love and care to each other.

In addition, in the afterglow phase, both lovers can experience a physical and emotional embrace that doesn't lead to sex but is rather an outcome of sexual contact. What a great time to hold and care for each other as a statement of mutual affirmation and tenderness that can build the marital bond.

Keep in mind that both of you have just been more completely "naked" in body and soul than at most other times in your relationship. You have experienced a sacred event designed by God to connect, bond, glue and strengthen your marriage together. Yay for you. Yay for your marriage. Yay for God.

Women and men may experience this phase in ways that are similar or that differ from one another. Women, for example, often feel more vulnerable after sex. After all, they have let their man "inside" in an act of ultimate vulnerability and openness. Men need to respect this and linger as an act of affirmation and statement of their love for their partner.

Tenderness, soft ways of holding one another, thanking each other for the gift they have just given, all of these are ways to think about afterglow.

It may last for minutes, hours or more. Staying in each other's presence and acknowledging the special privilege of sharing body and soul with your lover – what a unique way of affirming love and care for your mate. Relaxing in the afterglow of what just took place, mindful of how special sexual intercourse really is, honors God at the same time.

He invented it. Thank Him too.

AFTERGLOW
Review and Practice

- This is a time to linger and enjoy the experience that just took place.

- Two have become one. Emotionally and biologically, two spirits and bodies have joined together in a union created by God and unlike any other experience. Afterglow becomes a time to celebrate that experience.

- At this time, both lovers have the opportunity to reflect on, silently or verbally, what just took place as their bodies return to their original state, or just linger and hold each other.

- In the afterglow phase, both lovers can experience physical and emotional embrace that doesn't lead to sex but is rather an outcome of sexual contact. Keep in mind that both of you have been more completely "naked" in body and soul than at most other times in your relationship.

- Women often feel more vulnerable after sex. After all, they have let their man "inside" in an act of ultimate vulnerability and openness. Men need to respect this and linger as an act of affirmation and statement of their love for their partner.

- Staying in each other's presence and acknowledging the special privilege of sharing body and soul with your lover – what a unique way of affirming love and care for your mate.

- Relaxing in the afterglow of what just took place, mindful of how special sexual intercourse really is, honors God at the same time.

Exploring Together

- Take the time to learn more about each other sexually. This section will require more transparency and vulnerability than before but we encourage you to lovingly learn more about each to help you grow closer. Conversations about sex like these are best done out of the bedroom – vertically, not horizontally.

Below is a Sexual Response Table. Reflect on your own experience of yourself during the sexual phases. Note the changes your body and emotions go through. Write these down on a piece of paper. Share with each other your experience.

Atmospere	Arousal	Apex	Afterglow
Desire and Initiation	Excitement or Plateau	Orgasmic	Resolution

Desire and Initiation: (atmosphere):

- How do the two of you know when each other want to make love? What do you each experience? Who initiates? Are you happy with how initiation happens? If so, give each other a "high five" for that. If not, how would you like it to be different? What can you do to make it like you'd like?

Pleasuring: (arousal):

- When pleasuring each other sexually, what tends to stimulate you sexually? (gets you "turned on"). Do you like to talk during sex? Talk to each other about what kind of touch you find pleasurable (where, length of time, etc.). When does entry occur and who decides? Are you both happy with this? If not, how could it be different?

Letting Go: (apex):

• Describe your sensations of sexual release with each other.

For the woman: if you do not experience release, identify when your feelings start to lessen and what is happening at that point. How can your partner help you?

For the man: if you do not feel in control of ejaculation, describe what triggers ejaculation,. What have you tried to control? How can your partner help you?

  • Do you experience any blocks, inhibitions or anxiety during your lovemaking that keeps you from enjoying the process? Talk about them with each other and problem solve together how you can help each other overcome them. Is there anything you need from your partner to help you move through the challenge?

Afterglow:

  • What do you usually do and feel after lovemaking? What would you like your partner to do or say to make this time together more satisfying?

Take a moment to hug each other and thank each other for being so real and open. If you need reassurance or affirmation in any way, please ask for it from you partner.

Enhancing Your Marriage

  • This week, focus on affirming each other with touch and words that praise their attractiveness to you. Hand holding, hugs, pats on the back or knee as well as statements like "You look beautiful" or "You look hot." are good examples. Make a point to continue to affirm each other for their openness in the Exploring Together questions.

- Deliberately Plan a Bedroom Date. Carve out at least an hour together when you can be alone without distraction. Set the atmosphere using your "Five Senses List." Bathe together if you'd like and enjoy luxuriating sexually with each other, allowing your experience together to unfold naturally, remembering the goal is oneness and mutual pleasure – not orgasm. (Though by all means, enjoy that if it occurs.)

Pondering the Spiritual

When we think of God's plan for sex in marriage, we are faced with wonder – amazement at how He made our bodies, the supreme pleasure we can experience when we make love and how sex can bind us together emotionally and spiritually. Sex isn't just biological release – although that is involved. Sex isn't just emotional connection – although we do bond through the experience.

Ultimately, sex is about a kind of deep passion that comes from the creative heart and hand of God – a magnificent gift from God to lovers bound together in ways sometimes mysterious. Two become one – a connection of heart and soul that fuses two lovers together in harmony, pleasure and thankfulness for what He has done.

- Read together Song of Songs 8:6, "Set me as a seal upon your heart, as a seal upon your arm, for love is strong as death, jealousy is fierce as the grave. Its flashes are flashes of fire, the very flame of the Lord." Also, Proverbs 5:18-19, "Let your fountain be blessed and rejoice in the wife of your youth, a lovely deer, a graceful doe. Let her breasts fill you at all times with delight; be intoxicated always in her love." And in 1 Corinthians 7:3, "The husband should fulfill his wife's sexual needs, and the wife should fulfill her husband's needs." How do these verses support God's intent for both of you to experience pleasure and passion and excitement in your sex life together? How does this kind of pleasure help create the experience of oneness?

• Reflect, as you may have before, on how God created sex to be a "union" between husband and wife. How does that union mirror or point to the kind of special union God wants with us? Look at all the phases of sex we have discussed. How does each one contribute to becoming "one" in spirit and body? Spend time praising God for His marvelous work in your life and the way He created sex to be a bonding, union-like experience with your lover.

Some questions adapted from Penner and Penner, 1990.

PLEASURE AND EROTICISM

"Your two breasts are like two fawns,
twins of a gazelle,
That graze among the lilies."
SONG OF SOLOMON 4:5

What Comes To Mind?

THINK OF THE word erotic. What comes to mind? Pornography? Thoughts we shouldn't have? Dirty thinking? Something God wouldn't approve of?

We explored the initial phases involved in the sexual response cycle and addressed, in part, the question of what creates sexual excitement. When we talk about being stimulated to experience and seek out physical connection, what gets that going – besides biology and hormones? For many, one component of sexual excitement is engineered by erotic stimulation and input.

So what does this mean, to be or feel or enhance erotic potential in your passion with your spouse? Perhaps you haven't thought about the term and wonder what it means and how it applies to sex and sexual pleasure.

Often, the erotic is defined as something that tends to arouse sexual desire. A simple, consistent and useful definition we commonly find.

And so we see "erotic" scenes in movies, books and magazines. Maybe in the form of pictures or stories that ignite sensual feelings and affect our mood and openness to physical contact. Frequently, the "erotic" in movies and stories gets divorced from whether two people actually love one another or are in a loving, committed relationship.

Often, the erotic is defined as something that tends to arouse sexual desire. A simple, consistent and useful definition we commonly find.

The Negative Rap

We remember watching a movie a few years ago with William Baldwin and Cindy Crawford called Fair Game. An all-out action show with guns, explosives and near-death encounters along the way. At the end of the flick, we find Baldwin and Crawford having intercourse up against a car in public – as if they have somehow developed a bond of love during the journey and capped it all off with a daring, erotic sexual encounter. We thought it was stupid and ridiculous. Erotic? Not at all. Stupid and ridiculous!

Scenes like this are a testimony to the prevailing ignorance seen in movies and even amongst ourselves about what sex, erotic sex, is all about. We don't expect to see erotic sex in movies about two married partners of 20 years. Movies don't equate erotic experience with two passionate partners who love each other and have weathered the storms of married life over the years. No, indeed. They often abound in the context of forbidden lovers who barely know each other. Or shouldn't be engaged in intercourse because they are married to others or because there is some other taboo in place.

All the while, we have seen the frequency of compulsive sexual behaviors simply explode in our society. The best example is Internet pornography. Because the "erotic" often gets connected with pornography or some kind of meaningless sex in the movies or magazines, it gets a bum rap. When the word "erotic" is thought of, images that devalue healthy sexuality and even degrade men and women may not be far behind. That is unfortunate, since erotic simply means to focus on or tend to create and arouse sexual desire.

So the erotic often becomes synonymous with "pure sex drive and stimulation" that doesn't necessarily involve a shared experience with someone we love and adore. In fact, there may be no sex partner, since erotic fantasies and material often facilitate self-stimulation for those who choose to masturbate for sexual release. Not uncommonly, we associate "erotic" with that which arouses lust and sexual urges – any thought of love and commitment aside.

The best example is Internet pornography. Because the "erotic" often gets connected with pornography or some kind of meaningless sex in the movies or magazines, it gets a bum rap.

And so the topic is controversial, especially in spiritual circles where there may be resistance to any idea of sexual stimulation. When sexual purity is promoted and honored, we often don't know what to do with the idea of being super aroused, titillated or feeling sexy. Some feel guilty.

So we want to jump in and tackle the issue of erotic stimulation head on.

We want to take a close look at all the feelings and experiences that arouse sexual desire and help you understand them – including the erotic. You need to understand how erotic material, fantasies and events create arousal and how to think about eroticism and benefit from a proper look at its role in lovemaking.

Can erotic feelings and erotic passion be OK?

We believe the answer is a resounding yes!

We also believe that the erotic, as God designed it, is misunderstood, both as a concept and how to apply it to our lovemaking. That needs to be corrected.

Erotic stimulation flows from God's creative and loving mind.

We want to connect it to its real purpose – to generate passion and excitement between two committed, married lovers.

It belongs in the arms of two married lovers, soul-mates, bent on creating a garden of pleasure out of the fabric of a God-given capacity to feel sexy and aroused.

Let's advance the subject ahead a step or two. You might ask,

"If it's alright to feel sexy and even experience that with my lover, how do I get there, into that space where I experience myself as sensual and sexual?"

And assuming you are open to bringing erotic pleasure into your sexual expression with your lover, you might wonder,

"How do I get myself into that space of feeling excited and aroused and how do I help get my spouse there as well?"

Perhaps I don't look like George Clooney or Pamela Anderson but want to be the suave, seductive force that sends my lover into orbit along with a good dose of erotic pleasure.

On a note that always makes us chuckle, how many of us have ever even addressed this issue to begin with? Not like you hear it from the pulpit, local news or other media you can trust. Oh yes, we do see it explored vividly in porn magazines or even the typical ones you see at the checkout counter at the grocery store.

But trustworthy? We don't think so. In fact, we know so.

The Place of Erotic Experience in Sex – Is There One?

All forms of sexual excitement and expression need to be understood and considered. Especially those that enhance our love bond with our life partner and ultimately honor God in the process. Let's not throw out erotic desire as something to avoid before we know what it means, looks like and sounds like.

We want you to be explosive lovers with each other, able to create dynamite between the sheets. We want you to know, really get, what forms of arousal add fuel to the fire. To be able to burn up the bedroom with unquenchable love, infused with desire for one another that touches the heart and body from head to toe. How cool, how special.

Not that every sexual encounter sends off fireworks. Sometimes sex can be quick and even one-sided, especially if one is less wanting and decides to nevertheless take care of the needs of their partner.

But two lovers who know how to create and build sexual excitement – heated and fierce – can set the stage for multiple types of encounters. Some that set the room on fire and some less fiery.

This means growing in our capacity to feel and deliver an erotic message to our lover and ourselves. We want you to embrace erotic pleasure as a potential component in lovemaking – part of being sexy, feeling sexy and communicating sexy desire to the one you love and married.

And God wants this too. He created us with the capacity to experience maximum erotic pleasure. The Song of Solomon attests to this. Erotic, sexual expression between two committed lovers – well, He designed it all and made it possible.

We want you to embrace erotic pleasure as a potential component in love making – part of being sexy, feeling sexy and communicating sexy desire to the one you love and married.

John and Rita

When we first met John and Rita, we were impressed by their love for one another and commitment to creating a passionate love life together. John and Rita were on furlough from a missionary placement and planning to spend a few months in the States before returning to India.

They clearly loved one another but had reservations about their sex life. John felt greater sexual desire than Rita, who often experienced guilt about feeling sexual. Somehow, she knew God created sex and that it was supposed to be positive, but she couldn't get herself into an experiential place where she was able to let loose and surrender to the process.

John didn't know what to do with his own desire for his wife and so tried to bury his own feelings and resign himself to a more limited sex life with Rita.

Rita grew up in a missionary family. She witnessed little affection with her parents and sex was a taboo topic in the home. What she learned occurred in school and health education classes. Somehow she grew up believing that sex was something to be avoided or certainly not discussed.

John grew up in a home with many siblings and parents who divorced when he was about 10 years old. His home was anything but quiet. Rather, chaotic and unpredictable. Marrying "stable" Rita was a breath of fresh air for John. Yet he too had little understanding of how sex was supposed to be. He had a brief bout with pornography as a teenager and the stimulating pictures and scenes comprised his only education in the way sex was supposed to go.

So sex, for John and Rita, had become awkward, full of anxiety with challenges about what was really supposed to happen. During their five years of marriage, Rita had only one orgasm and it scared her as she wasn't sure if she was supposed to even feel "sexy" enough to reach that level of excitement.

She had trouble reaching out to John and even touching his genitals because arousing sexual desire in her mate was as difficult to imagine as manufacturing that for herself. She knew John was disappointed, leaving her self-esteem challenged, wondering if she was a good enough wife.

John, on the other hand, didn't know how to reach his wife. He knew something more was needed and that although he could become easily aroused, he had no idea how to reach out to Rita and get her excited and motivated to have sex. John believed that sex was a biological act, that most women wanted sex all the time and that he got short-changed with his wife — very much the result of his training with pornography. He loved Rita but felt helpless to change the situation.

Our work with both John and Rita centered on exploring the biology of sex and intercourse, especially the role of sexual stimulation in enhancing desire and passion. We explored the role of erotic desire with each of them, how to think of feeling sexy and bringing passion and excitement into each other's romantic experience.

We developed a crucial model for both Rita and John that not only highlighted the role of passion and arousal during intercourse, but also how sex is connected to intimacy and affection.

For Rita:

Just the permission to feel OK about feeling sexual desire and being "sexy" with her husband set the stage for greater openness to passion in the bedroom. This took some time as there were many fallacies about sex and her body that she was mistaking for truth. We gave her both specific exercises about how to get in touch with her sexual desire and ways to translate that into passionate behaviors that stimulated and aroused her partner.

For example, we encouraged Rita to spend time alone, in a comfortable setting such as in a warm bath, touching herself and letting herself feel arousal.

One misconception Rita had developed was that sexual stimulation occurs once a man's penis is inside her vagina. She didn't realize that most women experience sexual stimulation with their clitoris. In addition, she didn't know it was OK, and even helpful, to touch her clitoris during intercourse to aid stimulation. Alone she connected with her vagina and clitoris and practiced creating excitement by touch and feel.

So we gave Rita specific exercises on exploring her own body to increase her awareness and get more comfortable and confident with sensual feelings. (See Appendix F for more on this subject). Instructions about the role of her clitoris and how intercourse involves growing passion centered on body parts God created helped immensely. She learned to touch herself and explored her own imagination in generating "sexy" feelings that become part of love making.

For John:

John needed help understanding female sexual arousal and how his own sexual excitement probably happened at a different pace than his wife's or what Rita would likely experience in the future once she was more open to sex. For most men, sexual arousal comes more easily and the desire to go straight into intercourse and reach the mountain top quickly is more typical.

In some ways, sex is somewhat simpler for men emotionally. After all, men aren't penetrated – women are. A woman has much more to deal with. Someone is entering her body and, emotionally speaking, she can feel more vulnerable.

So John needed to slow down, become much more aware of his wife's pace in achieving arousal and find out what pleased her, especially at this delicate stage when Rita didn't have all the answers about her body and her own arousal to start with.

This meant being attentive to his wife's growing excitement during lovemaking. We taught him how to watch Rita's breathing, to see what makes her feel good during touch and arousal. We also instructed him to ask her what feels good and what she wants more of to help stimulate and create excitement.

For both John and Rita:

We helped them identify and let go of limiting beliefs about sex. John had to reconstruct his beliefs about his wife, what her reluctance in the bedroom meant and how to not personalize it. John also needed to learn what pleased his wife in an effort to influence her sexually, help her relax and provide a setting for stimulation to take hold.

Rita had to let go of her concern that she didn't measure up to her husband sexually and to learn that men are different in the pace they sometimes seek out in the bedroom. And that's OK. Different doesn't have to be threatening or disabling. We gave them plenty of permission to explore alternative ways to express passion in the bedroom, to enjoy one another's bodies and experiment with how to escalate their own desire for physical intimacy.

The results were positive to say the least. Both grew together in learning about this incredible gift God has given us – arousing one another and bringing excitement and passion into the spirit and soul, as well as the body. It became their new and favorite mutual interest.

Ben and Kim

Ben and Kim were, well, the flip side of the coin from John and Rita. Both had had extensive and not always positive sexual experiences before marriage.

For Ben, his involvement with pornography occurred during his key sexual development as an adolescent. He was sexually active during high school and assumed this was part of any dating relationship. He met Kim during his first year of college and after dating a short time, they became sexually active.

Kim also had several partners in her adolescent years and so sex with Ben seemed natural. Their relationship, one they believed was true love, was colored by early sexual experiences long before they really knew each other very well. Although Kim didn't find out until later, Ben actually had sex with a few other women while dating Kim, creating significant hurt they needed to deal with.

During their senior year of college, both attended an evangelistic rally and accepted Christ into their lives. Suddenly, they were Christians and sex before marriage became an issue. Interestingly, both were equally concerned about this aspect of their lives and so decided to commit to celibacy before marriage.

Once married, their sex life ran into problems and challenges they hadn't experienced before. Ben became less interested in sex and only infrequently pursued Kim, leaving her confused and wondering if Ben really loved her. Even whether the marriage had been a mistake.

Ben found himself back into the throes of Internet pornography. And so their marriage began to run aground, a stark contrast to the sex life they had generated earlier in their lives. The pain of the pre-marriage affairs became a topic that Kim would frequently bring up, wondering if Ben now had a lover and was finding sexual release outside of their marriage.

To complicate matters, Kim had recently developed a very close, friendly relationship with a male co-worker and just days before they came to see us, he had kissed her. She knew that was wrong but felt a kind of new life because of the interest this man showed her.

Obviously, Ben and Kim's marriage was in trouble. After five short years, they were on the brink of collapse. Although several areas needed to be addressed, we focused initially on their understanding of sex, intimacy and how to create true, loving passion in the bedroom with your lover, your mate. They missed this concept altogether and needed to revise it – the connection between intimacy and sexual excitement as well as the importance of putting firm boundaries around this sacred part of their marriage.

We want to pause here and ask a few key questions, vital ones that make a difference for all of us in creating an exciting, God honoring and deeply connected sex life with our partner.

PA⑪SE *and* PONDER

❋ **How would you describe the relationship between passionate sex and closeness between two partners in love? In other words, what is the connection between intimacy and sexual excitement?**

❋ **What do you believe was missing in Ben and Kim's sexual relationship? How did their sex lives before marriage influence their sex life together after tying the knot?**

❋ **Do you believe two lovers in marriage can have a thriving, passionate sex life without closeness, connection and intimacy? Why or why not?**

We can't overemphasize our deep and compelling belief that marriage represents a "whole" relationship where all the moving parts need to work together to create meaningful love. The tension between growing a close loving bond while simultaneously building a passionate erotic connection needs to be grasped and enacted in our love for our mate.

Imagine you are cooking your favorite meal. Some meat or vegetarian dish with the right spices, texture, preparation time, etc. Let's say you are going to barbecue a pork loin. You have options. But you are in a hurry, so you decide not to worry about the marinade or any other spices. You decide to forego any accompanying vegetables too. After all, you're in a hurry to eat.

So the pork gets no special treatment. You don't even pay attention to the juices, how long your prized meat stays over the heat. You just guess.

The result? No flavor, overcooked, no side dishes, no loving care for these 2 lbs. of potential delight to your palette.

Maybe a silly example, but how much better it would have been to have paid special attention to the pork, marinating it for hours in special spices you love the most. Taking the time to cook it to perfection with just the right amount of time on the barbecue. You see, the spices, the preparation, all of that becomes crucial even before the dish goes over the coals.

And as in marriage, so often we fail to nurture our love with our life partner. We fail to marinate and prepare and pay attention to the details that make love tasty, satisfying and lasting. The spices and preparation are as important as the cooking time and temperature we set. The "whole" process makes the dinner worth eating. And so it goes with love.

Back to Ben and Kim. So much of our work with Ben and Kim centered on developing their understanding of true intimacy and how to think of being "sexy" with one another, while cultivating a bond of friendship. Becoming soul mates in and out of the bedroom.

They needed to remedy past hurts, and put boundaries around their own behaviors that were hurting the marriage. They also had to create an understanding that sexual passion alone isn't enough to sustain a relationship. That true lovers need to love each other intensely in all areas of their lives. And they do this with specific skills and wisdom and with the intention of creating a vibrant bond with the one they love.

And as in marriage, so often we fail to nurture our love with our life partner. We fail to marinate and prepare and pay attention to the details that make love tasty, satisfying and lasting.

For Ben:

For Ben, this meant developing a real perspective on what creates vivid, lasting sexual arousal. Pictures on the Internet simply incite lust and as you will see later in this chapter, that is the erotic at its worst. Erotic doesn't mean looking at pictures that incite passion. Creating erotic passion means enveloping yourself in a sexual experience with your lover, soul mate and life partner that generates true excitement and desire.

Ben learned to get excited about all the ways he could bring closeness and joy into the bedroom, without focusing on just arousal through look and touch. Several skills helped him in the process, including a more comprehensive understanding about passion that involved touching Kim's spirit and learning what it means to become "one," while sustaining excitement and energy with his wife while naked.

Some key ideas Ben found helpful in his own growth process were:

- Learning the difference between lust and closeness as drivers for sexual excitement. Ben was able to embrace the idea that "lust" depends on maintaining a fantasy life that has nothing to do with real sexual passion. Instead, he learned to practice being attracted to the woman he loved, not the one he made up in his head.

- To do this, Ben began focusing on what it was like to be with and touch his wife in the bedroom without resorting to pictures in his head. He spent time thinking about how to value her as a sexual being by enjoying her body, their mutual gaze during lovemaking that reflected something about their friendship and wanting to bring her pleasure and even safety in their nakedness.

- Ben also concentrated on developing his own, new definition of intimacy. He focused on what this means between two lovers who know each other deeply, rather than pictures on the Internet with no connection between people.

He started listing ways he could tell his wife he loved her that would move her heart toward him and that would provide the bond necessary for good sex. Ben had to redefine what good sex really entailed.

- This meant defining what he needed, emotionally as well as sexually. Not just orgasmic relief but meeting deeper needs such as belonging, being dependent on the love of another, friendship, etc. as key components of sexual and non-sexual excitement.

For Kim:

For Kim, as well as Ben, learning what sex is all about – including passion, excitement and the role of intimacy – helped her define her needs more clearly and see how the sex during high school lacked depth and scope.

She reflected on her earlier sex experiences, the lack of closeness and even emptiness she felt, realizing she had often been used by men with no positive outcome for herself.

Some key ideas she found helpful in her own growth process were:

- Learning to define her needs for closeness and love and ways to get these needs met outside of sex. Her unconscious connection between sex and her own worth clouded many of her earlier sexual experiences, even those with Ben. When he became less interested in her sexually, it had tremendous impact on her security and the confidence Ben loved her.

- This also meant learning that intimacy and sexual excitement go together. Her longing for closeness and connection drove her sex life. Both go together in a beautiful God-created way but she needed to learn the deep tie between them. This helped her grow in her efforts to reach out to Ben in love and care, knowing that both of

their deeper needs for bonding and love would need to be
met before real passion could grow in their nakedness.

Once they both realized the shallow sex life they had created together
and with others in their sexual history, as well as how it really under-
mined what God wanted for them, they were motivated to create something different. Something that centered on a cherished love that feeds
true passion in their marriage.

This meant grasping what God wanted for them in marriage, how
he created sex to be something wonderful and how passion in the bedroom represented a real "communion" between the spirit of two lovers.
Not just biological release. We had them read Christopher and Rachel
McClusky's "When Two Become One" to reinforce these ideas.

They began to practice specific ways they could enhance passion and
arousal with each other. They cultivated their love in other ways by
how they treated one another in all areas of their life, prioritized each
other's needs and reached out with care and affection every day.

Both had to work on forgiveness. His involvement with pornography,
the past affairs and her growing connection to a male co-worker, had to
be understood as more than betrayals. Rather, these reflected immatu-
rity and a lack of understanding of their own needs and the ways they
attempted to get those needs met that don't work. Much as they had
attempted to get their needs for love and belonging through sex while
dating, they were now continuing that pattern outside the marriage
relationship.

Understanding the role of passion in their love life, how to create and
sustain sexual energy in the context of a loving, caring bond, helped
save their marriage.

True passion and deep connection never exists in the context of a
shallow relationship devoid of extreme love and commitment. Both
exist side by side.

Eroticism, a key element in creating and sustaining sexual desire,
becomes one leg of the stool and supports a relationship infused with

excitement and passion. Let's look more closely at the real story behind sexual desire that is fueled by what we call "eroticism" and the "erotic triad."

Eroticism – The Real Story

True eroticism, hot, sexy and piercing sexual encounters, can and should happen between two committed and married lovers. Throughout the span of their life together.

There is an entirely unique and wholesome way to view erotic behavior between two lovers in a committed marital sexual relationship that builds up the couple and enhances and strengthens their intimate life.

Committed, bonded married couples who share a passionate sexual relationship can capitalize on creating exciting, highly sensual feelings and moods with one another. What we call erotic passion.

THE EROTIC TRIAD

The Three Ingredients of Erotic Desire – The Erotic Triad

S O LET'S CONTINUE to explore what makes true sexual excitement happen. The kind that can buckle the knees, send shafts of energy through the pores of your sensual spirit and brings you to a level of excitement unparalleled in most other experiences of life.

Three distinct components give us a unique and comprehensive insight into the "erotic" – how we can capture this kind of energy and insert it into the fabric of our sexual experience. And honor God's intent in the process.

These are the need to fuse and lose oneself in the other, the need to actually experience, really experience, sensual, bodily excitement and the need to feel fully separate with the object of our sexual energy. Complicated? Somewhat, but we will explain and believe you will grasp a fresh way of thinking of sexual, sensual loving in the nakedness of your bedroom. The erotic kind!

These three essential dimensions of sexual experience form what we call the "erotic triad" and consist of **communion**, **sensuality** and **assertion**. These give us a broader, yet more exact understanding of eroticism and how to build this kind of passion into our sex life with the one we love. So hang on tight and get ready to peer into a misunderstood subject that needs light and clarification. Your love life will grow from these essential ingredients.

Communion

There is something special and unique about this word. It often conveys an experience we have in church we commonly call communion. We mean this respectfully and also spiritually. Communion is a sacrament God established that provides a present experience of union with Him. Biblical sex, although not a sacrament, also foreshadows the kind of communion we have now and will have with our Lord for eternity. Exciting, to say the least.

When we think of "communing" with someone we know or care about, the meaning we often share centers on a kind of deep connection, a merging of mind and heart, between lovers or even friends for that matter. Communion spells bonding – the sticky kind where two join one another – meaningful and sometimes even engulfing.

And now we apply the concept to creating sexual arousal, fulfilling intercourse fueled by erotic excitement. Especially during the arousal phase, we have the opportunity to experience profound pleasure and passion. One aspect of this involves passion that leads to a deep sense of communion.

A healthy marriage and one that involves a vibrant, thriving sex life has achieved the level of bonding that God intended for us to experience. One aspect of that connection involves the communion of two hearts and souls.

When God designed sex in marriage, He intended for sexual contact to include an experience of "oneness." "Two shall become one" has become a familiar phrase in Christian circles and reflects a profound, spiritual emphasis.

This oneness represents a unity of heart and soul that contains intensity, passion and deep satisfaction. The passionate experience of sex leading to climax symbolizes this union – a spiritual reality that defines and solidifies the bond two lovers have for one another. No wonder God wants this reserved for marriage.

A healthy marriage and one that involves a vibrant, thriving sex life has achieved the level of bonding that God intended for us to experience. One aspect of that connection involves the communion of two hearts and souls.

Any sexual experience with another human being that doesn't encapsulate a commitment toward this kind of unity is destructive at some level. God designed sex to create "oneness." That doesn't happen with a prostitute, a casual sexual experience or even a masturbatory one. Sex leads to oneness, or is intended to. We can use this as a model to evaluate any sexual experience, whether in the movies or on the Internet. It provides a guide and reminder of the importance of sex itself. It isn't a biological act alone. It is intended to create psychological unity and profound connection.

So we start with this truth – that the sexual experience between loving married adults involves a kind of bond and an emotional connection that we call communion. In that experience, we share a love for one another surrounded by safety, mutual consent and mutual adoration.

By focusing on "oneness" as one aspect of how we bring sensual energy and joy into marriage and the bedroom, we end up with the capacity to create and enjoy highly charged, erotic experiences with our mate. The act of surrender and closeness, inherent in God's design for two becoming one, helps create this kind of sexual energy.

Furthermore, the experience of oneness or communion can be deliberately enhanced and can also help develop a sense of the erotic side of the sex act. Yes, communion or oneness can actually enhance the experience of arousal, of becoming excited with passion and deep sexual "wanting" of the other.

By focusing on "oneness" as one aspect of how we bring sensual energy and joy into marriage and the bedroom, we end up with the capacity to create and enjoy highly charged, erotic experiences with our mate.

We want to take a look at 5 different elements of communion that we can incorporate into our marriage bond, "eroticism enhancers" forming crucial building blocks of an exciting, sexy life together. Passion at its best. These help us understand the experience of oneness we call communion.

Gaze

Both in and out of the bedroom, we have the unique opportunity to gaze into each other's eyes. During the act of sex, this can become an especially intimate experience. Sometimes intimidating. Choosing to look into each other's eyes intermittently during sexual contact can add to our experience of oneness and enhance the closeness we feel for our spouse. While we can feel very vulnerable in this place, it is that vulnerability that allows us to feel even more immersed in each other.

When you look into your lover's eyes, you convey the message that you see inside, want to get emotionally inside and care about what lies beneath.

Think of this for a minute. For a man, penetrating a woman gets them inside. Obviously. Yet how much more powerful when we peer inside the soul, step into an inner sanctuary of spirit and being, where the true person and their personality reside. Once in, we can say "I love you" with a deeper, more profound sense of meaning. Inserting the penis simply augments this reality. Now, I'm inside your vagina but first, I was inside your heart. A man who knows this and acknowledges this to his wife can create passion like never before.

For women, the gaze can be a surrender and acceptance of the man she will let in, that she has given him entrance into her deepest spirit and wants him there. How inviting and exciting for men, to be let inside, to be allowed to feel their way with penis and emotion into a sacred place of another human being. The most important human being in his life. Gazing into her eyes, staring into his, symbolizes deep connection, communion at its best, trust and love, safety and unity.

> *Now, I'm inside your vagina but first, I was inside your heart. A man who knows this and acknowledges this to his wife can create passion like never before.*

Breathing Together

As sexual excitement builds during sex, we can enhance the experience by *noticing* our breathing together as passion grows. We all breathe in and breathe out. But when this breathing is deliberately focused on during growing passion, watching our lover be swept away by our presence, touch and care, the result can be explosive and exciting. During intercourse, for example, we can move cheek to cheek and breathe together, in and out, in and out and even synchronize this with a man's penis, moving in and out creating rhythm. Rhythm, combined with feeling the tenderness of each other's skin, being inside, letting one inside, enhances arousal and sensuality in force. We can create a kind of erotic sexual dance together.

You may also notice that, as arousal and passion increase, breathing changes. Noticing the changes in our partner can enhance our connection with them.

Kiss

One of the most intimate acts in and out of the bedroom involves kissing. Learning to kiss "passionately" can enhance and grow our energy with one another. In addition, while making love, we can kiss one another while gazing into each other's eyes and breathing in sync, allowing the oneness to be experienced together – simultaneously. When a couple enjoys kissing passionately outside of the bedroom as well, it is a good barometer that intimacy is really alive.

Kissing, like other passionate experiences, lets your lover in – into heart, spirit and being. Learning to kiss, really kiss, can't be underestimated. Take the time to show each other how you'd like to be kissed and what kind of sensuous kissing you enjoy. We all have different kinds of kisses that we find enticing – tender, deep, meandering, etc. Kissing truly lets another person closer to your heart, embellishing a oneness that creates communion.

French kissing means inserting our tongues into a private space. Like men penetrating their wives with their penis (or even their tongue during oral sex), indwelling each other's mouths can be breath-taking. Two become one physically during the experience.

This kind of passion can be heightened during intercourse. A man, for example, can insert his tongue into his wife's mouth as he inserts his penis into her vagina. Matching stroke for stroke. She can return the experience, letting her tongue glide into his mouth as a representation of entering into his private space and person. Again, a symbolic representation of the willingness both share to commune, to become one deliberately, to say to each other "I trust you and want you inside me."

Holding or Touch Without Thought

The pleasure that comes from touch (and the softening of our defenses that so often happens with touch)) cannot be overstated. We encourage couples to practice holding and touching without thought or intent, without thinking about what will happen later. This can be a wonderful experience when we focus only on the sensations and experiences that come from physical contact. We can relax into the hold to feel more closely connected, breathing and relaxing more and more into each other.

In this experience, there is a letting go, a kind of surrender to pure experience that helps relax the mind and heart, while simultaneously building passion and excitement. Like the body doesn't know what to do – relax or wind up.

One way to think of this involves mindfulness, living in the "now." This can be so important in lovemaking. Just enjoying the sensation of holding and touching, without moving ahead in mind and heart to the orgasm that may be just around the corner.

. . . .

The pleasure that comes from touch (and the softening of our defenses that so often happens with touch) cannot be overstated.

. . . .

And letting go means we surrender to our own internal experience or willingness to feel deeply – to saturate ourselves with vibrant sexual emotion that paves the way for oneness, communion and deep mutual connection. The message we send our lover cannot be overestimated – "I love you, will feel with you, trust you enough to surrender to my own body and to let you know you are safe enough for me to plunge into a oneness where I lose, for moments, my sense of individuality." How sexy, how divine.

Excitement

The build-up of excitement can be enhanced by practicing all the areas of pleasure and arousal we have discussed so far. The goal of sexual contact centers, in part, on generating energy and excitement in the marriage bond. Exciting moments create exciting memories that encourage you back into the bedroom to experience more of each other and to maintain a life of intimacy together.

So many couples have grown apart and ceased experiencing much excitement in many areas of their relationship.

Couples who learn how to bring passion and energy into the bedroom, end up bringing this aliveness into all areas of their marriage. A focus on sexual pleasure, therefore, can be helpful and even instrumental in reminding couples of the need for excitement in all areas of their lives.

We encourage couples to actually focus on how they individually bring energy into life itself, into their key relationships and of course, into their marriage. This emphasis reminds us that life is meant to have energy. Even even spiritually, we are meant to have a life with meaning and momentum.

This sets the stage for a variety of experiences that include a more "erotic" component as we incorporate ideas about sensuality and assertiveness.

PAUSE and PONDER

❋ Do you feel like you are communing in the bedroom? What could make it more of an experience of oneness for you?

❋ Among gaze, breathing together, kissing and holding without thought, which has the most appeal to you? Would you like to try that out in the bedroom?

❋ Would you like more energy and passion in your bedroom? What do you think you could do to make that happen?

Sensuality

Sexual passion grows from a deep connection between two people who allow themselves to experience the bodily sensations that accompany desire and sexual contact. The ability to experience sensual pleasure in your own body and your capacity to make enjoyable contact with the body of your mate depend on a real appreciation for the senses and how they contribute to pleasure and erotic desire.

Remember that erotic involvement depends on a person's capacity to experience a wide range of emotions, urges and fantasies. This kind of freedom, to know one's own body and sexual feelings and to be willing to explore and know someone else's, forms the cornerstone of erotic pleasure.

When we think of sensuality, we highlight the five senses as we did in the pleasure chapter. Our senses are important to creating a passionate sexual experience as well. These are sight, sound, smell, taste and touch. Let's revisit them in light of our emphasis here on eroticism.

> *This kind of freedom, to know one's own body and sexual feelings and to be willing to explore and know someone else's, forms the cornerstone of erotic pleasure.*

Sight

This involves experiencing what our eyes see. This can be a look at one another's body or a gaze into the eyes of our lover. Many times, for too many couples, sex happens in the dark, with their eyes closed as if the whole experience needs to be hidden because it is shameful or too scary to be seen.

We can rob ourselves from being fully appreciated or fully appreciating the whole of our lover when we don't "check out," "take a peek" or better yet, "take a live, mental photograph for memory" of our partner. Taking each other in visually causes us to slow down and absorb and value each other when we are most vulnerable ourselves. Such an affirming act for both partners.

In addition, looking at our lover represents an act that others don't get to share. Friends and family don't get to see the nakedness of husband

and wife. So if we deprive one another of that, it makes no sense as it doesn't reinforce the gift we give one another of entry into the private space reserved for lovers and no other. We need to relish and delight in being naked with only one person in the world.

And God created us male and female. Interestingly, that means different body parts that create arousal. Kind of funny in a way. Why do men like seeing a woman's breasts, for example? Makes no sense. Some fatty tissue, yet it sends men into orbit.

> *We need to relish and delight in being naked with only one person in the world.*

Or a women's vagina. No real aesthetic appeal, yet men get aroused by a simple glance at the "secret hair" and want to touch and fondle it. Women seeing a man's penis? Well, a tubular trunk with no inherent interest. But it means something potentially exciting to women.

Our point? God created our whole body and its parts to help us want and desire one another. So we need to look, to have permission to peek, gaze and see the beauty of His creation and marvel at how this draws us close to one another. Communing with sight alone.

This also means gazing at your lover's body apart from the usual erotic suspects. The neck, ears, face, belly, etc., all have the potential to arouse and to send the message that only you get to fix your eyes on me, with sexual interest and desire. So explore all of each other's bodies and enjoy what you see.

Smell

Sex is accompanied by bodily smells that we may or may not find pleasant. We are conditioned to think that certain smells are "good" and others are "bad." Every individual finds different smells appealing. Allowing ourselves to notice each other's smells can stimulate and remind us of the unique place and time we find ourselves in – naked with our lover, odors that reflect an ambience of charge and excitement.

Women, in particular, need to understand that even the odor of the vagina can be exciting to their mate, with a smell that has pheromones in it – chemical signals that trigger a response in your lover. It is quite likely that you smell good to your guy because you smell like sex to him.

Still, some smells are not so pleasant to some people. Learning to somehow enjoy even unpleasant smells by connecting them with the pleasure we are about to experience can help. These may be odors unique to our partner that define them and that we may need to become accustomed to and honor.

At the same time, lovers need to be attentive to their own personal hygiene by deliberately setting the stage for a more pleasant experience by taking a shower or scrubbing body parts. Wearing cologne or perfume can help.

Or others may choose to create certain sensual odors through candles, incense and even lotions. An environment with the right smells can augment sexual excitement and move arousal forward.

Sound

There are many sounds that accompany the growth of real passion. This can be talking or whispering to each other during sex, noticing the sound of each other breathing and even soft music in the background.

We each make our own unique sounds in the process of lovemaking as well. They can be rather raw in their expression and that's okay. There is no need to be self-conscious about this. Moans, sighs and grunts are ways we tell each other how the things are going for us. As we get to know each other more and more, we come to recognize the deep expressions of pleasure that let us know that it's going great.

Often, individuals scream or moan at orgasm or during the buildup of arousal. Again, these sounds need to be honored. They are unique to your experience with one another and should be seen as part of the excitement of mutual passion and the oneness that communion and sensuality create. Oneness where it is OK to scream, moan and express deep emotion congruent with the exciting experience you feel with each other.

When you give one another and yourself permission to make sounds and moving expressions during lovemaking, you give testimony to the unique environment communing creates. No others get to hear this but the two of you.

. . . .

When you give one another and yourself permission to make sounds and moving expressions during love making, you give testimony to the unique environment communing creates.

. . . .

Taste

Sexual energy can be enhanced through taste. This can be the taste of your bodies such as your lips joining together or through oral sex, if that is something you mutually enjoy. Some chocolate or other yummy food can be a real treat for the two of you as well. A little creativity can go a long way here.

And a man's penis and surrounding area can have flavors that you might not order when dining out, but during sex, they can be enticing and sexy. Similarly, a woman's vagina can taste many different ways (and can even be affected by her diet and time of the month). In an informal survey by OB/Gyn Lisa Rankin, M.D., author of "What's Up Down There," when queried about what a vagina tastes like, men had a host of answers from: ripe mangoes, a battery, seawater, asparagus, lemon mixed with baking soda, tuna salad. So in this case, it may be a bit like dining out.

Learning to appreciate and even enjoy each other's tastes can go a long way in enhancing your sensual/sexual experience.

Touch

This one may seem the most obvious. How we learn to touch one another physically adds so much to the passionate experience. This can be a learning process in which couples express their own wants and needs to alert their partner to what feels good and what doesn't.

It's amazing and sad how many couples never say anything about what they want in terms of touch, out of embarrassment or concern they will hurt their partner's feelings or they will be judged or criticized. Or because (as is the case with too many women) they have been too scared, guilty or inhibited to learn about their own bodies through exploring all its parts and where and what kind of touch feels good, moves them and excites them.

All five senses are intimately involved in creating maximum pleasure in the bedroom and couples need to learn how to enjoy their own body as well as their partner's. By focusing on the five senses, we have an avenue for building a positive experience where we feel sexual, sensual and passionate.

PAUSE *and* PONDER

* **Which of the five senses do you feel create the most excitement for you in the bedroom?**
* **Which ones would you like to develop more with your mate to arouse and sustain passion?**
* **How do you use the five senses to create sensual feelings and passion with your lover?**

Assertion

Communion and sensuality form two key building blocks of eroticism. But there is a vital third — assertion. We mean really vital. Without assertion, we fail to capture the unique energy and dynamic passion that pulls out the "sexy," the "exciting," the "power" behind erotic experience.

With a spirit of communion in place and the mutual enlivening that sensual experience brings to the sexual encounter, assertion becomes the vital, third dimension necessary in creating eroticism.

Let's look at this in its simplest form. Take flirting, for example. This requires effort around specific behaviors where two individuals engage one another. This could be a coy glance, an engaging smile, and other messages that convey romantic interest in the other.

Remember, our focus centers on creating a potentially erotic experience. A dynamic passion that pulls out the "sexy," the "exciting," and in so many ways creates an erotic, sexy experience between two lovers. But assertion is perhaps the most challenging to understand and appreciate.

By assertion, we mean all the ways we deliberately bring attention to our wants and needs sexually and how we intentionally try to meet the sexual wants and needs of our mate.

So assertion involves two key themes — how we "take" what we want and need sexually and how we "give" in a way that focuses on what our lover wants and needs. Let's look at both separately. After that, we will explore a really important theme around knowing ourselves sexually, including our masculinity and femininity. What we will call our "Sexual Self."

- -

By assertion, we mean all the ways we deliberately bring attention to our wants and needs sexually and how we intentionally try to meet the sexual wants and needs of our mate.

- -

Assertion involves the ability to ask for what we want and also the capacity to reach out and "take" or "go after" our own pleasure, while letting ourselves experience the fullness of that pleasure and intensity of it. By that, we do not mean to "force" ourselves on one another. Rather, we can display assertive energy that lovingly, respectfully, and intentionally brings our bodies in contact with our mate in passionate embrace and touch.

Again, we use the word "take" with caution. What we don't mean is aggressively insisting or demanding that your needs get met and forcing your spouse to comply.

What we are focusing on grows out of the safe communion that has been created and the mutual pleasure that has developed.

> *Real communion sets up a stage of safety. Assertion doesn't destroy that but builds on the trust and connection that have been created. Communion makes healthy assertion possible.*

But in order to bring passion into each other's presence and experience the erotic together, we need the boldness that comes from assertive energy. And so we passionately reach out to our mate with confidence, with energy and with firmness that "takes" what has already been created and agreed upon.

If communion involves an element of losing ourselves in the other, assertion reclaims our individuality in the relationship. Communing never means endlessly watching ourselves give up our uniqueness in giving to our lover or being overly compliant at the risk of our own identity. With assertion, we guarantee that our "person" and "personality" stay alive and well. Even when we surrender physically and emotionally to our love partner.

In this model, we can also be passive and receptive to sexual advances. But assertion means we know what we want and we share an agreement to go after what we want from our spouse – even if one partner is more passive as part of their choice and agreed on by both. All of this is in the context of love and mutual adoration.

> *If communion involves an element of losing ourselves in the other, assertion reclaims our individuality in the relationship.*

We can't emphasize enough that sharing a mutually passionate experience means taking deliberate actions designed to grow passion and bring mutual pleasure and fulfillment. We can't simply jump in bed, lay there, and hope for the best.

So assertion becomes a dimension of eroticism that can't be ignored. And although we learn to go after and take from one another, this always comes from a spirit of mutual consent, playfulness and desire.

Gordon and Janet

We remember one couple with whom we worked for several months on developing their passion in the bedroom. Their marriage wasn't in trouble but their sex life had become mechanical and both wanted to know more about creating a more passionate intimacy together.

Among other topics, the issue of "assertiveness" in their sex life became one of our areas of discussion. Typically, Gordon initiated sex. Over the past 10 years of their marriage, almost every sexual encounter started with Gordon's inquiry and move toward his wife.

They had taken this for granted but interestingly, never really questioned the process. It was assumed Gordon would initiate and Janet would say "yes or no."

In one session, Janet told us that she had a fantasy of initiating sex herself. As we watched her face turn red and her husband's face light up, we explored this further. Janet always assumed she was supposed to "wait" for her husband's advances and that maybe it wouldn't be appropriate for her to suggest sex. Amongst other concerns, she wasn't sure her husband would see her as "feminine" if she pursued him.

Gordon was interested and eager to hear this. He shared with Janet his view that a woman's femininity meant, in part, that she "wanted sex" and was willing to "go and get it."

Gordon went on to share how he worried that initiating sex made him look too needy but more importantly, too aggressive. He always hoped his wife would want sex with him, enough to let go and ask for what she wanted. He admitted that her "wanting him" would be a real turn on and allow him to play a more passive role and enjoy the encounter from a different perspective.

As Janet became more assertive, their sex life was enhanced. This gave both permission to discuss their wants and needs in the bedroom and also to explore what "assertiveness" meant to both of them – finding safe and caring ways to go after each other and take what they needed.

At first, Janet felt awkward but soon discovered that reaching out more assertively gave her permission to feel more sexual, to experiment with her own sexual wants and to stop always feeling like she had to respond to his needs and often drown out her own. What a difference this began to make.

Give

Here, assertion takes on a different, yet vital dimension. Giving sexually means assertively reaching out to our spouse in an effort to enhance and rock their physical and emotional experience during lovemaking. Here, we attempt to be the consummate lover and to bring satisfaction, fun and electricity to the bedroom experience. It is less about us and more about our lover.

Even though this part of assertion is enjoyable to the "giver," the goal is to make a significant difference in the experience of our lover. To creatively and intentionally move them toward greater emotional and physical pleasure.

- -

Giving sexually means assertively reaching out to our spouse in an effort to enhance and rock their physical and emotional experience during lovemaking.

- -

Making the decision to "give" and touch our spouse emotionally and physically forms a needed pillar in how we assertively make a difference in his or her life sexually. Deliberately exploring our lover's body and, if they are open to it, trying out new "tricks" such as kissing new areas or touching their genitals in new ways or doing that sexy dance they have always wanted in an attempt to generate sexual feeling, warmth and momentum, become forms of assertive behavior. Purposely using your creative, sexual self goes a long way in giving to your lover.

Sexual Self

So what exactly do we mean by your "sexual self?" When we think of assertion as part of creating passion and excitement, we need to ask ourselves what we bring into the relationship sexually. Especially, what parts or aspects of ourselves do we bring into the bedroom and what parts do we leave out?

As lovers, we need to have full access to our own sexual and emotional feelings and sensations as we have discussed throughout this book. We need to be conscious lovers who are aware of our sensual feelings, thoughts and emotions. Each of us has a responsibility to touch our spouse with our whole self, including everything that makes us exciting and involved, both physically and emotionally.

One way to think of this involves a closer look at the concepts of masculinity and femininity. We won't fully elaborate on each of these because that would be another book. But let's look at those themes in general.

Masculinity and Assertion

As men, we need a way to understand ourselves sexually and what constitutes a masculine approach to sexual advances and touch with our mate.

Frequently, when we think of male assertion in sex, what comes to mind is the dire, destructive nature of forced sexuality – rape. Because of this, a proper discussion around male assertion rarely happens. We hope to undo that here.

First and foremost, we need to focus on bringing our whole person into the bedroom, not on a one-dimensional way of involving ourselves sexually with our lover. As men, we too often think of orgasmic relief as the end goal and we go through the same patterns of lovemaking that we did the time before.

The potential result can be a lack of excitement and a failure to bring our true sexuality, with all its variations, into our love life.

Bringing all of us into the bedroom means accessing our whole self. Our ability as masculine men to bring safety to our wives, power that doesn't hurt but excites, fun, tenderness, gentleness, forcefulness, passion, sense of fun, playfulness, etc.

It becomes vital personal work for men to discover and unlock all the ways they can influence their wives sexually and emotionally. See Appendix G "Intimacy - A Brief Primer for Men on How To Love."

Our point is that the more skill, knowledge and purposeful choices you make in heightening your lover's sexual experience, the more you are practicing an assertive, deliberate approach to creating a vibrant sexual life. This involves a "deliberate" mindset – that I am going to bring strength, positive energy and a safe kind of power into the bedroom – where my presence moves her. And allows her to feel and know her own femininity and how it has influenced her man.

Masculinity, at its core, is about creating this strong presence. Without this strength and way of being in the life of your lover, without learning to clearly incorporate your masculine strength into the passion of sexual contact, the feminine (her feminine) can't exist in its full expression. And without the feminine, masculinity doesn't exist in its full expression.

That is the amazing part of creation . . . masculinity and femininity creating passion, romance, deep connection and thrill.

Spend some time reflecting on these key questions and begin the journey of more fully identifying your masculine self.

PAUSE *and* PONDER

❋ How do I define masculinity and how do I relate this to sex with my spouse?

❋ What kind of presence do I have in the bedroom? What elements of sexuality and masculinity do I deliberately bring into my wife's life sexually? For example, do I intentionally bring in tenderness, safety, gentleness, fun, appropriate forcefulness, and excitement? How?

❋ How do I see myself inviting and reinforcing my wife's femininity? What do I do that encourages her esteem around her femininity and sensuality?

Femininity and Assertion

The issue of assertion and femininity is an interesting one. How can a "feminine" woman also be assertive? Understanding this concept gives you a window into your sexuality and your ability to create a vibrant, exciting sexual life with your husband.

Much as we do masculinity, when we reflect on femininity, we think of bringing into the relationship a complete set of emotions, inner strengths, passion, tenderness, etc. that define you as a woman. This includes softness, gentleness, seductiveness and the power you exert in your presence as a woman with a woman's body and soul.

Remember, you allow a man "inside." How you do this, as an expression of your connection with your own femininity and even seductiveness, makes a big difference. It takes a certain courage and intentionality to take him inside and to do so as a testimony to your enjoyment of yourself as a woman.

So, as with men, this means accessing your "whole self" – all the parts of you that you bring to the relationship that influence your sexual feelings and how you want to impact your husband's arousal and experience in the bedroom.

The more in touch you are with all of these aspects of yourself and how you sexually and emotionally influence your man, the more choices you have in the sexual experience. Again, we call this assertiveness because it represents a deliberate way of bringing your feminine self into the sexual experience.

PAUSE *and* PONDER

* How do I define femininity and how do I relate this to sex with my spouse?

* What kind of presence do I have in the bedroom? What elements of sexuality and femininity do I deliberately bring into my husband's life sexually? For example, do I intentionally bring in softness, seductiveness, excitement, and allure into the bedroom?

* How do I make sure my femininity is felt and experienced by my lover with forcefulness and ultimately with an invitation to be "taken" by him?

* How do I see myself inviting and reinforcing my husband's masculinity? What do I do that encourages his esteem around his masculinity and sensuality?

A Word to Men and Women

It is easy in this fast-paced world, especially as a relationship becomes more complex with kids and other commitments, to find ourselves limiting what qualities and strengths we bring into our marriages. Including the bedroom.

It is easy to become one-dimensional in our approach to one another and cease to be in touch with our masculine and feminine sides. And so what we give each other lacks focus, intentionality, scope and depth.

Focusing on our masculine and feminine personalities and the essence of our sexual self, sometimes causes us to radically re-think how we reach out to one another. If we do this in a deliberate, skillful way, we bring in a dimension of assertiveness that captures the heart and passion of our lover. We can begin to transform the bedroom experience in profound ways.

PLEASURE AND THE EROTIC TRIAD
Review and Practice

- We want to take a close look at all the feelings and experiences that arouse sexual desire and help you understand them – including the erotic.

- Because the "erotic" often gets connected with pornography or some kind of meaningless sex in the movies or magazines, it gets a bum rap.

- Erotic stimulation flows from God's creative and loving mind. We want to connect it to its real purpose – to generate passion and excitement between two committed, married lovers. It belongs in the arms of two lovers, soulmates, bent on creating a garden of pleasure out of the fabric of a God-given capacity to feel sexy and aroused.

- Two lovers who know how to create and build sexual excitement – heated and fierce – have set the stage for multiple types of encounter – some that set the room on fire and some less fiery.

- We want you to embrace erotic pleasure as a potential component in love making – part of being sexy, feeling sexy and communicating sexy desire to the one you love and married. And God wants this too.

- We need to understand the close relationship between passionate sex and deep, emotional closeness in the marriage relationship.

- Committed, bonded married couples who share a passionate sexual relationship can capitalize on creating exciting, highly sensual feelings and moods with one another – what we call erotic passion. There are three key elements that go into eroticism – communion, sensuality and assertiveness.

- **Communion**: A healthy marriage and one that involves a vibrant, thriving sex life has achieved a level of bonding that God intended for us to experience. One aspect of that connection involves the communion of two hearts and souls. Communion or oneness can actually enhance the experience of arousal, of getting excited with passion and deep sexual "wanting" of the other.

- With communion, we can focus on these elements to enhance the experience: gaze, breathing together, kissing, holding and excitement.

- **Sensuality:** Sexual passion grows from a deep connection between two people who allow themselves to experience the bodily, physical sensations that accompany desire and sexual contact. Elements of sensuality focus on sight, smell, sound, taste and touch.

- So with a spirit of communion in place and the mutual enlivening that sensual experience brings to the sexual encounter, we now look at a third, vital dimension necessary in creating eroticism – assertion.

- **Assertion:** By assertion, we mean all the ways we deliberately and intentionally bring attention to our wants and needs sexually and how we intentionally try and meet the sexual wants and needs of our mate.

- With assertion, we learn ways to appropriately take and give in our sexual contact with our lover. Taking involves being intentional about reaching out to get my needs met – in ways that are appropriate and safe.

- Giving means how I reach into my lover's life sexually to rock their world.

- Knowing our sexual self means a high level of awareness about what we bring into the bedroom sexually and emotionally. We need to be conscious lovers aware of our sensual feelings, thoughts and emotions. Each of us has a responsibility to touch our spouse with our whole self, including all that makes us exciting and involved physically and emotionally.

- Knowing myself sexually as a man means developing a working definition of masculinity.

- Masculinity, at its core, is about creating a strong presence. This involves a "deliberate" mindset – that I am going to bring strength, positive energy and a safe kind of power into the bedroom – where my presence moves her.

- When we think of femininity, much as we do masculinity, we think of bringing into the relationship a complete set of emotions, inner strengths, passion, tenderness, etc. that define you as a woman.

- Focusing on our masculine and feminine personalities causes us to sometimes radically re-think how we reach out to one another. If we do this in a deliberate, skillful way, we bring in a dimension of assertiveness that captures the heart and passion of our lover. We can begin to transform the bedroom experience in profound ways.

Exploring Together

We realize the concepts in this chapter may be new and challenging to absorb. The following questions may be difficult to answer but we want you to begin exploring them with one another. No one is a sexual expert. These are concepts you can grow with over time.

- Spend time discussing what you think the importance of eroticism is in your sexual experience with one another. What does it mean and how is it different than what the world defines as eroticism?

- Share together your understanding of *sensuality, assertion and communion* and how these combine to create healthy eroticism.

- Wives, talk about how you think of bringing femininity into the bedroom as an expression of *assertion and also as a component of the passion you want your husband to experience.* Husbands, talk about how you think of bringing masculinity into the bedroom as an expression of *assertion and as a component of the passion you want your wife to experience. Note* how that's different than *aggression.*

- What does it mean to each of you personally to take responsibility for bringing your *sexual self* into the bedroom, being highly conscious as lovers of your sensual feelings, thoughts and emotions and how you share these with your lover during sex?

Enhancing Your Marriage

In this chapter, we talked about how communion can be enhanced through gaze, holding, breathing together and kissing.

Below is an exercise for each of these. Choose one at different times (outside the bedroom at first and then, if you're pleased with the results, as part of your love-making experience at a later time). After each exercise, talk with each other about what you experienced.

- **Gaze:** In a comfortable place, turn toward each other face to face. Gaze lovingly at each other. Calm yourself if need be so you can observe the feeling in your partner's eyes. Focus on communicating love through the way that you look at each other.

- **Holding:** Comfortably recline together on a bed or couch with one of you propped up against the other (like you might if you were in a roller coaster car together where one's back is up against another stomach). The person in the "back seat" wrap your arms around your partner. Allow time (10 to 15 minutes at least) to relax together and experience the comfort of holding and being held. If you feel anxious at all, calm yourself with loving thoughts and settle down by focusing on your breathing or your partner. Switch positions and repeat.

- **Breathing Together:** Prop yourself together as you did in the holding exercise. Focus on your breathing and your partner's breathing. Calm yourselves and inhale and exhale together. Notice the rhythm you create as you breathe in sync.

- **Kissing:** Take turns practicing kissing. Kiss your partner lovingly and passionately and show them how you like to be kissed. Practice trying on new ways of kissing one another. Talk with each other about what you enjoyed.

- Talk together about how you would like to make your bedroom experience more fulfilling and erotic. Is there some activity you would like to try? Are you both willing to try it?

- Plan an erotic time together. Talk about what it might look like and then try it out. Remember sex is adult play so have fun.

Pondering the Spiritual

- Since God created us as sexual beings, how do you think He would define eroticism as a distinct element of our sexual passion for one another?

- Spend time together reading the "Song of Solomon." In fact, read it out loud in your favorite version of Scripture. Note specific verses that capture the author's delight in his or her lover. What elements of erotic passion do you find?

- God created us male and female, with the expectation we would bond together sexually with passion and excitement. Discuss how this passion is an example of the devotion and energy he wants us to have with him!

- Read Deuteronomy 10:12-22. Find Scriptures, including this one, that support the expectation God has that we would love Him with our whole heart, with passion and devotion.

AFFIRMATION

*"When we reach inside the heart and soul of our partner
and leave even the tiniest trace that we have been there
– loving and caring – we change their world."*
DOUG & LESLIE GUSTAFSON

Shaping the Heart

How do you mend a broken heart? Speak to the insecurities of a child? Touch someone's soul with your presence?

How do you let someone know they matter, really matter? That you believe in them, hold them near your heart and that your life would be empty without them?

How do you cleave to your lover and leave an indelible imprint of your affection, your desire – while you suspend your own interests in favor of theirs?

How do you saturate your life partner with respect and protect them from feeling insignificant – that you see them more valuable than all the rubies in the world?

How do you make your lover feel special, the kind of special that *sends chills up your spine and leaves you glowing, warm and even on fire?*

What holds love together and knits two souls into a perpetual bond of friendship?

How do two lovers become "soul mates?"

Penetrating questions, yet more significant than you may imagine. What happens to a love relationship when we entrust our heart and spirit to the care of our lover and we end up disappointed, hurt, or experience indifference?

Love can die from lack of care and attention to what gives life and passion to the human soul.

Amazing intimacy doesn't happen by accident. Needs feeding, dished out with diligence, perpetuated by a determined lover's presence, to sweep their partner off their feet. In and out of the bedroom. Full-time care, not part-time lovers.

So what happened to Darren and Kim?

Darren and Kim

In the middle of a stormy, winter afternoon, Darren and Kim came to see us. Their marriage was in shambles, as dark as the clouds outside, full of disappointments and frustration. They described several years together of hurt and pain and an inability to forge anything new out of the rubble. They had no children, having decided early on to discontinue trying after a few years of failed attempts.

They both complained that there was little affection between them and not much motivation, other than their faith, to continue trying. Seeing us was a last ditch attempt to save the marriage — a skeleton without flesh and bones, unable to stand.

Conflicts had escalated over the past few years. Darren shared his frustration over their bickering, noting that they never fought about anything too important. Just little things that didn't make any sense.

Their sex life had become nonexistent and Darren had started looking at Internet pornography as an escape and substitute for the intimacy that was missing with his wife. He justified this on the basis of his needs as a man, but felt guilty and wished he had a better relationship with Kim and that his sexual needs were met with her. She found him on the Internet a few times, but her complaints went nowhere. Deep inside she felt rejected, that she wasn't sexy enough for him and that he simply didn't want her. She felt increasingly alone and isolated, with no answers. Only hurt and pain.

One evening Darren found Kim chatting online with an old boyfriend from high school. Although she denied any wrongdoing, she did tell Darren that they had been talking for the past few months. She remembered the attention this boy gave her when dating and that he had always cared about her. She was flattered. In anger, she told Darren that the man gave her more positive attention than her own husband, stormed out of the room and refused to talk about the issue any further. After all, she noted, at least she wasn't fantasizing about sex and watching naked men online.

Darren was crushed but recognized that there hadn't been much love between them lately; he felt confused and helpless. This led to their first appointment with us and the work we began doing together.

Both ended up in tears during our first meeting. We asked them how their relationship started out and what happened to end up where they were today. They each described a positive connection early on in dating and during the first few years of married life. Sex was frequent, they had date nights and seemed to get along fine, with occasional minor conflicts.

Yet over time, they had drifted apart. Almost imperceptible, the kind of drifting you don't notice until the pain and hurt mount. Then you feel it crashing down, eventually like an avalanche and you're left bewildered and in shock.

Now they were both dealing with feelings of betrayal, that they had cheated on each other in their own way and found other outlets to boost *their feeling of significance and being cared for or important. In essence, they discovered ways to feel alive, to experience energy and passion, even if not directly with someone in bed or in any way physically.*

"I felt important and special, something I haven't had for a long time," Kim shared, while tears streamed down her face.

Darren admitted he enjoyed porn and masturbation, that it gave him something to look forward to and helped with sexual release. "I was looking for an outlet and maybe a way to experience my anger toward Kim. So it became easy to justify."

Neither one could explain why they didn't solve this together, discuss their needs for love and attention and try to figure out how to rebuild their love for one another. Things just drifted along and they ended up not solving much at all.

One of our key questions early on centered on finding out how they expressed love and care for one another in the beginning of their relationship and what got in the way of reaching out to one another.

Interestingly, both agreed that they just "drifted" apart. The "Little things we used to do for one another, just kind of ended" Darren lamented. "But I want her back" he cried, pounding his fist on the coffee table in front of us. Kim actually reached over and grabbed his hand. And that was the beginning of their move forward.

We decided to keep our focus on the "little things" they used to do for one another and gave them assignments to resume these behaviors. We asked them both to personally commit to reaching out to one another and try to restore and build love in their relationship once again. All this with the assumption they would discontinue acting out with old boyfriends and Internet pornography.

Interestingly, they did in fact start making real and ongoing attempts to show care and interest in each other. Darren, for example, arranged a date night, going to dinner at one of their favorite restaurants with a walk along the beach afterwards. They even chose to hold hands during the walk, feeling a bit awkward but staying with it nonetheless.

They were excited to tell us of their progress and we praised them for their diligence in creating time and space for one another and reaching out with care and attention. Within a few weeks, they resumed their sex life, although both felt apprehensive and ambivalent about being that vulnerable and open to getting hurt. What they did realize, however, is that somehow they had let their relationship fall apart from lack of attention, care and failure to reach out.

As we discussed our work with Darren and Kim, we were struck by one of their comments that resonated with us and with them. Kim noted that "We used to think of being each other's soul-mate in life. Now we believe it's possible again."

That really stuck in our minds. Being "best friends," "soul mates" – words that speak of the incredibly unique place two lovers, in a vibrant healthy marriage, hold in each other's hearts.

Happens automatically? No. No indeed.

Becoming soul mates takes work, effort and careful attention to creating love and affection. At the heart of this kind of friendship, we find two lovers who regularly "affirm" one another.

Affirmation. Simple word but perhaps the single most important ingredient two lovers share together. Means touching each other's hearts and minds with actions, words and experiences that convey acceptance, respect, adoration and a deep affection for the identity and heart of your mate.

Consistent and genuine affirmation creates "soul mates," an enduring love and a marriage that withstands the winds of adversity – of any kind. Creates amazing intimacy.

Defining Thoughts

So we define affirmation as *all the ways we verbally and non-verbally support and reinforce the value and worth of our mate.* And demonstrate our love for them. Yes, demonstrate! Affirmation involves action – deliberate ways we cultivate and initiate love and care in our partner's life to bring visible support and reinforcement into their world.

We hopefully marry someone who becomes our best friend, soul mate, passionate lover, confidant and partner in life's unpredictable ups and downs. Acts of affirmation feed all of these. Without affirmation, we live in an emotional desert.

When we affirm one another in marriage, we intentionally think of ways we can reflect and recognize the value of the other person. When we focus on the uniqueness of our spouse and what we love about them, the results can be incredible.

So we define affirmation as all the ways we verbally and non-verbally support and reinforce the value and worth of our mate.

Types of Affirmation

An essential ingredient of a thriving marriage comes from loving each other with consistent and meaningful acts of affirmation. We divide these into several distinct categories or ways of incorporating affirming behaviors into our married life.

In our work with Darren and Kim, we helped them integrate all of them into their unique ways of reaching toward the other.

Verbal Praise

One way we affirm one another comes from words of praise and thankfulness. This means creating communication patterns that reflect our care for our mate, how we value them and how we appreciate their uniqueness.

It's amazing how seldom we use verbal praise, the kind that comes from the heart and touches your lover, right between the eyes, soul and spirit. Penetrates to the core. Through ears and into the recesses where lovers store memories of affection and memories of what it's like to be truly valued.

But you have to say it. Isn't automatically known. Not an "ESP" experience. Not stuff each other knows because you said it in a card last anniversary, birthday or other holiday.

Let's ask some crucial, specific questions along these lines.

PAUSE *and* PONDER

* So how do you praise someone? In other words, how do you verbally show you care for your mate? What specific words do you use to tell them they are valued and loved?

* How consistently do you give verbal and behavioral praise to your lover?

* In what ways do you affirm the "uniqueness" of your mate? What words convey this kind of affirming love?

* Do you spend time thinking of ways to verbally let your spouse feel truly "it" – your girl, your guy?

Affirmation talk – needs to be built into the fabric of how you think of your mate and certainly how you reach out to them. It can be enormously helpful to think of your lover the way God does. As so valuable, He died for him, died for her. Revolutionary thinking for some but the real meat of what creates and sustains love and friendship.

When we take these powerful thoughts about our lover, not the last annoyance or conflict embedded in our brain, but who he/she is in their essence, and translate those ideas into words they actually hear, actions they see and feel, real healing, growing and building love occurs.

The other side of the coin? Words that hurt, demean or become so vanilla-flavored they don't convey love and care.

Words can hurt. May take several positive words of affirmation after one negative, painful comment to our lover to reverse the damage. The power of words cannot be overestimated. They can move us to soar, reach the highest mountains, or bury us in the debris of a shattered self-image, the rubble of disappointment that our lover doesn't really care – thinks less of us – maybe even wants to hurt us.

Ask these questions.

PA(II)SE *and* PONDER

✶ **What is your language like? Do you inspire your lover by verbal praise and thankfulness that they are in your life? Or do you criticize, belittle or even crush his/her spirit?**

✶ **Do you withhold praise and verbal affirmation? Unwilling to take the risk to send love messages by speaking into his/her heart?**

Be honest. You know your style. Your words have more power than you imagine. You can build love with your voice and turn a marriage of doubt and conflict into a meadow of flowers and vibrant life.

Touch

You can use physical touch to affirm your spouse. Even a quick hug can send the message that you value your mate and care about them. A quick caress, a meaningful touch on the shoulder, both communicate thoughtfulness, a way of reaching out that says "I know you're there, care about you and want you to know."

Yet touch can be tricky. For some men, touch means "groping" their lover's body, genital contact that focuses on sex, not necessarily intimacy.

Touch needs to be "wanted" and affirming, as defined by our mate. But touch needs to happen. We need to find mutual ways of consistently embracing one another that reach into the heart, deeply and suggest "I love you," "You're my girl, my guy."

The right physical expression, in and out of the bedroom, can move a man or propel a woman into an experience of being recognized, valued and special.

The great news? Touch is free. Not like buying flowers, an expensive dinner or unique gift. And touch can happen all the time. No time limits, statute of limitations, red tape to untangle. You just move forward, bound ahead, and reach out.

Amazing that something that costs nothing could stir the soul to such depths, affect the heart with such profound meaning and say so much, without a sound.

We need to find mutual ways of consistently embracing one another that reach into the heart, deeply and suggest "I love you," "You're my girl, my guy."

Non-verbal Communication

A glance or warm look can send a message of love and affirmation. Finding ways to affirm one another without words and without touch can bring a creative force to our love relationships.

In our marriage, we often "wink" at one another, lip sync "I love you" and feed each other glances that only two lovers could possibly share. Probably looks silly to the onlooker but nice to get the occasional "You must be newlyweds" from those that don't know us.

One thing for sure, it isn't hard to figure out how to reach into the spirit of your lover from 10 yards away. You have to be creative, but lack of proximity doesn't deter two people from expressing themselves.

And facial expressions? Wow! They convey so much. A frown can communicate displeasure and even disgust. And a meaningful smile can say "You mean the world to me."

We know from communication theory that when we communicate with someone, much of the meaning comes from non-verbal cues and facial expressions. Much more than the "content" or actual words you use.

Taking responsibility for our non-verbal cues, especially our tone of voice and the expression we wear on our faces, goes a long way in creating meaningful, loving exchanges. Practicing ways to notice our tone of voice, for example, and shaping it to send clearer messages of love and care can turn a marriage around – sometimes overnight.

Writing

Brief notes, text messages, letters, emails, cards and other forms of written communication can bring joy and warmth into our marriages. Finding creative ways to briefly touch base, even in a busy day, can be reinforcing and tender and meaningful.

As we develop consistent patterns of loving each other with a variety of affirming ways, our love grows exponentially.

How to Demonstrate Love to One Another

One useful way to think about effectively loving our spouse centers on becoming experts at their love language. What turns them on – especially other than being naked and pleasing one another physically in bed.

What sends clear and consistent "I love you" messages to your mate. Ones they receive, internalize and believe deep down inside represent being truly cared for and valued. Often the way to communicate love and passion to your life partner means figuring out how they want to be loved.

Yes, HOW they want to be loved – what really works for them, touches their heart and sends "You are special and I love you" reverberating through their mind and spirit. Think of it this way. Bringing joy and energy into your marriage depends on excelling at loving behaviors. These acts of love can be thought of as specific ways you bring pleasure to your spouse, deliberately and passionately. Ones they truly enjoy, connect with and speaks their language.

To do this we can identify what we call our "love language" – and come closer to defining the kind of intimate connections we can have with our mate.

Love Languages

We all have the hope of being loved. But did you realize you actually have a love language, a preference for being loved in certain ways? Some of you may already familiar with love languages, but they may be brand new to others.

Gary Chapman, in his book *The 5 Love Languages: The Secret to Love That Lasts*, has outlined 5 different love languages or styles that we can select from that help us define how we want to be loved and how our spouse hopes to be loved★. These are:

Quality time

Touch

Gifts

Acts of service

Words of affirmation.

Quality Time

Somewhat self-explanatory, this way of being loved means spending actual meaningful times tog ether. These could include date nights or other ways of recognizing the value of time together nurturing the marriage.

★ Adapted with permission of Northfield Publishing from *The 5 Love Languages: The Secret to Love That Lasts*. Copyright ©2010 by Gary Chapman. www.5lovelanguages.com

For us, even going to the coffee shop and talking, reading or just silently "being with" one another can be quality time.

Walking around the mall (sorry, guys) can create unique shared experiences.

And of course, special dates, ones that don't have to be expensive, can fill your time with loving memories and make a statement that "I want to be with you, spend time with you" because I enjoy and love you.

Quality time often means finding babysitting for the children and devoting your time, affection and attention to one another. Only each other.

For the one whose love language is quality time, setting time aside for the purpose of just being together means the world. It is, after all, the most important way they feel really loved. May not be their only way, but ranks up at the top!

Touch

Some hope for actual touch as a means of experiencing love from their partner. This can be hugs and other ways we express physical love.

We have discussed this above, but it is worth mentioning that this is actually a love language. Some value "touch" more than others. We could be discussing sex here but mostly we are focusing on the kind of touch that exists with our clothes on. The kind of touch that sometimes makes us feel naked and vulnerable, but no intercourse or sexual contact is involved.

Touch that says "I love you," I "see you," "I feel you." Sometimes this speaks more deeply to one partner more than the other.

Gifts

This involves actual gifts, large and small, that help you feel loved and valued. We define gifts somewhat broadly. This could be an insignificant item in terms of expense but one that means much to your partner. Some feel so cared for when their lover has purposely found a token, an item or even something as simple as a note to let them know they have been thought of and that you wanted to show that in a tangible way.

Acts of Service

Included in this category are behaviors where you reach out by "doing" things for one another. This could be help with the laundry, making coffee, or any myriad of actions that denote care and attention.

Again, this often means more to one spouse than the other. Figuring out if this is your love language is important.

Words of Affirmation

Some feel loved when their spouse provides words that affirm them and reinforce their love and value.

Again, we covered this earlier but include spoken words here to remind us that for some, this is their love language. It means more than anything to be verbally praised, cared for and affirmed.

What it Means

By identifying your love language, you give your partner a window into how you hope to be cared for and what "touches" their heart. Often the language that you are using to love your spouse is your own love language.

Do you like to get her car washed and filled with gas? Or take the kids to the park when she is tired? Then, perhaps you long for Acts of Service towards you. Times where she pours your coffee, or organizes your office for you.

Do you like to sit close to him and eagerly await to give him a hug at the end of the day? It is quite possible you desire to be touched to feel loved.

Do you find yourself buying him a little something when you are at the mall? Maybe you are overdue for a gift from your guy, because that makes you feel special.

Do you often tell her she is beautiful or an awesome Mom, but you wonder if you'll ever feel appreciated by her with words of praise? Quite likely your love language is verbal affirmation.

Finally, do you often always find yourself trying to get him to spend time with you on the couch, talking and connecting? Then you likely thrive and feel loved by quality time.

Once you know the love language of your spouse, you can make more informed choices about loving them and creating the kind of connections that grow your relationship. It really make loving each other easier and less complicated.

Now comes an interesting dimension to all we have discussed. Frankly, affirmation, as easy as it seems, often hits roadblocks for some. It centers on the fact that true, genuine acts of affirmation involve becoming vulnerable to one another in some way. It is vital that we identify what may be stopping us from developing consistent patterns of affection and affirmation toward our lover.

Remember, becoming best friends, soul mates and each other's lover means creating consistent actions that say "I love you" and "You are my best friend." Actions.

So it becomes vital to understand what stops or hinders us. Amazing intimacy needs the fertile soil of partnership and friendship to blossom. Let's look at some challenges that get in the way.

The Challenges in Affirming Our Partner

Several challenges affect our ability or willingness to affirm our spouse. All of us, to some degree or another, experience some resistance to regularly affirming others.

Following is a short list of possible reasons behind this, kind of the "usual suspects" that stand in the way but can be dealt with and eliminated.

Family of Origin

Affirmation may have played a very small role in our lives growing up. We may have little experience in receiving verbal and non-verbal praise, including a lack of positive reinforcement and recognition growing up as children.

Even well-intentioned parents can fail to build a consistent way of reinforcing the worth and value of their children into their words and actions.

Some families promote negativity and even abuse their kids, eliminating any chance of developing the sense of self-esteem that can be a model for healthy behavior in the future.

But more often, parents don't spend time thinking of all the ways they can impact the lives of their children by being more intentional about how they praise and reinforce their personalities and behaviors.

Past Relationships

Or perhaps we have been in other relationships, even former marriages, where praise and reinforcement died or was absent.

So we bring in the "ghosts" from our past that influence how we see our partner and ultimately what we expect will happen in the marriage. We have trouble letting go of past hurts and wounds and this affects our willingness to love and open ourselves up to our partner.

Negative Patterns and Habits

The process of affirming one another depends on creating a positive marriage on all fronts. Marriages experiencing stress and anger and any kind of deterioration often cease to bring mutual praise into the partnership.

We frequently develop patterns in our marriage that don't include finding ways to honor and cherish one another.

Part of this involves "complacency," a killer in the realm of intimacy and closeness. We all get busy in our lives and often deal with the daily operational concerns that are necessary for running a home.

So we develop relational habits that reflect the stress we live under. We don't necessarily take time to build moments of closeness into our fast-paced existence. So out of habit, or lack of developing habits, we economize in our relationships and only share what is necessary and timely.

And so we begin to "neglect" engaging our partner in all the positive ways that reinforce our love for them, verbally and in our actions. It is not uncommon to hear about lovers who spent considerable time reaching out to one another during courtship but eliminate many of these positive behaviors once they are married.

Affirmation needs to become an intentional habit and pattern each person in the marriage commits to and brings into the partnership.

Otherwise, love can die.

Vulnerability

Third, affirmation can be experienced as a kind of vulnerability. It can feel a bit scary. To praise someone means to speak and act from a very genuine, heartfelt place. Individuals frequently struggle with this kind of tenderness and authentic honesty. And so fail to develop ways of communicating that bring affirmation into the open.

In other words, some lovers struggle with affirming one another, which again has to do with the challenges in "opening up" to another human being. To softly tell our partner we love him or her requires reaching into a part of our heart and soul in a way that creates a certain vulnerability, tenderness and softness to be believed.

This openness, with couples who have frequent or high levels of conflict, becomes almost impossible. To be vulnerable means potentially getting hurt emotionally.

For others, however, just the act of opening up and letting their heart be known represents a skill and experience that is hard to create. The "know how" may not have been developed. Learning to be vulnerable, to expose our heart and being to the life of another, requires a level of understanding and even expertise that may be hard for some. Sometimes we have to learn how.

This review is not comprehensive, but gives us a way to understand the resistance we sometimes experience in reaching out. In our chapter on "Presence," we discussed several key issues also related to this topic that may be worth reviewing.

Affirmation and Relationship Growth

So practicing the many ways we can affirm one another and personally committing ourselves to engaging our spouse in affirming ways can revolutionize our closeness and even our sexual lives.

It certainly turned around Darren and Kim's lives. Headed for divorce and all the hurt and grief that come alongside, they both found a way to soften their hearts and imagine engaging one another in loving, caring ways. Actions that spoke volumes.

Consistent, intentional acts of support, encouragement and caring become the basis for true relationship growth and development. On the other hand, removing or ignoring the power of affirmation can cause love to die.

We often liken this to planting and caring for your garden. We often tell couples we work with this brief, hypothetical story we call "The Garden."

The Garden

Imagine that you and your partner just re-landscaped your back yard. You planted new flowers, trees, put in a new lawn and turned it into the beautiful garden of your dreams.

You added all the ingredients you've always hoped for in a beautiful yard, complete with all the live vegetation and all the colors you imagined were possible. After looking at your new creation, you and your lover say to each other, "This looks amazing. Let's come back in a year and see how it's doing."

Obviously, without water, with no one pulling the weeds and no consistent attention to caring for the plants and flowers, it would all be mostly dead.

Would you turn to each other in complete surprise and say, "Wow – I can't believe everything here has died?" As if surprised and shocked by what you discovered? Overall, the dead or dying flowers, trees and plants would not be of much surprise.

But you might turn to your mate and say, "Why haven't you cared for and watered and weeded our beautiful back yard?"

And so it often goes in the marriage relationship. Couples frequently seem shocked that the marriage has deteriorated or doesn't produce the life and passion once thought possible. Yet who has tended to the entire garden? Who has ensured, in word and deed, that weeds didn't grow, that flowers blossomed with water and the bushes and shrubs were pruned and tended? In short, we commit our lives to someone we love and the question is whether or not we spend the time and attention needed to grow and sustain the relationship.

Affirmation becomes one of the key ingredients for growing and sustaining the garden of love that two people commit to in the marriage relationship.

Building a solid, meaningful plan that you intend to carry out in loving your mate creates the fertile ground that sustains the love and passion between two people for life.

Affirmation and the Uniqueness of My Spouse

By loving one another, we have a special opportunity to affirm each other's uniqueness and individuality. Being open to the uniqueness of our spouse and finding ways to encourage the expression of our differentness is love in action. Implicit in this is a deep recognition of each other's separate identity.

We each have a unique identity forged out of God's hand in our life and our unique personal experiences. Our success in marriage depends, in part, on feeling positive about our differences, not threatened by our lover's uniqueness.

Yes, some individuals in marriage are threatened by their spouse's uniqueness and differentness. They see it as a threat to the oneness they hope for in the bonds of love. Usually this happens when someone fears abandonment, possibly due to childhood experiences and often reflected in a bonding style that is less than secure.

Yet being able to maintain and express individual differences becomes central to any person's mental health and to the growth of the relationship. We are all created differently with unique attributes and personalities. When a spouse attempts to curb their partner's individuality out of fear, it diminishes the other and stalemates the growth of the partnership.

On the other hand, affirming and valuing our partner's unique identity can be a significant way of expressing love and care. In the early stages of courtship, we generally value each other's differences. They can, however, gradually become threatening, usually because the relationship hasn't grown the depth it needs to for both to feel secure.

It is our differences, in part, that keep a relationship interesting and alive. In fact, in large part. How boring it would be to be married to ourselves.

Affirming Our Partner's Individuality

So, how do we actually affirm our partner's unique identity and personality? Let's take a closer look.

First, ask yourself these questions.

PA(I)SE *and* PONDER

* ❋ "How am I unique? How would I describe my own identity?"
* ❋ "How is my partner unique and how would I describe their identity and individual characteristics?"
* ❋ "How is our differentness expressed in our marriage?"

❋ **Do our differing personalities end up creating conflict or do we enjoy each other's unique characteristics?"**

❋ **How did my partner's unique identity contribute to my interest in and love for him or her?**

A sign of maturity and success interpersonally depends on developing an appreciation for individual differentness and honoring these in the bonds of a love relationship.

And we really mean "honoring" these. It is vital to champion the individuality or our mate. To find ways to express joy in them rather than seeing their differentness as threatening or something we are unwilling to understand.

One example of this comes from our own marriage. And this involves art. Art is a true passion of Leslie's.

Me? (Doug) I'm color blind. I can barely draw a stick man. If my artistic talent were a measure of my maturity and mental health, I would be psychotic and in a psychiatric hospital.

Don't get me wrong; I like art. I'm just not gifted at creating it and seeing the variegated colors that make up most positive works we see.

My wife is a gifted artist. I want her to spend time painting and I want to champion her efforts and work.

So we go to art shows. I examine all her art projects as they progress. I even weigh in with my "color blind" opinion. I know she really values my opinion and viewpoint (although maybe not on the color issues).

I want her to soar in her work and development as an artist and will do almost anything to see her enjoy this part of her life. Even when it means time and attention away from me and my interests.

So, does this make me a hero? Not my point at all. But I did have to cultivate a way to be involved in an aspect of her life in which I have no skill or talent.

Why? Because I love her and, more importantly, want her to experience and express her individuality and uniqueness. It is God's gift to her and how He created her. I want to champion that. What do I get in return, not that I expect anything? More than you could imagine.

There is something about believing in our lover and wanting them to soar and our willingness to find ways to express this to him or her that creates love and trust in the relationship.

And, it goes both ways. I, Leslie, have had to come to acknowledge and appreciate that my sweetheart Doug has a mind that won't quit - I think he is brilliant, quite frankly☺. But Doug has more ideas and visions of ways to better other's lives than anyone I have ever met. I am a lot more Type B than he is, so I have to purposely practice affirming who God has created him to be – a gifted thinker and visionary.

Is it hard sometimes? Absolutely! His creative mind can tire me out. But it means the world to me to see him thrive and be who God created him to be. When Doug is in his creative thinking zone, he is full of joy and inspiration. I see him come alive and feel valuable and happy. It brings tears to my eyes and joy to my soul when he experiences this. Because I love him and this is who he is and it's a beautiful thing.

Take some time to fill out this brief questionnaire and then share it with one another, "Identifying Your Lover's Unique Self."

Identifying Your and Your Lover's Uniqueness Self-Questionnaire

I am a unique and distinct person in the following ways. (List characteristics that you feel define you as a person).

My spouse is unique and a distinct person in the following ways. (Again, list characteristics that you feel define your partner as a person).

Take turns sharing this list with one another.

Define why you love your partner based on these differences. Take each unique characteristic and complete this sentence: I love that my lover is _____ because _____.

Take turns sharing this with one another.

Once you develop a mindset affirming and honoring your lover's differentness and see these individual personality characteristics as ingredients of your love for one another, your marriage will grow.

From this mindset, you can begin to commit to ways to honor these differences verbally and by your actions to reinforce your belief that you truly love each other. Not because you are the same, but due to your appreciation for each other's personality and attributes.

Final Thoughts

So what do you think? Can you imagine developing a new style that incorporates an intentional way of affirming your mate?

Perhaps this means a closer look at your own uniqueness and that of your spouse. What makes you feel loved and valued and what makes them feel special.

Affirming one another becomes the ingredient that creates and sustains love. Keeps love from dying, from degenerating into the abyss of inattention. Keeps love alive, abundant and visible.

Visible.

AFFIRMATION
Review and Practice

- So we define affirmation as all the ways we verbally and non-verbally support and reinforce the value and worth of our mate. And demonstrate our love for them.

- Affirmation involves action – deliberate ways we cultivate and initiate love and care in our partner's life to bring visible support and reinforcement into their world.

- Affirmation – touching each other's heart and mind with actions, words and experiences that convey acceptance, respect, adoration and a deep affection for the identity and heart of their mate.

- Consistent and genuine affirmation creates "soul mates," enduring love and a marriage that withstands the winds of adversity – of any kind. Creates amazing intimacy.

- There are many ways we can affirm our lover. Through verbal praise, touch, non-verbal communication, and writing, to name a few.

- One way we affirm one another comes from words of praise and thankfulness. This means creating communication patterns that reflect our care for our mate, how we value them and how we appreciate their uniqueness.

- You can use physical touch to affirm your spouse. Even a quick hug can send the message that you value your mate and care about them.

- A glance or warm look can send a message of love and affirmation. Can't underestimate the power of non-verbal cues you give off to your partner.

- Brief notes, text messages, letters, emails, cards and other forms of written communication can bring joy and warmth into your marriage.

- One useful way to think about effectively loving your spouse centers on becoming experts at their love language. These include quality time, touch, gifts, acts of service and words of affirmation. Knowing your and your lover's love language is essential in order to reach out to them with care and affirmation that resonates.

- Affirmation can come with some roadblocks because genuine acts of affirmation involve becoming vulnerable to one another in some way.

- Some of these challenges can include:

  › Family of origin issues: Affirmation may have played little role in our lives growing up.

  › Past Relationships: Perhaps we have been in other relationships, even former marriages, where praise and reinforcement died or was absent.

  › Negative patterns and habits: We frequently develop patterns in our marriage that don't include finding ways to honor and cherish one another. Part of this involves "complacency," a killer in the realm of intimacy and closeness.

  › Vulnerability: Affirmation can be experienced as a kind of vulnerability. It can feel a bit scary.

- Consistent, intentional acts of support, encouragement and caring become the basis for true relationship growth and development. On the other hand, removing or ignoring the power of affirmation can cause love to die.

- By loving one another, you have a special opportunity to affirm each other's uniqueness and individuality. Being open to the uniqueness of your spouse and finding ways to encourage the expression of your differentness is love in action. Implicit in this is a deep recognition of each other's separate identity.

- Some individuals in marriage are threatened by their spouse's uniqueness and differentness. They see it as a threat to the oneness they hope for in the bonds of love. Yet being able to maintain and express individual differences becomes central to any person's mental health and to the growth of the relationship.

- A sign of maturity and success interpersonally depends on developing an appreciation for individual differentness and honoring these in the bonds of a love relationship. And we really mean "honoring" these. It is vital to champion the individuality or your mate – to find ways to express joy in them rather than seeing their differentness as threatening or something you are unwilling to understand.

Exploring Together

- Do you see evidence of your husband/wife affirming you? In what ways? If not, ask your partner if they believe they are affirming to you.

- Are you affirming of your sweetheart? How so? How could you be more affirming? Ask your partner for ideas if need be.

- If you have not already, take a moment to identify your love language. Share these with each other. Describe how reaching out to you in your love language affirms you.

Enhancing Your Marriage

- Make a focused attempt this week to love your partner in their love language. Check in with each other at the end of the week to see how it went. Do you feel more loved?

- Take the time to get together or go on a date and deliberately affirm each other using what you learned in your "Exploring Together" time. Make a choice not to talk about negative topics or areas of conflict. Talk to each other about how it felt to be affirmed by the other.

- Here is a fun exercise to make each of you feel affirmed and special. It's called "King and Queen for a Day." Allow each other one whole day where you each get to be treated like a King or Queen. On that day, it is your job to lovingly serve your sweetheart - do nice things for them, anticipate their needs if you can and make it your point to convey to them how very special they are by how you treat them. Make sure you each get your own day. Enjoy!

Pondering the Spiritual

- God's love for us is almost unfathomable. He chooses us to be His and showers us with blessings. Psalm 18:19, says "He brought me out into a broad place; he rescued me, because he delighted in me." Spend time in prayer together thanking Him for loving and affirming you.

Include thankfulness for the life and purpose He has given you.

- Reflect on how God sees you – your identity in Christ. Find Scriptures that support who you are "In Christ." Spend time this week discussing what your identity in Christ means and how this can shape how you view and see each other. Some verses to get you started, are: Jn. 1:12; Jn. 15:15; Rom. 5:1; Eph. 1:3-8; 1 Cor. 6:17; 1 Cor. 6:19-20; Col. 1:13-14; Heb. 4:14-16; Rom. 8:1; Rom. 8:31-39; Col. 3:1-4; Jn. 15:16. Spend time in Bible study, finding more passages that show how God loves you and affirms your person and identity.

Next, we turn to our final attitude, bringing God and spirit completely into the equation. We call this Awe.

AWE

"O LORD, I have heard the report of you, and
your work, O LORD, do I fear."
HABAKKUK 3:2

"Much dreaming and many words are meaning-
less. Therefore stand in awe of God"
ECCLESIASTES 5:7

I N THE FALL of 2010, our family drove through Zion National Forest. What an experience. We were struck by the majestic rock forma- tions, overwhelmed by the beauty and grandeur of panoramic can- yons, deep red, sky-high rock carved out of what must have been the very hand of God.

We stood in awe, breathtaking scenery suffusing all our senses with what felt like a divine presence. A handiwork that seemed impossible to conceptualize as a result of random chance. We moved from the cement- covered highway to the monumental corridors of this extraordinary cre- ation, where we could absorb the Master's incomprehensible touch.

With juniper and pine trees carefully nestled in sometimes unexpected places, between jagged walls of stone, unmovable and a silent testimony to ages ago when life came into being. Towering rocks and cliffs, formed out of what seemed like red clay, watching over us. Travelers privileged to witness grandeur, majesty and brilliance.

The kind of scenery that makes you gasp, makes your heart skip a beat and sends an unfolding peace through your body and spirit.

Surprisingly, only a few months later I (Doug) went in for emergency open heart surgery. I was about to die and didn't know it, with major blockages in three of my heart's arteries. I have learned more about the heart over the past several months than all the years of my life before.

The heart is an amazing work of art. Hard to believe that one muscle powers the human frame in such a fluid, remarkable way. Inspired by a surgeon's scalpel and what feels like a second chance on life, I have a renewed interest in the miraculous. A deep curiosity about how goodness and virtue and spiritual power get enacted in my own little world.

When we pondered writing this book, we wanted to speak to your hearts in a special way. To send you a message of hope for more, anchored in truth and in guiding principles that beg to be implemented in your marriage. Ones that make a huge difference in the love you experience so you could see just how "amazing" intimacy can be.

We hope and pray you will be able to create a Zion within your own hearts and that you will believe in the miraculous power of love to stir the soul and etch its way into the deepest patterns of your marriage, affecting how you care for and reach out to one another.

Our picture of this involves grasping and internalizing spiritual resources and ideas that revolutionize our soul and help make us new. New on the inside. We see God as a being who brings us light and Who stands for virtues that we can make our own; in ways that create a riveting, inspirational marriage.

Our idea of God stems from our belief in the Judeo-Christian God of the Bible. We believe in a God who makes Himself personally known and desires to reside in our own being in such a way that we are transformed by His power and values. A God who revealed Himself in Scripture and created a gospel that centered on His son, Jesus Christ.

We realize, however, that as a reader of this book, you may not share the same perspective. But we hope you will read what follows with an open mind and consider embracing a connection with greater forces that lie beyond, that can add resources to your life and marriage that truly empower you. A belief in principles inspired by more than what comes from the human spirit alone, that provide an essential framework for loving others thoroughly and even unconditionally.

And this is where awe comes in. Our idea of awe comes from our belief that a great marriage can be better carved out of the jagged rocks of our own history if we rely on more than just ourselves. This happens when we add spiritual truths and light that come from outside our finite being. And we then stand amazed at what they can do. What love can accomplish; how compassion and forgiveness can transform our hearts; how tenderness can melt walls and bring a new day. Just to name a few.

As you move into this chapter, spend some time pondering the questions below. Think of your own spiritual life and how you bring light and love into your personal experience and into your marriage. Think of how you embrace spiritual realities and virtues that give you the capacity to love, truly love others – especially your wife, your husband.

PAUSE *and* PONDER

* "Where do you draw strength, wisdom and love for your partner from?"
* Do you depend completely on yourself to be able to love others?
* "What truly inspires you in your life?"
* "Do you live by spiritual principles and energy that guide how you reach out to your mate?"

* **"What do you worship?"**
* **"What is the motivation for your life?"**

Questions like these challenge us to think through what moves us. What makes life worth living; where we draw strength and inspiration from; why we're alive; how we expect to make love and relationships work; how and why we feel capable of reaching out to another human being, our life partner, with a love that truly counts and makes a difference.

These questions challenge us to look beyond and reflect on what we appreciate most, what we stand in awe of. It makes all the difference in the world.

The Meaning of Awe

Awe is defined as follows:

> *"An overwhelming feeling of reverence, admiration, fear, etc., produced by that which is grand, sublime, extremely powerful, or the like: in awe of god; in awe of great political figures."*

At some level, awe directs us to gaze at God and draw from Him our energy, capacity to love and care for our partner. To internalize what He has defined as most important; to lead a life characterized by inspiration and a desire to love others completely. "Awe" means we stand in amazement at all the blessings available to us from the light of His person and Spirit that give us the capacity to grow and expand as human beings. Especially in our capacity to reach out and thoroughly love others, including our mate.

Everything you choose in life can be thought of as a mirror of what you deeply believe inside – your core thoughts and conclusions about the meaning of life, what is most important and worth dying for and how you grow and develop as a person. This includes what empowers and motivates you and keeps you centered in love and compassion for yourself and your mate.

In many ways, this means understanding our spiritual center, knowing that what comes from *within* is fed and cultivated by *light from above*. In a very real sense, God inhabits our being and life in a way that magnifies the possibility of loving from the whole heart, with consistency and power. Ultimately, this attitude focuses on the reverence and awe we have toward God's amazing grace and His plan for each of us. A plan reflected in His desire for us to sexually and intimately love one another.

And yes, God desires that you experience maximum intimacy with one another in marriage, best seen in how you love each other sexually and emotionally. And all part of His design for marriage to be truly "amazing."

> *In many ways, this means understanding our spiritual center, knowing that what comes from within is fed and cultivated by light from above.*

Culture versus God's Intention

The media and our culture portray love and sex in so many ways that miss the mark. Virtually no attention is given to spirituality as a force connecting two loves. Love and sex are disconnected from God and His presence in a person's life. Even the union and closeness sex creates between two lovers as an amazing, spiritual experience is virtually never addressed.

There seems to be an agenda in our culture to portray love and sex as separate experiences. Love involving emotion and commitment, sex involving physical desire at times associated with love and commitment, but not a necessary link between the two.

This leaves us socially with a vision of intercourse and intimacy that becomes detached from specific values and beliefs other than personal ideas of morality and right and wrong.

Yet true intimacy has been clearly defined by God as more than a mere extension of biologically driven urges and wants. Real intimacy is created out of the bedrock of biology and spirituality, where two become one in all aspects of their relationship. Intimacy between two married partners becomes a reflection of the closeness He wants with each of us individually.

If you see your marriage relationship and the intimacy you can achieve as part of God's creative magnificence and you are truly amazed at how He made us male and female, you will take your affection and sexual passion down a different path with your mate.

In fact, once you see His grand design in creating us male and female, related to how you bond affectionately and sexually, your amazement at His generosity and creativity become expressed in how you treat each other.

> *If you see your marriage relationship and the intimacy you can achieve as part of God's creative magnificence and you are truly amazed at how He made us male and female, you will take your affection and sexual passion down a different path with your mate.*

Sustaining true love and lasting passion toward your mate requires an understanding of the need to live spiritually. This means you work at carving out a path with a clear focus on the spiritual truths that bring joy, compassion and care into your own heart and ultimately to the life of your partner. A path that reflects an abiding respect for how your own attitudes and behaviors emerge from the divine blessings we receive from above.

Awe contains a component of shock and amazement at God's creative mind and just how deeply He wants us to love each other with passion, fervency and consistency.

When we think of awe, we reflect on the reality that love, compassion and any of the virtues that reflect light and goodness fill us up in a way that impact our personal life and relationships. These virtues inspire and empower us to live differently. We have the privilege and responsibility to invite them in and let them take residence in our heart, mind and soul.

Sustaining true love and lasting passion toward your mate requires an understanding of the need to live spiritually. This means you work at carving out a path with a clear focus on the spiritual truths that bring joy, compassion and care into the life of your partner.

Your Spiritual Center

One way to explain all this is to think of yourself as having a spiritual center that drives what you believe and what you feel. It is composed of all the beliefs about love and care that empower you to reach out to your mate and that grow your bond together.

Think of it as a vast well you draw from, with virtues such as joy, peace, forgiveness, compassion and love feeding your heart and mind in a way that gives you direction, motivation and the drive to construct an amazing life. They compel you to reach out to others, to bring light into your personal life and to create a bond in marriage full of love.

How do you fill up that center? Imagine for a minute that your heart has a door. When opened up, as you sit in reverence for God's blessings, you allow light, the Spirit and the divine inside. You let in the brilliance of love, forgiveness, compassion, and other virtues that shape your heart and spirit in powerful ways. In ways that help you reach out and connect with your lover and that further define your core, your spiritual center.

Think of yourself as having a spiritual center that drives what you believe and what you feel. It is composed of all the beliefs about love and care that empower you to reach out to your mate and that grow your bond together.

Because we stand in awe of God and the blessings of light He bestows on us, and because we invite the presence of all He stands for into our hearts, we can live a richer life. We find ourselves shaped by all the virtues that move us to higher ground and that make an incredible difference in the love we create together.

Reflect on these thoughts and questions.

PA(U)SE *and* PONDER

❋ **How do you define "light" in your life, including the virtues that guide how you reach out to your mate? Name some of these virtues.**

❋ **Think of your "spiritual center." What do you do to become more aware of spiritual truths that bring light into your life and direct how you think and behave?**

❋ **How do you open the "door" of your heart to fill your being up with light?**

When we focus on expressing love and care out of a spiritual center that we cultivate and grow, our marriages are influenced by principles that have a huge impact.

And awe makes this all happen. Our attitude and disposition about God and the divine blessings and light He brings to us make all the difference in the world.

Awe and Your Better Self

When we bring light into our heart and let it drive how we think, feel and behave, we develop and have access to a better self. Our best self is the one that lives by virtues and divine blessings and reaches out in love to those around us. Including, of course, the lover we have married.

The challenges of building and sustaining love in your marriage require you to have access to your *better self*. Knowing God and internalizing His truths and ways into your life provide a way to live on a higher plane, to use supernatural resources to change how you think and relate to your lover.

When we bring light into our heart and let it drive how we think, feel and behave, we develop and have access to a better self. Our best self is the one that lives by virtues and divine blessings and reaches out in love to those around us. Including, of course, the lover we have married.

This access to a better self allows you to create a new and exciting relationship with your life partner. And this better self provides the very real capacity to bring into your marriage several vital themes that can transform how you love and relate to one another.

We find it helpful to focus on different topics that help us understand how to bring virtues and goodness into our heart. Think of these as disciplines or guideposts that you can explore to help enrich you in your growth and in your ability to bring light into your spiritual center. We have limited our discussion to just a few and encourage you to explore additional areas that promote love, goodness and virtue in your daily life and that will help you reach out to your lover.

Wisdom

Wisdom is a resource that guides us in life and brings power to all our decisions. It influences how we think of our world and how we view our marriage. With wisdom, we can reach out to one another intelligently and with focus.

In the book of James, chapter 3, verses 17 & 18, we read,

> *"But the wisdom from above is first pure, then peaceable, gentle, open to reason, full of mercy and good fruits, impartial and sincere. [18] And a harvest of righteousness is sown in peace by those who make peace."*

The benefits from bringing into your marriage peace, gentleness, willingness to yield your desires to the other, mercy, positive deeds, sincerity, etc. impact the quality of your love for one another more than you can imagine.

Proverbs 16:16 tells us,

> *"How much better to get wisdom than gold!*
> *To get understanding is to be chosen rather than silver."*

We think of wisdom as a huge resource that affects the choices we make, how we approach others and what we end up prioritizing in life. Wisdom anchors us in truth, in sound decisions and provides ways to think through how to love our mate.

And of course, wisdom is anchored in the truths that God Himself has defined, found in Scripture. We find wisdom, also, in the writings of those He has gifted and motivated, when those truths are consistent with the written Word. Growing in wisdom happens when we pray for this blessing in our life and when we commit to study wisdom writings, especially God's word and authors who write on topics consistent with Biblical truth.

We trust that the principles found in this book are consistent with God's truth. Our prayer while writing *Amazing Intimacy* has been to honor our Maker with principles that will guide you into a deeper, even profound love for your mate. We truly want you to experience amazing intimacy – all that God intended. Ultimately to glorify Him.

Thankfulness

Scripture teaches us to be thankful in all things.

In 1 Thessalonians 5:16-17a we read,

> *"Rejoice always, pray without ceasing, give thanks in all circumstances."*

This includes thankfulness for your mate, despite their plusses and minuses, which gives you a proper attitude that carries you through difficulties. In addition, being thankful reminds you that your mate is a blessing from God, a gift. Appreciating the person God gave you as a life partner results in a sometimes profound shift in your attitude toward that person.

In many ways, thankfulness is a kind of heart disposition. In other words, thankfulness means we look at the world and God as a source of blessings, even with the ups and downs that circumstances bring our way. Thankfulness shapes our heart and mind. And it extends potentially to a deep gratitude for the blessings God has provided us in life.

Standing in awe of God, His light and the resources He provides causes us to rejoice in all the ways He blesses us, empowers us and guides us. It gives us an overwhelming attitude of gratitude. Thankfulness can be thought of as a natural response to his goodness.

Thankfulness means we look at the world and God as a source of blessings, even with the ups and downs that circumstances bring our way.

Forgiveness

The key to relationship growth and strength, in part, centers on your ability to forgive your spouse. In marriage, conflict can result in wounds and hurts that get buried if not dealt with.

Forgiveness provides a model for how you orient yourself toward your spouse when there is dissonance and a need to clean the slate to move ahead.

When we struggle to forgive others and harbor anger and resentment, our spiritual center becomes clouded. Light and blessings get replaced with hurts and wounds, making it difficult to reach out and love our spouse. Both partners in a marriage need to commit to keeping resentments from building by striving to forgive each other, complete with apologies and repentance for the wrongs we can create.

Letting Go

Closely related to forgiveness, letting go of hurts and pain becomes important in keeping a love relationship fresh and alive. God's active presence in your life gives you the ability and motivation to let go, to give each other new chances at repair and keeps you emotionally current. Holding onto grudges and hurts, on the other hand, keeps you in bondage to anger and resentment.

Letting go implies that each partner works at solving problems with a desire to keep love fresh and hurts at a minimum.

Mindfulness

This theme suggests a reflective posture in life – that you think about what you are saying and doing and feeling moment by moment and make wise, careful decisions about how you respond to your mate and reach out to touch their life.

Living with an ongoing awareness of the light in your life and desire to bring godly virtues into your thoughts and behavior, creates a richer, more focused way of loving your mate. You can imagine experiencing the blessings that come from above moment by moment and having these affect how you love, how you reach out and how you behave.

In Philippians 4:8, we read these inspiring words by the Apostle Paul,

" Finally, brothers, whatever is true, whatever is honorable, whatever is just, whatever is pure, whatever is lovely, whatever is commendable, if there is any excellence, if there is anything worthy of praise, think about these things."

This really focuses on the possibility of filling our minds with positive, spiritual light. A true example of mindfulness! Staying centered on what is true, honorable, right, pure, lovely and admirable gives us a spiritual path and way of living that have profound, positive consequences.

Imagine you fill each moment of each day with a contemplative awareness of bringing light and love into the life of your soul-mate, your spouse. What a difference that would make. We believe that it's possible to work on our own mindset and keep love and compassion and all the blessings of light in our awareness much of the time. And that we can take this ongoing insight and convert it to all the ways we reach out to our mate day by day.

Compassion

Nothing impacts the heart and mind of another human being more than compassion. This skill and capability represents a vital theme that can transform a marriage from bad to good to great.

We all need compassion. Someone to see into our vulnerabilities, not take advantage of our weaknesses and hurts, and attempt to provide healing and protection. Compassion is a "soft" people skill but also a matter of the heart.

Individuals rich in compassion have had their hearts and emotions shaped by others who have loved them unconditionally. And certainly by God Himself.

Self-Care

Absorbing light and the love that flows from it allows us to see ourselves as vital. This gives us a want and capacity to care for ourselves. It is critical that we care for ourselves to be sustained over the long run.

Bringing light into our lives is as essential as the food we eat. Living in and being mindful of light shifts our focus from circumstances to the presence and healing benefits of divine blessings. These blessings give us peace and reassurance. Our load is truly lifted when we move from worry and strain to valuing what our Maker provides.

Self-care involves deliberate practice. It means we prioritize our time and that we find deliberate ways to seek out the blessings God provides. Then, by faith, we can learn to let go of anxiety and stress.

In Philippians 4:6-8 we read,

> *"Do not be anxious about anything, but in everything by prayer and supplication with thanksgiving let your requests be made known to God. And the peace of God, which surpasses all understanding, will guard your hearts and your minds in Christ Jesus."*

A life focused on God and His spiritual blessings finds rest and peace. Our self-care depends on surrendering to a new life with a focused, spiritual path that allows us to take care of ourselves emotionally and mentally.

Enduring Pain

This may seem like an odd one, but we truly believe that out of our own woundedness and personal pain, we can find joy. So often we grow in our maturity and perspective about life and relationships due to the hardships we have encountered through which we have persevered. Or perhaps are currently in the middle of.

It is often in our suffering and struggles that we are motivated to seek out spiritual light and guidance. Letting light into our spiritual circle and center often happens when we face adversity and have to wrestle with solving issues less independently. We frequently seek God and His help during chapters in our life filled with challenges.

We also have opportunities to reach out to others who suffer or are wounded with the light we have found in our own darkness. And sometimes we are in a marriage that is struggling and is creating pain between two partners. Finding a path out of a deteriorating marriage means incorporating the principles found in this book and seeking light and goodness and all the virtues from above to heal, move forward and create new patterns with our lover.

In James 1:2 we read,

> *"Consider it pure joy, my brothers and sisters, whenever you face trials of many kinds, because you know that the testing of your faith produces perseverance."*

The stories and lives we find in the Bible, from beginning to end, reflect this theme. God made us to stand trials of all kinds, to persevere and to come out the other end more whole and mature and closer to our partner and God.

Prayer

Perhaps one of the most important ways we let light into the depths of our spirit and mind is through prayer. In our prayer and meditative life, we draw from resources beyond and above by opening the door to our heart to all that is good, and truthful. We invite in God's presence, power and virtues to live out a life that goes beyond our mere human talents.

His indwelling presence and power create motivation and the capacity to reach out in love, even unconditional love, to our mate. We ask for His filling and then depend on the resources He provides to live differently.

In Ephesians 6:18a we read,

"Praying at all times in the Spirit, with all prayer and supplication."

The Bible is full of prayers offered to God for assistance, trusting in His goodness and everlasting love to strengthen and help those who call on him. We find this repeatedly in the Psalms and elsewhere.

Even Jesus encouraged us to pray and modeled ongoing prayer with His Father. In Mark 11:24, we read,

"Therefore I tell you, whatever you ask in prayer, believe that you have received it, and it will be yours."

Prayer opens the gates of heaven to our requests. And it opens the portal to our heart and spirit, transforming us as we bathe in the light God offers. No wonder the apostle Paul told us to "pray without ceasing." (I Thessalonians 5:17).

Also, two lovers who pray together regularly bring great power and increased intimacy into their marriage. Praying together can be intimidating for some. It can help to remember that prayer is simply talking to God and doesn't need to be fancy or eloquent. We encourage you to set aside time each day, perhaps before going to bed, to pray for one another and issues and people important to you. The bond created in your prayer life together can be quite meaningful and incredible.

A Final Word

Amazing intimacy has deep roots in all the principles we have suggested in this book. We have ended with awe to give your journey a sense of hope, completion and promise. For with light from above, you can create magic in your love for each other without the burden of feeling alone in your effort to build an awesome relationship. Your internal well gets filled with God's presence and light and this makes the journey all the more incredible.

Our hope, grounded in faith and the love and power we know God presents to each of us, is for you to soar. High above the canyons of

Zion. Far beyond what you ever dreamed possible. Together finding the way of love as you reach deep into the mind and heart of your lover, blessing them with your presence and forever strengthening the bond you share in marriage.

Thank you for joining us on this journey, one of hope, knowing that it is possible and even probable to create the marriage of your dreams. Intimacy that is amazing and lasts a lifetime!

We close with these inspiring words, a brief story, a reflection of a life lived under the umbrella of God's magnificence and majesty – in true "awe" of His person.

Coram Deo

Recently a friend asked me in all earnestness the same question. He asked, "What's the big idea of the Christian life?" He was interested in the overarching, ultimate goal of the Christian life.

To answer his question, I fell back on the theologian's prerogative and gave him a Latin term. I said, "The big idea of the Christian life is *Coram Deo. Coram Deo* captures the essence of the Christian life."

This phrase literally refers to something that takes place in the presence of, or before the face of, God. To live *Coram Deo* is to live one's entire life in the presence of God, under the authority of God, to the glory of God.

To live in the presence of God is to understand that whatever we are doing and wherever we are doing it, we are acting under the gaze of God. God is omnipresent. There is no place so remote that we can escape His penetrating, loving gaze.

To be aware of the presence of God is also to be acutely aware of His sovereignty. The uniform experience of the saints is to recognize that if God is God, then He is indeed sovereign. When Saul was confronted by the refulgent glory of the risen Christ on the road to Damascus, his immediate question was, "Who is it, Lord?" He wasn't sure who was speaking to him, but he knew that whoever it was, was certainly sovereign over him.

Living under divine sovereignty involves more than a reluctant submission to sheer sovereignty that is motivated out of a fear of punishment. It involves recognizing that there is no higher goal than offering honor to God. Our lives are to be living sacrifices, oblations offered in a spirit of adoration and gratitude.

To live all of life *Coram Deo* is to live a life of integrity. It is a life of wholeness that finds its unity and coherency in the majesty of God. A fragmented life is a life of disintegration. It is marked by inconsistency, disharmony, confusion, conflict, contradiction, and chaos.

The Christian who compartmentalizes his or her life into two sections of the spiritual and the non-spiritual has failed to grasp the big idea. The big idea is that all of life is sacred. To divide life between the sacred and the unsacred is itself an affront to God.

This means that if a person fulfills his or her vocation as a steelmaker, attorney, or homemaker *Coram Deo*, then that person is acting every bit as spiritually faithful as a pastor who leads others to Christ week after week. It means that David was a religious man when he obeyed God's call to be a shepherd as he was when he was anointed with the special grace of kingship. It means that Jesus was every bit as religious when He worked in His father's carpenter shop as He was in the Garden of Gethsemane.

Integrity is found where men and women live their lives in a pattern of consistency. It is a pattern that functions the same basic way in church and out of church. It is a life that is open before God. It is a life in which all that is done is done as to the Lord. It is a life lived by principle, not expediency; by humility before God, not defiance. It is a life lived under the tutelage of conscience that is held captive by the Word of God.

Coram Deo ... before the face of God. That's the big idea...

R.C. Sproul
THAT'S AMAZING INTIMACY.

AWE
Review and Practice

- Awe is defined as follows: *"an overwhelming feeling of reverence, admiration, fear, etc., produced by that which is grand, sublime, extremely powerful, or the like: in awe of god; in awe of great political figures."*

- "Awe" means we stand in amazement at all the blessings available to us from the light of His person and Spirit that give us the capacity to grow and expand as human beings.

- Everything you choose in life can be thought of as a mirror of what you deeply believe inside – your core thoughts and conclusions about the meaning of life and how you grow and develop as a person.

- In many ways, this means understanding our spiritual center, knowing that what comes from *within* is fed and cultivated by *light from above*.

- The media and our culture portray love and sex in so many ways that miss the mark. Virtually no attention is given to spirituality as a force connecting two loves.

- If you see your marriage relationship and the intimacy you can achieve as part of God's creative magnificence and you are truly amazed at how He made us male and female, you will take your affection and sexual passion down a different path with your mate.

- Sustaining true love and lasting passion toward your mate requires an understanding of the need to live spiritually. This means you work at carving out a path with a clear focus on the spiritual truths that bring joy, compassion and care into your own heart and ultimately to the life of your partner.

- One way to explain all this is to think of yourself as having a spiritual center that drives what you believe and what you feel. Think of it as a vast well you draw from, with virtues such as joy, peace, forgiveness, compassion and love feeding your heart and mind in a way that gives you direction, motivation and the drive to construct an amazing life.

- How do you fill up that center? Imagine for a minute that your heart has a door. When opened up, as you sit in reverence for God's blessings, you allow light, the Spirit and the divine inside. You let in the brilliance of love, forgiveness, compassion, and other virtues that shape your heart and spirit in powerful ways. In ways that help you reach out and connect with your lover and that further define your core, your spiritual center.

- Because we stand in awe of God and the blessings of light He bestows on us, and because we invite the presence of all He stands for into our heart, we can live a richer life. We find ourselves shaped by all the virtues that move us to higher ground and that make an incredible difference in the love we create together.

- When we bring light into our heart and let it drive how we think, feel and behave, we develop and have access to a better self. Our best self is the one that lives by virtues and divine blessings and reaches out in love to those around us. Including, of course, the lover we have married. This access to a better self allows you to create a new and exciting relationship with your life partner.

- We find it helpful to focus on different topics that help us understand how to bring virtues and goodness into our heart. Think of these as disciplines or guideposts that you can explore to help enrich you in your growth and in your ability to bring light into your spiritual center. Some of these are:

- **Wisdom:** Wisdom is a resource that guides us in life and brings power to all our decisions.

- **Thankfulness:** This includes thankfulness for your mate, despite their plusses and minuses, which gives you a proper attitude that carries you through difficulties.

- **Forgiveness:** When we struggle to forgive others and harbor anger and resentment, our spiritual center becomes clouded. Light and blessings get replaced with hurts and wounds, making it difficult to reach out and love our spouse.

- **Letting Go:** Closely related to forgiveness, letting go of hurts and pain becomes important in keeping a love relationship fresh and alive.

- **Mindfulness:** This theme suggests a reflective posture in life – that you think about what you are saying and doing and feeling moment by moment and make wise, careful decisions about how you respond to your mate and reach out to touch their life.

- **Compassion:** Nothing impacts the heart and mind of another human being more than compassion. This skill and capability represents a vital theme that can transform a marriage from bad to good to great.

- **Self-Care:** Absorbing light and the love that flows from it allows us to see ourselves as vital. This gives us a want and capacity to care for ourselves. It is critical that we care for ourselves to be sustained over the long run.

- **Enduring Pain:** This may seem like an odd one, but we truly believe that out of our own woundedness and personal pain, we can find joy.

- **Prayer:** Perhaps one of the most important ways we let light into the depths of our spirit and mind is through prayer. In our prayer and meditative life, we draw from resources beyond and above by opening the door to our heart to all that is good, and truthful.

- We have ended with awe to give your journey a sense of hope, completion and promise. For with light from above, you can create magic in your love for each other without the burden of feeling alone in your effort to build an awesome relationship. Your internal well gets filled with God's presence and light and this makes the journey all the more incredible.

Exploring Together & Pondering the Spiritual

- Spend time together reflecting on what "Awe" means to each of you personally. How does standing in awe of God and your perspective on God's goodness and majesty influence your spiritual life? And how does it influence the kind of marriage you can create together?

- How would you describe your spiritual life and the kind of spiritual "center" you feel you have? How do you bring virtues and goodness into your own center and how do you reach out to others with the spiritual light you experience?

- Read 2 Peter 1:1-11. Look at all the virtues listed. Where do these virtues come from? If you applied these to your relationship in marriage, how would each of them enrich the quality of your life together?

- What are some of the challenges that keep us from opening the door of our heart to blessings, virtues and light? How, as a couple, can you encourage each other in your spiritual journey and walk with God?

- Reflect on the "guideposts" or themes listed above – *wisdom, thankfulness, letting go, mindfulness, compassion, self-care, enduring pain, and prayer.* What meaning does each one have for you personally and how can you apply these to the growth of your marriage?

- Spend time together praising God for the wonders He provides. Thank Him for what He is doing and will do in creating a marriage for you that thrives and is filled with love and passion. Ask Him to bless you with a marriage beyond your dreams. One filled with love, laughter, passion and strength. One where intimacy is truly amazing.

Appendix A

THE WHEEL OF LIFE

Wheel of Life

Take a few minutes to complete the "Wheel of Life." As you complete this, you will each find out about your own goals and satisfaction with your life across several dimensions. Share with each other what you learn. Remember, the focus ultimately is on what you want out of life, and more specifically, what you want in your life together. And what it means to set goals in an effort to reach your true potential to create love and passion together.

NAME: _____ DATE:_____

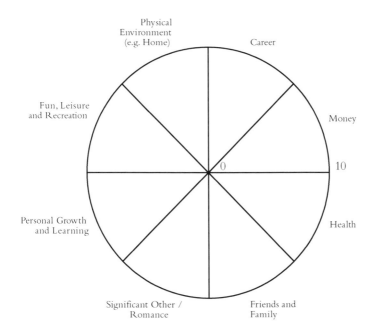

Wheel of Life Instructions

The 8 sections in the Wheel of Life represent balance.

- Please change, split or rename any category so that it's meaningful and represents a balanced life for you.

- Next, taking the center of the wheel as 0 and the outer edge as 10, rank your **level of satisfaction** with each area out of 10 by drawing a straight or curved line to create a new outer edge (see example)

- The new perimeter of the circle represents **your** 'Wheel of Life'. Is it a bumpy ride?

EXAMPLE

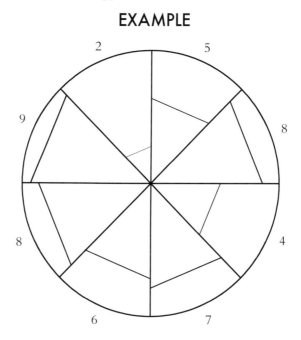

Detailed Instructions:

1. Review the 8 areas on the Wheel of Life. The Wheel must, when put together, create a view of a balanced life

for yourself. If necessary, split categories to add in something that is missing for you. You can also re-label an area so that it is more meaningful for you. The usual suspects are:

1. Family/Friends
2. Partner/Significant Other/Romance
3. Career
4. Finances
5. Health (emotional/physical/fitness/nutrition/ wellbeing)
6. Physical Environment/Home
7. Fun/Recreation/Leisure
8. Personal Growth/Learning/Self-development
9. Spiritual wellbeing (not necessarily religion – can be sense of self)
10. Significant Other/Romance
11. Others could include security, service, leadership, integrity, achievement or community.

2. Think about what success feels like for each area.

3. Now rank your level of satisfaction with each area of your life by drawing a line across each segment. Place a value between 1 (very dissatisfied) and 10 (fully satisfied) against each area to show how satisfied you are currently with these elements in your life.

4. The new perimeter of the circle represents your 'Wheel of Life'. Ask yourself, "Is it a bumpy ride?"

5. Now, looking at the wheel here are some questions you can answer to take this exercise deeper:

1. Are there any surprises for you?

2. How do you feel about your life as you look at your Wheel?

3. How do you currently spend time in these areas?

4. How would you like to spend time in these areas?

5. Which of these elements would you most like to improve?

6. How could you make space for these changes?

7. Can you effect the necessary changes on your own?

8. What help and cooperation from others might you need?

9. What would make that a score of 10?

10. What would a score of 10 look like?

6. Now share your answers with your partner. Focus on each area in the circle.

7. Take time to answer the area of the circle related to your significant other (spouse) and romance. How did each of you assess this area of your marriage? Discuss how your relationship can grow.

Appendix B

WHAT'S MY INTIMACY STYLE?

1. I feel good about myself most of the time and find my partner to be trustworthy.
   T   F

2. I wish my partner was more available so I could feel more content.
   T   F

3. I try hard to make sure my partner is happy and feel nervous when they are not.
   T   F

4. I would rather keep a safe distance from my partner.
   T   F

5. Strong emotions make me feel anxious or uncomfortable.
   T   F

6. I feel very content when my spouse and I are emotionally close.
   T   F

7. When my spouse is busy doing things, I feel angry.
   T   F

8. I often feel insecure and disorganized.

T   F

9. I believe if my partner were happier with me, I would finally feel content.

T   F

10. I start to feel suffocated if I am close to my partner for very long.

T   F

11. It angers me that I don't have all the love I need.

T   F

12. It is easy for me to focus on making my partner happier than me.

T   F

13. I feel preoccupied with feeling loved and cared for.

T   F

14. I enjoy time with my spouse and I also enjoy alone time.

T   F

15. I feel happy with myself and my partner most of the time.

T   F

16. I prefer time away from my partner – it's easier.

T   F

17. I worry too often that my partner will leave me.

T   F

18. I am not sure my partner's love is real and I pull away in anger as a result.

T   F

19. I feel myself desiring to be close to my partner and also resistant to being close.

    T   F

20. It seems I have always been concerned with keeping those I love pleased with me.

    T   F

21. I most often feel unsafe, unsure and uncomfortable with myself and my partner.

    T   F

22. I find I feel the best when I am in control of those around me.

    T   F

23. I experienced abuse as a child and it makes me feel very insecure in my relationship.

    T   F

24. I often wonder when and if my partner will really be there for me.

    T   F

Circle the ones below that you answered "T".

Secure	1, 6, 14, 15
Avoidant	4, 5, 10, 16
Invisible	3, 9, 12, 20
Angry	7, 11, 18, 19
Anxious	2, 13, 17, 24
Chaotic	8, 21, 22, 23

DISCOVERING YOUR COMPASSIONATE SELF

H OW WOULD YOU rate yourself on the dimension of compassion and the degree to which you truly care for the well-being of others?

Spend a few minutes taking our "Compassion Assessment." And discover how far you've come in knowing and giving over your compassionate self in your key relationships, especially your marriage.

Circle the number that best describes you

I view others through the lens of sympathy and care for their well-being.

1 not at all   **2** sometimes   **3** frequently   **4** most of the time

I view my spouse, their personality and their actions without being critical of them.

1 not at all   **2** sometimes   **3** frequently   **4** most of the time

I seek to understand my lover's thoughts and feelings in order to maintain my loving connection with them.

1 not at all   **2** sometimes   **3** frequently   **4** most of the time

I strive to be less critical of myself, reaching for self-acceptance and self-respect.

1 not at all   **2** sometimes   **3** frequently   **4** most of the time

I believe we all need significant levels of support and mutual appreciation to get by in life.

1 not at all   **2** sometimes   **3** frequently   **4** most of the time

I make it a point of paying attention to my partner's well-being each and every day.

1 not at all   **2** sometimes   **3** frequently   **4** most of the time

I see others as unique and special and try to convey this attitude in how I accept and treat them.

1 not at all   **2** sometimes   **3** frequently   **4** most of the time

I believe love is built on the habit of reaching out to my spouse with care and affirmation.

1 not at all   **2** sometimes   **3** frequently   **4** most of the time

People would describe me as compassionate and giving of my heart, emotions and time.

1 not at all   **2** sometimes   **3** frequently   **4** most of the time

My spouse would describe me as giving and caring and that I accept them completely for who they are.

1 not at all   **2** sometimes   **3** frequently   **4** most of the time

Score

35–40   The Mother Teresa of Compassion

25–35   Compassionate much of the time

15–25   Occasionally compassionate but needing more growth in this area

1–15   The Donald Trump of Compassion - much work needed

What is Compassion? – A Primer.

We define compassion in a number of ways. Perhaps the most useful is to think of how you view others and even yourself from the standpoint of several key dimensions:

Sympathy – The experience of feeling for someone else, understanding their pain or suffering and wishing to alleviate their burden. So, can I feel for someone who is struggling or hurting or be concerned about their general welfare? Do I desire for them to suffer less?

Empathy – To know and feel what someone else is experiencing – to put ourselves in their shoes. So, do I have a genuine desire to understand what someone is feeling and thinking and to know them as a person? To share in their suffering by attempting to experience their world and pain? This can involve feelings of personal pain or discomfort at someone's plight.

Non-judgmental attitude – Letting go of any criticism of what someone else experiences and trying to simply understand their experience for what it is. So, am I able to let go of my own personal concern or even hurt and see others without criticism?

Mindfulness – The practice of paying attention to inner and outer experiences intentionally and regularly. Do you allow yourself to experience and bring kindness and compassion into all your relationships in your daily life?

Compassion – A Closer Look

Compassion can best be defined as a set of behaviors and actions designed to support, nurture, soothe, protect, soften, embrace, and deeply care for another. Compassion for our mate involves those very choices to continue to reach out and touch their being with ours – in tenderness and desire to touch their lives.

Compassion comes from deep inside our own center, and can be cultivated through meditation, mindfulness and prayerful contemplation. Ultimately, our personal growth involves an ever-increasing experience of care for the heart and soul of another. And a desire to see them thrive, not suffer.

Prior Experiences

Our entire life experience, including family of origin, shapes our capacity to care and see others through the eyes of compassion. Our ability to empathize with others, see them less critically and more supportively, comes from our own journey – whether or not we have been loved and supported in this kind of way.

How have your experiences in life shaped how you care and see others through the lens of compassion?

Interestingly, the story of God in our lives can be understood as a continued covenant of love that the Bible often refers to as His "loving kindness." We have no greater example of compassion than that of an eternal, perfect Being accepting us unconditionally and showering us with love and grace at every turn.

Compassion Themes

Several themes can be identified that gives us a closer look at the meaning of compassion. Our corresponding questions provide a way of measuring our own lives in how we do, or don't, live out this vital virtue we call compassion.

Spiritual light and potential – *How do you view God's impact in your life in creating compassion, especially as you see each other through His eyes?*

Perspective about human life – *Does your perspective of life, our common frailties, our challenges in suffering and the struggles of life give you sympathy for human beings?*

Acceptance – *Do you practice acceptance of others and letting go of criticism and judgment toward them?*

Choice in this journey – *Do you make it a habit to "choose" compassion in your outlook toward others and your partner?*

Self-Compassion – *How do you treat yourself? With love and grace or criticism?*

Practicing Kindness – *Do your habits and actions reach out to others with kindness?*

Ultimate empathy – *Do you strive to understand others and see life from their perspective?*

Forgiveness – *Are you able to forgive others? Is your life characterized by acts of forgiveness, giving grace to others for their mistakes and letting go of wounds and hurts you hold on to in the relationship and need to let go of?*

Growing Your Compassionate Self

There are several avenues for cultivating passion in a person's life. We will mention several strategies that may help you grow this dimension of your life. The question becomes, how do we move forward and cultivate a meaningful path to greater compassion in our married life and relationship with others?

Here we will outline a simple 5-fold path.

1. *Choose Compassion*

Exercising and growing compassion toward others in our life depends on choosing to do so. In other words, compassion is a lifestyle borne out of decisions we make to view others in certain ways and reach out to them with specific compassionate actions.

Take a closer look at the key themes above and identify those you want to incorporate more fully into your life. Set goals for integrating these into your thoughts and actions as you reach out to your mate more intentionally.

2. *Enlist Your Imagination and Fantasy*

How do you "imagine" yourself feeling and acting as a more compassionate person in your marriage? You can also identify key role models in your life that have exhibited high levels of compassion toward you and others and seek to pattern your life after theirs.

Then, visualize how you would treat your spouse and others using your growing vision of what a compassionate person does and feels. Be specific about the internal feelings and actual behaviors that would characterize your way of involving yourself with your lover.

3. *Develop Self-Compassion*

Practice compassion for yourself. Again, using the "Compassion Themes" above, imagine reaching out to yourself with greater acceptance, less criticism and more hope. What would that look like and feel like?

4. *Create a Spiritual Path*

True compassion comes from above – feeding ourselves with themes of love and care from a higher source than our own limited perspectives. Can you identify a spiritual path for yourself by imagining reliance on God and His role in feeding your capacity to love, forgive and truly care for others?

5. *Practice Mindfulness*

Mindfulness and compassion go hand in hand. With mindfulness, we often think of tuning into immediate experiences without agenda, criticism or evaluation. In other words, develop awareness of what happens in each moment without judgment or need to evaluate what's happening with labels or conclusions. Just let the moment be.

We take this a step further and argue that mindfulness involves the conscious desire to bring compassion for others into our ongoing awareness each moment, each day. Practicing God's unique presence in our lives also helps ground us in the ultimate spiritual resources He has to offer. Remember, He is a God of loving kindness and infusing our experience with His power and Spirit gives us a tremendous capacity to bring compassion into our lover's life and the life of others.

Hopefully we have provided a roadmap, however brief, to create a journey forward toward a more compassionate lifestyle. One that will change your life and that of your spouse forever.

Appendix D

ATTITUDE OF OPENNESS QUESTIONNAIRE

Choose the response that best applies to you, answering either true of false. After you have finished, compare your answers with summary at the end.

1. I feel calm and present when my partner and I solve problems together.
   T   F

2. I find I become alert and guarded when my partner and I talk about our real issues.
   T   F

3. When we don't see things in the same way, I find it difficult to listen to his/her viewpoint.
   T   F

4. When my partner is speaking, I find myself thinking about my response and not hearing.
   T   F

5. I like the experience of hearing what my partner thinks and feels about issues.

   T   F

6. I am able to gather my thoughts and speak clearly about my perspective with my spouse.

   T   F

7. I avoid talking about our problems – it's uncomfortable.

   T   F

8. I look forward to the times when my spouse and I can share how we really feel with each other.

   T   F

9. I feel freed up and able to share my feelings, thoughts and opinions with my partner.

   T   F

10. When my partner and I disagree, it seems neither of us even hear each other's perspective.

    T   F

Defensive **2, 3, 4, 7, 10**

Open   **1, 5, 6, 8, 9**

Are you more open or defensive with your spouse?

Appendix E

HAVE I GROWN UP? ASSESSMENT

Rate yourself on the following key statements:

1. I am able to identify my feelings and emotions and use these to better communicate.
   T   F

2. I am willing to listen and understand my partner's thoughts and feelings, even if they are different than my own.
   T   F

3. Am I able to stay calm during conversations, especially if there is conflict?
   T   F

4. I am able to temporarily set my own needs aside in order to better understand what my spouse is thinking and feeling.
   T   F

5. I care deeply for my spouse's welfare and regularly find ways to let her know this.
   T   F

6. I appreciate my spouse's uniqueness and do not feel threatened by our differences.

  T   F

7. I am able to listen to my partner without anger and irritation dominating my experience.

  T   F

8. I am willing to bring up unresolved conflicts in order to process them more effectively and get closure.

  T   F

9. I seldom let my emotions get the better of me or let them impact my spouse in negative ways.

  T   F

10. I am able to feel deep levels of love for my spouse.

  T   F

11. I seldom put up walls and have no trouble getting close in my love relationship with my mate.

  T   F

12. I am not easily injured and tend to get over hurts soon.

  T   F

13. Most often, I listen to my spouse and don't wait for my spouse to repent before giving love.

  T   F

14. I am more interested in understanding my spouse than being understood.

  T   F

15. *I seldom feel threatened when there is conflict and most often see it as an opportunity to grow.*

  T   F

16. *I seldom try to avoid my feelings and have little trouble hearing other people's emotions.*
    T   F

17. Most of the time, I do not feel anger and resentment.
    T   F

18. *I seldom avoid being close to my spouse.*
    T   F

19. *I often reach out to my spouse and most often don't wait for them to reach out to me.*
    T   F

20. *I mostly identify positive experiences in my life and don't focus on the negative.*
    T   F

Scoring

T   15-20 Surprisingly mature

T   10-15 Growth needed

T   1-10 Much growth needed

ORGASM MADE EASY – A 4 STEP GUIDE FOR WOMEN

OU ARE NOT alone. Many women have difficulty having an orgasm or have never had one. That is unfortunate and frankly pains me as there is so much good that sex and orgasm have to offer a woman. As Lisa Rankin, whose book we've previously mentioned, says, these include many health benefits as well as self-esteem, self-confidence and feeling wonderfully feminine, just to name a few. God intended women to enjoy and experience full pleasure in the bedroom. Just think about it; God definitely knew what He was doing when He created sex - when we feel good in the bedroom, we want to go back there and feel good some more, which keeps us motivated to maintain a consistent sex life.

And as you no doubt know now, sex is glue for your marriage. It keeps a couple bonded together, and satisfied with their marriage and each other. When it's just so-so – or feels like a "have - to" or is downright disappointing or a negative experience – it is very hard to keep wanting to have more.

So my intention here is to make orgasm easier for you. YAY! That said, I realize this topic may be new to some of you and a bit scary. I will be speaking honestly about sexuality and teaching sexual technique, which may be surprising at times, but hopefully not shocking. I want to deliver this information in an uplifting, edifying and playful way. At times though, you may need to "hang on to your seats" so you can get to the end of the ride. I am writing in this style for a reason.

Most of the books I have read on the subject, while very informative, are heavy on explanation and very clinical – which for some can increase anxieties instead of putting them to rest. If you would like more insight and ideas, then I recommend "For Yourself" by Lonnie Barbach, Ph.D. Also helpful is "The Celebration of Sex" by Douglas E. Rosenau. Both of these helped inform this guide.

So bottom line, orgasms are possible and your body was made for them. You likely just need some helpful, clear instruction and practice so you can discover your orgasm or have them more often. So here we go. Woo Hoo!

STEP 1 – Preparing

Becoming orgasmic requires a commitment on your part to try. I know, commitment can be a big word, but it's a necessary ingredient. In order to try, you must set aside private time to practice. The more you practice, the more likely you are to learn how your body works and find your orgasm. Some say even an hour a day most days is the way to go." Kind of like going to school, but the subject is your body.☺ Douglas E. Rosenau recommends at least 3 times per week. Whatever amount of time you put forth is going to move you forward. The more often it is, the easier it will be for you as it seems to help keep women in their "sensual zone."

Mental preparation is also critical. Way too many women have lots of different kinds of mind obstacles that can get in the way of giving themselves permission to learn to try and stay the course. A range of fears, negative messages about sex, moral untruths about sex, untruths about enjoying sex, shame and guilt about their bodies – and the list goes on – all constitute potential challenges to enjoying and experiencing orgasms.

Everyone is individual in this, with their own unique histories, but the obstacles tend to fall into these categories: fears, untruths, negative messages, negative thoughts and harsh feelings about your body and sex. These are not your friends.

At this point, it would helpful to write down your own fears, negative thoughts and beliefs you have about sex and your body and see how they compare to these truthful statements:

> *"I am created by God and He loves every part of me and calls it good. He wants me to appreciate and enjoy what He has given me and make use of it to keep my husband and me close, bonded and connected."*

Or,

> *"Sex is pleasurable, helps my marriage and I am deserving of being able to enjoy the fullness of lovemaking with my husband."*

Or,

> *"My marriage needs to thrive to last a lifetime and sex is an important part of that. Being able to enjoy my own pleasure in the bedroom will help make that happen."*

If your own beliefs, thoughts and feelings about sex contradict these truths and you think they are getting in your way, then they need to be continually dismissed, thrown out, ignored or confronted (talked back to) to lessen their power. If that is too hard, then finding positive affirmations to put in their place can help too. Here are some suggestions:

> *"My body is perfect in God's eyes."*

> *"My husband thinks I am hot and even if I am not sure about that, I am going to believe him and act as though it's true."*

> *"There is nothing sinful or unnatural about me and my desire to feel good sexually."*

"My thoughts and fears are not me and are not the truth about the good God wants for me."

"I will find my way to orgasm if I put in the time and effort."

"I have believed lies about sex and my body, but I am free to let them go and experience pleasure in my body now."

"I was not in control of the bad things that happened to me as a child, but I get to be in control of my sexuality now and it is for me and my husband only."

"I am learning to embrace my femininity and look forward to feeling more and more sexy."

"I have girlfriends who like and enjoy sex and I want that too. No reason I should not."

"Sex is good for me and feels good and I want that."

"I look forward to the time when I can really enjoy sex like my husband does."

These are just some ideas. Write others that come to mind so you can have them in your arsenal when the old thoughts or fears rear their ugly heads.

In addition to preparing by giving yourself permission to try and committing to it and getting your mind into the right frame is the need to create a sensual space for yourself. Find a safe place in your home where you can retreat and make it beautiful for yourself. A place that is comfortable, filled with sensual delights that make you feel sexy. You can use your list from the section on the erotic triad to help you out here. Whatever you need to create an environment where you can begin to relax and settle into your own "little world."

Okay, let's move on to Step 2.

STEP 2 – Exploring and Self-Pleasuring

Yes, that's what I am talking about. Step 2 is about getting to know your body and exploring its parts as well as learning to self-pleasure. Some women get concerned about self-pleasuring and wonder if it's okay. Not only is it okay; it's critical. Only you know what your body feels like when it is touched.

You are the expert of your body (or are on the path to becoming one☺).

If you don't know how your body works, what feels good and what does not and what it can do, it will be real hard to let your husband know.

Some women are also bothered by the solo nature of self-pleasuring. If that's so, just hang in there. We will be bringing your husband into the picture soon. And, if you both are comfortable with it and it's not distracting to you, or too arousing for him, you are free to have him hang out with you, observe or just lay close to you while you practice during this stage. Although, if he becomes a hindrance and makes you feel too self-conscious at this point, or wants to move things in a sexual direction, it would be wise for you to have you own "study time".

Some women prefer their husbands do that touching and that's fine as long as you guide the process and let him know what does and does not feel good.

There are 3 sessions to this stage and you can repeat each of them as much as you'd like before you move on the next. Becoming comfortable in each session, being able to relax and have a positive experience lets you know you are ready to move on to the next stage. Keep your expectations at bay and appreciate each time you have to practice this new kind of self-care.

The goal is not to produce orgasms but to learn about your body, discover what it feels like to touch yourself and begin to find where you feel pleasure. Don't be surprised if you feel little when you first get going – it takes time. Viewing these sessions like your own special "spa" time may help and spending at least 20-30 minutes each session will help you experience what you need.

Session 1 - Discovering

Here is your chance to get to know your body more and start to feel what it's like to be touched in the way that you want. We're not focusing on genitals yet so no need to go there.

Prop yourself up comfortably with pillows and begin to move from the top of your head to your face, ears, neck, shoulders, breasts on to your tummy, etc. and all the way down your body. Notice what kinds of touch feel good – soft, firm, circular, back and forth stroking. You may not like touch on some parts at all and that is okay and good to know. Spend time appreciating each part that you touch. Remind yourself how wonderfully you are made and how amazing it is that you can enjoy touch. Get to know each body part. As you are moving down your body, don't forget your inner thighs, legs, calves and feet.

If you start to feel anxious or tense at any point, take a minute or two to practice some deep breathing. Draw the air through your nose as you feel the depth of breath into your belly and let the air out slowly. Calming statements like "I will be fine, this is good for me," "relax" or simply concentrating on your breath can help. Repeat the breathing and calming until you feel relaxed again and start touching where you left off. If there are specific negative or fearful thoughts in your mind as you are relaxing and breathing, picture the thoughts floating away in a bubble – farther and farther and farther away. You can also use your affirmations to keep yourself encouraged.

All over exploration, relaxation and body appreciation are what we are after here. When you have repeated this session as many times as you need to feel like it was a positive experience, where you have discovered some kinds of touches that feel good and where and you are comfortable with being touched, move to the next session. Yay for you.

If you have included your husband in the process, you are welcome to have him touch you all over as you guide him or have him just be with you. However, he must be informed that moving forward to anything sexual is not allowed. He is simply there to support and get to know you. Some men cannot do this at all because the experience is too arousing and that becomes counter-productive to you getting to know you. If this is the case, having him sit this one out is the best way to go.

Session 2 - Getting to Know and Touching the Hot Spots

Now it's time to get a little more personal. It's time to learn about your genitals – what they look like and how they feel. There is a time for everything in life, right?☺ If you have included your husband, you might want him to be waiting nearby for the first part of the exercise where you will simply be exploring yourself and gathering facts.

Propping yourself up again with pillows, get a small hand held mirror so you can take a look at your genital area. I know this may sound a little uncomfortable or scary to you but remember to breathe, calm and affirm yourself if you need to before you begin.

Become a scientist of sorts; put on your observational skills and remember you are on a "fact finding mission" at this point if that helps. As you hold the mirror up to your vulva (a fancy word used for the whole genital area), notice its size, shape, colors - which range from your skin color to various pinks, brown and even purples and textures that feel velvety soft, slightly but softly rough and crinkly. Put your experience into your own words too. Your vulva is kind of like a snow-flake – no two are alike.

Begin noticing and exploring all the different parts – the outer lips (labia major), the inner lips (labia minor), the vaginal entrance, the ure-thra that is just above the vagina and the clitoris above that which is a hooded-looking part. Touch all the parts to know what they feel like.

Look in the mirror and check out the whole clitoris. This is the number one "hot spot" for women and it deserves your time and atten-tion. Notice and feel the clitoris and pull back the hood on top. Take a good look and feel around some more. Pause a moment or two to simply appreciate the detail and wonder at this interesting creation designed for pleasure and marriage building. You can even give your genital area a cute or sexual name. Have some fun with it.

When you feel like you have done enough "scientific exploration," you might want to take a quick break, get a sip of water or do some more deep breathing and relaxing so you are ready to move on.

Settling back into the exercise, re-prop yourself or lay down flat, just so long as your newly named vulva is in reach of your hand. Your husband can join in here if you'd both like and be the "toucher." You may want to introduce him to your vulva.☺ Begin touching all parts of your perfectly designed vulva and travel around the different areas trying on different kinds of touch like you did in Session 1 with your whole body.

Where does it feel the best and with what kind of touching? Do some parts not really feel much while other parts give you a warm tingle? Focus on touching (not stimulating) the clitoris to get a feel for what feels good and the kind of touch you like - firm, light, tickling, just on the hood, under the hood, around it but not directly on it?

Try some repetitive stroking to see how that feels. If you start to feel aroused, don't get alarmed; affirm yourself about how wonderfully you work and enjoy the feelings of arousal. If you don't get aroused, don't worry. You will have lots of opportunity to repeat and explore with these sessions as you need. Repeat as much as you need to increase your confidence and prepare yourself for Session 3.

Session 3 - All Over Touching

In this session, you get to put together what you have learned so far and combine the all-over touching and genital touching. Prop yourself up, lay flat again or create any other position that allows you the full range of your body and all its special parts. Begin at the top of your head and travel all over your body with your favorite kinds of touches, working your way to your genitals. Encourage yourself along the way with loving thoughts about what wonderful progress you are making and how you can feel yourself getting more feminine and sexy all the time. Breathe and relax as need be when unnecessary tension surfaces in your body.

When you get to your genitals, focus your time here and use the kinds of touches that you like on the places that you like to experience pleasure and feel warm and tingly or aroused. Focus your mind on the sensations as they come and go. Enjoy the experience of feeling aroused and if you feel like you would like to do more stimulating touching, move onto to Step 3. If not, just bask in the luxury of your own touch (or your husband's). As in previous sessions, when you feel ready to move on to Step 3, go ahead and do so.

STEP 3 – Winding Up and Letting Go.

Doesn't that sound fun? Anything that winds up and lets go is exciting. Think of a spinning top or those little plastic toys that you wind up and watch walk or hop. Or instead of winding up, how about a bottle of coke or champagne that you shake up. As you pop the cap off, the soda bursts out or bubbles over. Sometimes there are squeals of excitement and delight.

That's what an orgasm is like. When we get our bodies wound up, "shook up" and excited, they can't help but "bubble over" or let go. Sure, not all orgasms are this exciting. Some are more like champagne fizz as they range from warm tingly with light vaginal contractions to a more explosive release with intense vaginal contractions. But they ALL feel good and provide pleasure.

So this step is all about allowing your orgasms to occur naturally. One cannot make an orgasm occur by willing or overexerting. Orgasms are reflexes that happen spontaneously when there is adequate stimulation to the vaginal area, particularly the clitoris, and we have experienced enough bodily tension, build up and passion. We women do need to be "wound up," which means providing or receiving adequate stimulation. While the rest of our bodies stay fairly calm and we focus our minds on the increasing sensations and pleasure (or appropriate fantasy), we can simply "enjoy the ride" and let out bodies do their thing.

Romantic or sexual fantasies can be wonderfully helpful in allowing ourselves to fully enjoy our intimate experience. Fantasy for adults is "playing pretend "with our minds. Like children who use their imagination to create scenarios to aid their play and make it more fun, so it can be with adults in the bedroom. Fantasy helps enhance our arousal and helps "tip our cart" so to speak, from arousal into orgasm. Women's fantasies tend to be more romantic and less blatantly sexual but both can help enhance your experience and ultimately your lovemaking. Let your imagination go, picturing wonderful scenes of you and your husband touching each other in sexually stimulating ways and types of sexual interaction. You can create a range of sexually arousing images that excite you and help increase the sexual tension.

Fantasies need boundaries though to be healthy for marriage. The argument is that not all fantasies are created equal. Some enhance the bond and glue we share with our mate and others don't.

When our fantasies are about our husbands, they build up our sex life. But when they begin to be about other people or past lovers, that does not enhance your lovemaking and oneness. We want to remember that that is the goal – enhancing oneness, creating solid glue between two lovers, husband and wife. So being creative and using our imaginations – of perhaps our husbands treating us certain ways or doing certain things with or to us, or sexual adventures we'd like to have with him that we find sexually enlivening – these can add you the deep connection we want with our life partner, our spouse.

It can be helpful to take some time to ponder these to get your mind primed. Some women have never thought of or allowed themselves to fantasize so this can be a new skill that you are developing. Wonderful. This will help expand your sexual inner life and your marriage. These can keep your experience and your lovemaking interesting, novel and wanted. For more information about this topic, "A Celebration of Sex" does a great job exploring the topic. For now, I want to give you permission to use your mind creatively to conjure up lively mental pictures or perhaps revisit sexy romantic memories of you and your hubby in the past. You'll have the chance to do this in your next session.

Session 4 – Allover Touching with Intention

This is your opportunity during your "spa time" to increase your arousal. Beginning with all over touching and your relaxation skills, settle into your own sensual experience. Touch yourself all over in the spots that you have learned feel good to you. As you continue to get to know your body more and more, you will hone in on those areas that seem to love your touch (or husband's). Touch and explore your genitals and begin to focus more and more on the spots in, on or around your clitoris, that you have identified feel the best. Spend more time on your "hottest spots" and increase the rubbing in repetitive way and tune into the sensations you feel. Relish the feelings if you are able.

Now (if you have not already) let your mind dwell on sexual images and fantasies that are pleasing to you while you continue to rub. You may start to feel more and more aroused, which can make you feel uneasy, but don't let that deter you. If fearful thoughts start to get in the way, breathe and calm yourself and tune back into the warm tingly feelings in your body. As you are getting more and more aroused, feel free to add more clearly sexual images into your experience. You may find your body releases and orgasm happens or it may not. Either way is good as you are moving forward and learning to "come into" more and more sexual pleasure.

This session can be repeated as often as you need for you to find your orgasm. Vary the exercise to your liking, combining different mixtures of touch and fantasy in aim of increasing your pleasure.

Some women get help from adding Kegel exercises as a daily practice to condition the vagina to experience vaginal contractions, which mimic a part of orgasm. Kegel? What is a Kegel? I know, I know, funny word. Kegel exercises are exercises for the vagina. Yep. It turns out exercise is good for ALL parts of our body.

Have you ever had to urinate and there is no place to go so you had to "hold it in?" When you did, you had to squeeze the muscles around the vagina to stop yourself until you could find a restroom. That's a Kegel – the squeezing of the PC (Pubecocous muscle). Practicing this kind of squeezing repetitively strengthens this muscle. If you have lifted weights before, this is the same as "doing sets" on an exercise machine. Further, some women are helped during their sex sessions by doing Kegels as they are getting more and more aroused. Give it a try.

If you have kept up consistent practicing of this session (and your own variations of it) over a number of months and orgasm still eludes you, it would be wise to consider seeking help from a qualified and competent sex therapist. They are trained to be able to help you with the process or discover if there might be emotional issues or blocks from your history that are getting in the way.

If you have been able to experience orgasm at this point and feel comfortable enough to move on, you are ready to start Step 4. Yay!

STEP 4 - Sharing

Now it is time to bring your husband into the picture, if you haven't already. After all, your sexual life together is a shared experience and this is a mutual sharing/pleasure opportunity. You will be showing him what you have learned and teaching him how you work. As well as letting him be a part of your process. If you have not been open about what you have been doing so far, he likely has been wondering what you been up to when you lock the door for your sessions. It's time to clue him in.

If you have been solo up until now, I know it might be intimidating to consider being this intimate with your hubby. But it must happen. The good news is, you get to be in charge of the pacing of it all. I'll tell you more about that shortly. It is so important that you have a supportive, loving and safe husband who is willing to be part of the process. Most men are eager and excited to grow their sex life, though there are some men who may be threatened by your new sexuality. If he is, working through that first so he can get over it would be very helpful.

The one thing that will allow the two of you to have positive experiences in these sessions is the attitude you bring to them. Being open, playful and recognizing that the novelty of doing new things together will make it somewhat awkward. That's OKAY. The journey together is way more important than the outcome. These sessions are about enjoying your experience together, getting close and learning some "new tricks." Remembering that sex is adult play will help you through this newness and discovery.

Now, give yourself a sincere pat on the back for "working" so hard and making it this point. And affirm yourself for having the courage to continue . . . You rock!

Session 5 – Showing Him the Way

Yes, it's time to show your sweet hubby what you have been up to. Prop yourself up comfortably like you have before and create your sensual "spa" environment. Your husband gets to observe you enjoying your body and climaxing if that is possible. If not, no worries. It's more about getting comfortable in his presence and being able to grow more increasingly free with showing him your sexual growth.

To some degree, self-consciousness is to be expected but if his presence is highly distracting, then you have the power of proximity. What is the power of proximity you say? You get to decide where he can be located. Do you want him sitting away from you in another part of the room? Next to you? Nearby but not touching you? Cuddling up close? Or outside the door? You need to be able to get used to him being in the picture and that is not always easily done.

Wherever you decide to put him depends on your ability to get into your own experience and stay your own course. As you get more and more comfortable, you can ask him to move closer and closer. When you are close together and able to self-pleasure to climax, with him observing, you are likely ready to move on. However, feel free to repeat this session as much as you need to grow more and more confident with this new experience. There is no rush so make sure to enjoy this new kind of relating with your sweetheart. A supportive husband will be pleased to know you have made this kind of growth and it will likely be quite arousing for him. But this is not the time for full intercourse yet so he will need to "pull on the reins" for now.

Session 6 – Getting a Helping Hand

Now that you have been able to climax with your hubby observing, it's time to teach him how you work. This time, spend some time settling in with each other by giving and receiving non-genital massage of each other's bodies. As you relax together, begin touching your genitals and explaining what you are doing and how it feels. Then let him try. Give him ongoing feedback and guide him to what feels good- "A little harder honey", "Slower and more rhythmic", or, "What you are doing now, that feels great." Continue to explore together and enjoy the novelty of doing this together.

Here is another helpful strategy to guide your husband into helping you arouse and move towards climax. Have him sit propped up with you sitting in front of him – also propped up (your back to his tummy). Have him reach around your waist and put his hand atop of yours as you stimulate yourself. This allows him to get the feel of the motions that feel good to you first hand (no pun intended). When you both feel like he is ready to fly solo, remove your hand as he continues touching you. As before, let him know how he is doing and give him guidance.

Also, allow yourself to stop guiding and tune into the wonderful sensations and fantasy images that you have found useful in previous sessions. Relish in your husband's touch, the sensations and the fantasies. Tighten up your vagina like you have with your Kegels before, if you found that helpful. Continue to focus on the intensity and building passion. What beautiful sexuality.

You may find your body releases into orgasm. No biggy if it does not since you have ample opportunity to repeat this session and gain increasing confidence together. Besides, look how much you have accomplished so far together, already creating new passionate moments together and glue for your marriage. Eventually your body will naturally spill over into orgasm.

Another position for this exercise that some couples find helpful is to each be on their sides with her back to his tummy, also known as "scissors." If you lean back into him and fling a leg over him, he has good access to your vulva area. Playfully enjoy this new "trick" together. It can allow you both to be in a more relaxed position with each other.

Session 7 – Putting It Altogether

If you made it this far, Wow. Good for you. You have accomplished your goal of having an orgasm with your husband. Amazing. Fantastic. Kudos to you both.

Now it's time to learn to orgasm during intercourse.

As in other exercises, feel free to practice this one as much as you need to in order to get comfortable and find your rhythm with each other. Because you have already experienced orgasm together, this is really just adding one more step;, that is, having an orgasm while your husband's penis is in your vagina.

Begin this session as you have in the past, getting comfortable with each other through all over and sexual touching to increase arousal. You can choose who will provide the clitoral pleasuring – either your husband or yourself. Sometimes, it is easier at the beginning to be the self-pleasurer so you can control your own arousal. When you are feeling ready, ask your husband to slip his penis inside you as you continue to increase your arousal and he begins to thrust. Allow your mind to enjoy and experience the intense sensations.

Don't worry if your husband can't always wait for you to orgasm, as this can be very exciting for him. However, as the two of you journey together, he may need to try different strategies to hang in there so you can have the opportunity to experience orgasm during intercourse.

Monitoring his own arousal and tuning into you instead of his own physical experience can help him postpone ejaculation; and his pulling out and decreasing his own arousal until he can try again can also help.

Maintain clitoral stimulation as needed as you pair your touching with his thrusting. You are learning to become orgasmic during intercourse. Let your mind turn to the fantasies you have practiced imagining before and the tension and friction you feel will lead the way as you relish the feelings and allow your body to respond naturally to the experience.

If you prefer to have your husband be your pleasurer, you may find that being on top or in the scissors position allows him a range of freedom to touch you most directly. These positions will also free you up to move as you need to control the thrusting. Have fun with it and try out different positions, taking turns touching you while he is moving inside you to discover what you most enjoy and gets you the results you are after. Keep practicing together over as many sessions as you need to really embrace the experience and let yourself go.

When you have reached the point where you have experienced orgasm with your husband during intercourse, take the time to celebrate together. What a wonderful, bonding, oneness you have had together.

Session 8 – No Hands Intercourse

Oh wow, another step? I know, I know, you thought you were done and have accomplished it all. You have! This session is really only for those who want to expand their sexual repertoire. It is possible to have intercourse without direct clitoral stimulation. However, most wives do not have orgasms without it. So those of you who would like the option of trying for a "no hands" vaginal orgasm, I have thrown this session in to help guide you.

Begin with a position that allows you to practice Kegel exercises as well as stimulating the clitoris. Build the tension and arousal to near orgasm and then switch to vaginal thrusting alone at the point of climax. Use your mind and imagination to picture the thrusting in a way that is exciting to you. Switch back to clitoral stimulation to increase tension if need be, and then focus again on the thrusting alone and enjoyment of the increasing arousal. Immerse yourself in the fantasies and thrusting and experiencing the orgasmic triggers – increasing tension, muscle contractions, warm, intense feelings.

Some positions will allow for more contact and stimulation (without hands) to the clitoris. Experiment with different positions: man on top thrusting with contact of his pubic bone to your clitoris may be work well for you; or you on top so you can control the contact of your clitoris to his pubic area.

As you keep practicing these different combinations, switching from clitoral stimulation to vaginal thrusting alone, don't be surprised if you find yourself exclaiming, "Look, honey, no hands." ☺

Appendix G

INTIMACY MODEL –
A BRIEF PRIMER FOR MEN
ON HOW TO LOVE

'M SOMEWHAT EMBARRASSED to admit that on occasion, I have fantasies of being a sports legend, having set phenomenal records in 3 point plays on the basketball court, having won the NBA by a last minute, unbelievable jump shot no one suspected would fall through the net.

Or winning the Masters, sinking a 40-foot putt to clench victory. The crowd going nuts, yelling "You're the man" while overpowering the announcers as my wife runs across the green to hug me and celebrate. Tears run down her cheeks as she sees her hero best his opponent, sending him down in the agony of defeat.

Admit it, men. You have done the same. Perhaps you have sent a final 90 mile-per-hour pitch across home plate while the last batter succumbed to your right arm, surrendering the World Series to your team. Again, your wife runs across the field to embrace you, tears flowing, doubtless feeling deeply about your manhood and stature.

All of a sudden, you're ten feet tall, invincible and you have finally convinced her that you deserve the white horse you ride into her life each day.

Oh, what thoughts we entertain as we envision the role of hero, our wives trembling at the side of the "man of her dreams" – while we glow from the romantic dust we have stirred up around us.

Now imagine with me, for a moment, we have the potential to become that very hero. Not with an invisible, supersonic pitch, remarkable shot at mid-court or a smooth-as-silk putt no one else could sink from so far away.

No, a hero because we touch her heart with actions and bright-as-light intentions that place her first, rescue her like a princess and embrace her wildly as her special lover and the passionate guy who has swept her off her feet. Not a professional win, but a relationship victory that comes from deliberate guy-strength, more gripping that a 3 point at-the-buzzer basket. A heart-stopping insurgency that topples boredom, passivity and makes her think she's a queen.

So, imagine with me for a moment – feeling deeply in love with your spouse. Make it an imaginary experience of delight, closeness, passion. Include all the crucial ingredients you believe form a picture of intense, priceless union. Don't hold back.

Create a motion picture in your head and become the hero.

Picture all your actions and emotions saturated with a vision of true romance. Bring to mind all the ways you would treat your lover, what you would be doing to touch her heart and spirit and how she would respond.

Keep going. Develop a clear, mental snapshot of what it means to love another human being with intensity, masculinity and desire. See her melt in your arms. Watch her as she fantasizes about you – of who you are as a lover who has enveloped her with your presence.

What does she look like and what do you look like as a lover, friend, confidant, protector, supporter, giant-in-her-eyes type of guy that has swept her off her feet and into the power of your influence and care?

The hero you become rises from the ashes of misconception and ignorance by embracing a wild, even reckless, desire to know her intimately. You create a burning love, centered on a deep, influential understanding of intimacy and what it takes to be an intimate man.

So what does it take? To be an intimate man? Let's explore this together and glimpse at some of the basic ingredients that form deep connections with our lover, our spouse. We will name only a few.

Intimacy – A Definition

Let's provide a brief definition. Intimacy involves all the unique and ongoing ways we express love to our partner that keep us close, connected and our love growing – without losing our individuality.

Intimacy involves a close, affectionate relationship with our partner in which we deeply and regularly touch each other's heart and soul.

Intimacy at its Core

At the core of intimacy, we find three key ingredients:

1. A heartfelt *desire* to reach out and have someone experience our love, affection and care. This involves internal motivation and a caring heart. Ultimately, this means we carry a *mindset* that aims to consistently reach out to others, especially our mate, with tenderness and behaviors that bond us together. This mindset seeks a sense of ongoing connection or attunement to our lover.

2. A real or growing *capacity* within ourselves to love others. This capacity springs from an awareness and connection within us around what it means to love another and to be loved. Such a connection inspires and directs our understanding of care, affection and what our partner needs to

feel cherished and valued. It implies that we value growth, transformation and an ability to develop and sustain meaningful bonds with others.

3. *Actions* that translate our capacity and desire to love others into specific, discrete *events* that become meaningful experiences for the one we love and for ourselves.

This triad insures that we look in the mirror and assess our *intent and mindset, ability to love* and patterns in how we *reach out*. And *reaching out* involves moving toward our partner consistently with intimate actions and behaviors.

Intimacy in Marriage – Key Elements

To take this further, intimacy in marriage is a relationship term that refers to the exclusive, ongoing experience and bond of love two people share together, created and sustained by several dimensions that form the substance of intimate events discussed above. A close and ongoing look at these dimensions gives us additional understanding of our intent, ability to love and the ingredients of each intimate act that we choose to initiate. These include, but are not limited to:

- emotional closeness
- emotional touch
- physical touch
- spiritual touch
- trust
- physical passion & desire
- mutual attention
- compassion and affirmation
- healing words and experiences

- mutual respect

- genuineness and transparency

- surrender of self/self-sacrifice

Each of these helps us form a composite picture that unmasks the complexity of what makes a relationship "intimate" – by defining qualities that form the substance of a close, loving bond between husband and wife. These allow us to translate "intimacy" into actionable items or events that convey meaning to the one we love. Our love partner needs to "feel" our attempts to be intimate. They need to experience us.

A Short Definition of Each Element

Emotional Closeness

This refers to the feelings of love and affection two partners share, cultivated and sustained by reaching out to one another over time. Although feelings come and go during the moments of the day, consistently bringing each other affection and care results in a secure bond that transcends conflict and other temporary setbacks.

Achieving emotional closeness implies that each has the capacity to know and feel deeply for the other and that there are no significant limitations in their ability to bond and connect. And each has developed his or her ability to love deeply, regardless of past experiences or even relationship wounds.

Equally important, each lover has a secure identity apart from the relationship. Both need each other but not to heal self-esteem, establish a personal identity or confer worth.

Emotional Touch

Intimacy involves touching someone's heart and mind and soul – emotionally. Volumes could be written on this topic but the essence here addresses the vital issue of how to make someone "feel" and "experience" the love we have for them.

It's one thing to say "I love you," yet quite another to prove it.

As in all aspects of intimacy, however, proving it means we have something to offer to create a difference in our partner's life. We must be able to imagine the gift of touch coming from our own heart and mind experientially, before we have it to give our lover. Let me repeat that idea. We need to develop within our own hearts and minds and imaginations a sense of what it means to impact the life of the one we love, creating within them warmth, connection and care. We need confidence we can "reach" our lover and impact their feelings.

So ask yourself these questions:

What does it mean to touch your lover emotionally?

How do you touch your lover emotionally?

Take a few minutes to jot down what comes to mind.

What actions do you choose in reaching out to her that you believe create positive, loving emotional experiences for your mate?

Physical Touch

Intimacy involves touching someone's life physically – outside the bedroom and inside. Later I will discuss touch on the inside. There are many forms of touch that include reaching out with our hands, kissing our lover, stroking their hair or face, hugging, etc.

When we touch, we need to have something in mind besides physical contact. Intimacy involves touching with a purpose, imagining our lover being influenced by our warmth and also our desire for closeness with them. Touch becomes a vehicle for care, connection and closeness to be communicated.

Ask yourself,

"Am I able to access my own desire to be close to my lover and am I therefore

able to convert that into a meaningful physical contact that conveys this feeling and experience?"

Spiritual Touch

This involves recognizing that our mate has been created a spiritual being and in Christian terms, made in the image of God Himself. Touching our mate's life spiritually means seeing each other as God does including how He loves us, sees us as unique and desires the best for our lives.

It means watching out for and caring for our mate as someone we learn to cherish and love and providing direction spiritually in the home. Bringing spiritual leadership into the home through attention to God's active presence in the life of your family and in the life of your spouse involves prayer, looking to God for direction and a variety of other "faith" practices that bring in light and goodness.

This means attention to our own growth and letting God's Spirit invade our way of being and the choices we make. As we learn to hear God's active voice in all we say or do, we can bring wisdom into the center of home life and into the heart of our mate's life.

Trust

Intimacy depends on two lovers creating deep levels of trust. Both need to believe that their partner intends to be present, involved and consistent in their love for the other and that this love only belongs to them.

When trust is broken, through sexual and/or intense emotional contact with others outside the marriage, deep fractures in trust have to be restored for the relationship to survive. Restoring trust involves intentionally developing all the elements of intimacy being discussed – perhaps all over again – in order to create a fresh, thriving belief in the credibility of the person who has betrayed the marriage. Restoring trust means creating emotional and physical closeness that will not be violated again.

One of the greatest ways to build trust is through consistent attention to our partner where we are trying to impact their life with intimate actions, convincing them of our deep love, care and appreciation for them.

Ask these questions,

"Do my actions, values and lifestyle build trust with my lover?"

"Are there times when I violate trust by my behaviors?"

"Does my life reflect a deep set of core values around integrity that I bring into my lover's life? What are those values?"

Physical Passion & Desire

Two lovers in marriage share a desire for one another that is exclusive and represents a passion kept alive by romantic effort and regular physical contact. Ultimately, physical intimacy in marriage is a reflection of the quality of life and care two lovers build outside the bedroom.

Physical passion, to enhance intimacy, must be thought of as 24/7. You can't expect to generate excitement about love-making when you have treated each other poorly during the day or week.

Sex is a confirmation of what is special about your love and connection, grown on the bedrock of daily interactions and tangible acts of caring outside the bedroom. Physical intimacy then provides a unique energy that confirms your bond and creates passion that no one else shares.

Mutual Attention

Intimacy occurs when two lovers focus on building love together. Achieving high levels of mutual attention involves ongoing care and consideration for each other, concern about how the other is doing and attempts to check in and find out what the other is thinking and feeling.

Mutual attention also implies that we focus on how to create caring moments as an ongoing habit and that we seek consistent, positive inter-actions with our lover emotionally and verbally. We sometimes call this "attunement" or "involvement," referring to staying deeply connected with one another, even if we are physically apart. It's kind of like two people tuning into the same radio frequency, with no distortion and hearing clearly. It means developing habits that keep us dialed in, such as email and text or other reminders that at some level, we are one.

Compassion and affirmation

Seeing our lover through the eyes of compassion, acceptance and appre-ciation establishes an approach that insures the deepest qualities of love and care possible. Compassion means seeing ourselves and our partner realistically, without expectations that they become something super-human. It means we see each other with grace and are willing to forgive their mistakes or when we feel they have hurt us.

Compassion, in many ways, represents a focus on all of life. It implies we have a generous way of evaluating others, without criticism or unre-alistic expectations. And it means that we reach out with sympathetic arms and love our partner for who they are – complete with wrinkles and flaws. Knowing we too have deficiencies and issues that may hinder us.

Compassion implies tolerance for the weaknesses of our mate and an acceptance that our own weaknesses contribute to misunderstandings and challenges in our love for one another.

Ask yourself,

> *"Does my behavior toward others involve tolerance, compassion and a desire to see them not suffer?"*

> *"Do I see others through the eyes of criticism or care and tenderness?"*

> *"Do my actions demonstrate tolerance, forgiveness and a humble belief that we all need grace and forgiveness?"*

Amazing Intimacy

Healing words and experiences

Choosing our words so they reflect care and respect and even a desire to be a healing influence in the life of our partner honors and grows love and connection.

Being willing to apologize and accept responsibility for issues that come up becomes an important ingredient in creating bonds of love.

Saying, for example, "I love you and don't want you to hurt – let's talk it out" would be an example of an open attitude that seeks closure and a desire to see healing.

Ask these questions,

"How do I speak to others when I know they are hurting?"

"Can I put myself aside and reach out, even if I'm hurting too?"

"Do my own emotions prevent me from speaking and communicating in caring ways with my lover to clear the air, reach appropriate compromises and re-establish a loving bond together? Or do I hold grudges, stay angry and become distant or build walls between me and my partner?"

Mutual respect

Intimacy involves a commitment to treat each other with respect and dignity, despite faults. This means both continue to pursue a life style that honors and values integrity and believes in the other person's worth and intrinsic value. Behaviors that compromise anyone's ability to respect the other need to be acknowledged, worked out and corrected. Intimacy means a commitment to actions and values that always uphold mutual respect.

Genuineness and transparency

The bedrock of an intimate connection centers on being real. Intimate actions must be sincere, heartfelt and come from an honest place inside

338

our heart. Some individuals have trouble expressing themselves in genuine ways and behaviors come across as artificial or even contrived.

Practicing communication and sharing loving words and touch must be delivered carefully. This means connecting within our own heart first to insure that what we want to communicate comes from a meaningful, soft and tender place. Intimacy exists in soft places within our being. Loving takes place first in our own person, before we give it away to another.

Close your eyes and take a moment to reflect on the feeling of being loved and valued and even cherished. For some, this may be hard to do because of lack of these experiences in their lives. For others, being able and used to finding that softer center inside has never been attempted.

Once you begin to identify inner experiences of love and being fully accepted, imagine reaching out to your lover and trying to create these types of feelings inside of them. If you stay with your own internal experience of love and tenderness, you will likely reach out in genuine ways that are powerfully felt by your partner.

Surrender of self/self-sacrifice

Finally, intimacy involves a willingness to sacrifice our time and often our own self-centeredness to give to someone else. Loving often means setting ourselves aside – not in destructive or co-dependent ways – for the sake of focusing on the needs of someone else.

Giving to another often means I lose myself in the process of reaching out. My effort is to rock the world of the one I love by focusing on their person and needs.

Exercise

Spend some time taking each element of intimacy and imagine how you would make this happen in your life. How you would take the idea, make it your own and use it to reach out to your lover?

Once you develop concrete ideas about how to understand intimacy and how to package it behaviorally in reaching out to your lover, you can better establish patterns that sustain love. That makes you a person who strives to build and grow bonds of love with your partner.

The Story of Clark and Alice

Clark and Alice had been married for 13 years, with two kids and a dog. Clark historically didn't really value emotions and "touchy-feely" stuff. He loved his wife but thought she simply ought to know this and never occurred to him to that ongoing work and effort were needed to grow and sustain their connection. After all, an occasional date should serve to keep his wife happy and at peace.

Over time, however, fights went unresolved and both were feeling neglected and unimportant. Sex became infrequent and neither one knew how to turn things around. Alice had her own set of issues and chose to withdraw, while Clark busied himself with work, coming home later and later and feeling more and more resentful.

Both needed a new path and direction on several fronts, one being their understanding of the ingredients of intimacy and connection – how to grow these and sustain them over time.

Clark began focusing on the idea of emotional closeness and emotional touch – that his wife had the need to be heard and that he needed to develop more warmth in the relationship. This part was really difficult, but he was determined to improve his ability to love. He felt kind of soft, wasn't sure men should do all this, but decided to commit to new behaviors he hadn't tried before.

He began hiding notes she would find later in the day that commented on her beauty and how much he appreciated her efforts in the marriage. He tried to focus on what he loved about her and decided to invent ways to communicate this, sending occasional flowers, loving emails and setting up date nights.

During the process, he tried to focus on what love feels like – what the experience of being loved really means. He then chose to honestly reach out to his wife, hoping to help her feel alive and loved. He even told her he wanted her to really know deep inside how much he appreciates her. These words began a real process of healing between the two of them.

Alice chose to focus on mutual attention, realizing she had withdrawn significantly in the relationship and had not shown much respect for Clark over the past few years. Much of this due to her anger and hurt. Using healing words and surrender, she apologized for her distance and embraced him with physical touch to reinforce her desire to have him feel warmth and value. She began to realize that intimacy must be communicated with specific, intimate actions and that she needed to choose to do this regularly to establish new patterns in how she reached out to her spouse.

Over time, new patterns did indeed emerge and their love for one another grew. Each decided to maintain their part in growing their love and the results were profound.

Summary

As stated in the beginning of this brief discourse, intimacy involves all the unique and ongoing ways we express love to our partner that keep us close, connected and our love growing. Without losing our individuality.

Intimacy has to be operationalized. We need to understand how. And to fully comprehend the "how," we have to have an idea of the ingredients that go into making intimacy come to life in how we love our partner. Intimacy must have legs.

So, this has been a brief outline of some key features that describe what intimacy is all about. Intimacy involves a desire and mindset that seeks closeness. It means developing and growing in our capacity to give and receive love. And importantly, it involves actions that package key elements experienced by the one we love and that make intimacy true intimacy.

Intimacy is complex and multifaceted. This brief description doesn't capture all that we need to understand to master the concept and develop a path to better patterns of closeness in our love life. But it's a start and helps us get hold of a frame of reference we can build on.

Take these concepts and build on them. Love will then grow and intimacy will flourish.

References

Hybels, B. (2002). *Courageous Leadership.* Grand Rapids: Zondervan

Gottman, J. & Silver, N. (2000). *Seven Principles For Making Marriage Work.* New York: Three Rivers Press.

Rosenau, D. (2002). A *Celebration of Sex.* Nashville: Thomas Nelson, Inc.

Masters, W. & Johnson, V. (1966). *Human Sexual Response.* New York: Ishi Press International.

McCluskey, C. & McCluskey, R. (2004). *When Two Become One: Enhancing Sexual Intimacy In Marriage.* Grand Rapids: Fleming H. Revel.

Penner, C. & Penner, J. (2003). *The Gift of Sex: A Guide to Sexual Fulfillment.* Nashville: W Publishing Group.

Rankin, L. (2010). *What's Up Down There: Questions You'd Only Ask Your Gynecologist If She Was Your Best Friend.* New York: St. Martin's Press.

Chapman, G. (1992). *The Five Love Languages: The Secret to Love That Lasts.* Chicago: North Fields Publishing.

Barbach, L. (1975). *For Yourself.* New York: Bantam Doubleday Dell Publishing Group Inc.

Sproul, R.C. & Lingonier Ministries. *Tabletalk.* Sanford: Ligonier Ministries.

"Awe." Dictionary.com Unabridged. 2013

2570564R00196

Made in the USA
San Bernardino, CA
08 May 2013